Y0-DVA-604

Authenticity and How
We Fake It

Authenticity and How We Fake It

*Belief and Subjectivity in
Reality TV, Facebook
and YouTube*

AARON DUPLANTIER

McFarland & Company, Inc., Publishers
Jefferson, North Carolina

WINGATE UNIVERSITY LIBRARY

ISBN (print) 978-0-7864-9849-9
ISBN (ebook) 978-1-4766-2523-2

LIBRARY OF CONGRESS CATALOGUING DATA ARE AVAILABLE

BRITISH LIBRARY CATALOGUING DATA ARE AVAILABLE

© 2016 Aaron Duplantier. All rights reserved

*No part of this book may be reproduced or transmitted in any form
or by any means, electronic or mechanical, including photocopying
or recording, or by any information storage and retrieval system,
without permission in writing from the publisher.*

Front cover image of social networking © 2016 Rawpixel Ltd/iStock

Printed in the United States of America

*McFarland & Company, Inc., Publishers
Box 611, Jefferson, North Carolina 28640
www.mcfarlandpub.com*

For my wife, parents and brothers.

Table of Contents

Preface

A preoccupation with authenticity does not incur a reaction from us nowadays. It is commonplace. Fakery will not stand, be it of the Hollywood or Washington, D.C., variety (both are equivalent, we'll say). Skepticism directed at the productive forces which deliver our goods is just as common, banal, even. Any single person who knows Walmart is the world's leading retailer does not hesitate to guess they have at least one closet full of skeletons. Yet consumption, in the capitalist vein, reigns supreme despite our defenses being hoisted higher than ever, and that is because consumption has changed. Digital products, social platforms for the self, the democratization of our consumption experience has given consumers false consciousness insofar as they have anointed themselves the new rulers of consumer capitalism, even when this is not at all the case. As such, consumerism has been imbued with a sacred quality because now it is "consumer led." Yup, the corporate giants have finally relented! Gabe Newell, one of the founders of video game behemoth Valve Corporation, gave a speech at the 2013 D.I.C.E. Summit where he emphatically announced, "The customer has defeated us. Like, not by a little, but by a lot," as if there were some elaborate conflict afoot where somehow the companies were not always the victor of every skirmish. No, customers have not won, but they sure do enjoy hearing that they have. Makes them want to buy more stuff!

This book came to me amid a contradictory mixture of attitudes I encountered largely among my students. I use pop culture in my classroom, some of which might be considered, at best, trash. After watching a clip from MTV's *Jersey Shore*, which was part of a unit on ethnic identity, my students preferred discussing how bad the show was as opposed to the hyperbolized identities of its characters. "That show's so fake. It's obvious," was the gist of their evaluative judgment. "How is it fake?" I asked. "No one acts like that in real life. There's a script," etc. Weirdly, whenever I have one these discussions, they usually occur within close range of someone whose cousin or buddy worked on a reality show and confirmed it was all fake and staged. *Jersey Shore* was by no means rejected by the viewing public, and in fact was a wild success for MTV partly because it drew an audience ascribing to the same model of consumption as my students—the majority of my students admitted to watching the show, to be clear. Even if *Jersey Shore* was staged, its audience did not seem to mind, and could even revel in that notion. Worse still, *Jersey Shore*, which had a short run from 2009 to 2012, suffered a comparably low degree of producorial manipulation. A show I discuss in Chapter 1, truTV's *Lizard Lick Towing*, is deeply, hopelessly staged. So, yes, all reality TV is staged to a degree—so is much of 21st-century life. Social media, the prevailing mode of self-referentiality today, provides us with a direct means of "stage managing" ourselves (see "mediate" ourselves). We seem to gloss over that fact as we skewer the reality TV shows delivered to us on a silver platter by the productive forces we distrust. That is the grand paradox of my students' consumption habits: They are quick to isolate fakery and staging at every turn, but uncritically mediate themselves via Instagram, Twitter, Facebook, and all the other emerging social media platforms. They genuinely believe there is a difference between social media self-fashioning and reality TV participation and consumption, or at least their perceived difference is so profound that my students cannot grasp that relation.

Nearly all of what we say and do on Facebook is entirely predicated on Facebook. However, because Facebook draws from our reality outside that social medium, users generally do not believe that to be true. When my aunt posts a photo of her dachshund on Facebook, my kneejerk reaction is not somehow "This is fake. It was staged." No, I accept it at face value because Facebook's intrinsic relationship to the lived reality I know and cherish is undeniable. If I doubt social media's authenticity quotient, it is after the fact, if ever at all, even while my own Facebook posts are only ever conceived in relation to Facebook. And that is at the core of the mysticism which Facebook's content arrives to us upon; Facebook, then, has always been thus, as opposed to inauthentic reality TV shows which have the cultural reputation of being complete and utter fabrications with little relation to a known reality. A family photo taken specifically for Facebook is of course informed by Facebook. Just because I recognize those people in the photo does not mean that the photo is exempt from similar criticisms I might levy against an episode of A&E's *Duck Dynasty*. On a greater scale, every social event, and even moments of isolation, are underwritten by the possibility that a photo, or remark, or whatever else might end up on social media—against our will, often, in a perverse sort of natural surveillance Jeremy Bentham could never have imagined. That paradigm itself means our behaviors and attitudes will be stage managed in accordance with the media platform for which they will eventually arrive, no different than the filming of a reality show informed by the platform of television which consists of commercials, a target demographic, etc. What appears on reality TV is shaped by TV. What appears on Facebook is informed by Facebook. Yet there are degrees of mediation to be considered.

I am not arguing reality TV and Facebook are mediational equivalents, no. Surely MTV's demands for the mediation that occurred prior to and during *Jersey Shore*'s production did not somehow mirror my aunt's as she photographed her dachshund wearing a bumble bee costume. My aunt's mediational standards are socially-oriented, while MTV's are monetarily-oriented. There is a difference, but not necessarily one in quality. In truth, we could easily argue the version of reality that arrives to us via MTV is far more engaging, vibrant, and easy to digest than the one we might receive on Facebook, which often does not account for audience reception in the way conventional television does. In this regard, social media usually gets a free pass because people don't expect much from social media's productive laborers, who just so happen to be their friends, colleagues, family members. So given the prevalence of all these social networks, it seems counterintuitive that consumers nowadays get hung up on evaluative distinctions, or what I call "the quality problem." Certainly reality TV often does not fare well in light of these evaluative distinctions, but they also distract consumers from the deeper questions reality shows and social media, in conjunction, present to them. As such, it behooves consumers to consider platforms that fail the quality sniff test from the outset, such as amateur YouTube production. No one would mistake social commentary shot in a seventeen-year-old's bedroom on a low-fi webcam for the quality of scripted television, or even reality TV. Still, YouTube amateur video hazardously teases our evaluative tendencies. We can only excuse so many lapses in authenticity, but that's a precocious, albeit annoying, seventeen-year-old on the screen—is it fair to judge? Yeah, we still judge. Better, YouTube amateur video draws from an accepted, lived reality we accept at face value, just like social media. Therein, YouTube allows us to bridge the gap between fake-up-front reality TV and more "authentic" social media. What YouTube offers is the confluence of social media logic and more suspect reality TV production practices—this, in turn, sheds light on both platforms and YouTube itself.

And so is the tripartite focus of this media study: reality TV, Facebook, and YouTube. My choice to focus on these three platforms was not arbitrary. They complement each other, and offer insight into much larger cultural issues. Each platform is embroiled in what I consider *an impetus for authenticity*, one that engenders their viewers, producers, users, consumers (whatever designation the scenario calls for), susceptible to their machinations. Susceptible, I should say, such that their selfhood is beholden to those platforms. A concern about authenticity is truly about belief: We believe in the authentic thing, so we internalize it through our acceptance of it, and it consequently shapes us. Social media, for instance, is a very powerful means of self-orientation and producing subjectivity. People, young people especially, put a lot of faith in social media for their representation; faith that is often axiomatic. The customer has won, after all—distrust television, sure, but I decide what ends up on my Facebook page! And I can trust myself (right?). Out of this, faith in social media is also conceived under the guise of some amorphous notion of individuality, what many cultural critics these days see as an outgrowth of deeper and deeper narcissism among Millennials (this position has always been a red herring). MySpace, the failed social media platform which predates Facebook, banked on young people seeking individuality in their representation online, offering them a highly-customizable interface which could reflect their uniqueness. The isolated soul in front the computer screen, cell phone, tablet—that's the sort of dubious social creature Sherry Turkle is wary of in her book *Alone Together*. Facebook does not allow people to customize the site's interface as MySpace did, and for good reason. How am I supposed to know where to locate a person's religious affiliation or music interests if it is not in the places I am used to seeing it? Facebook's notion of individuality goes as far as your Facebook profile picture and cover photo—they are more concerned with grouping people together, making you the same, all the better for advertisers.

This book, then, isolates and details the emergent subjectivities of these platforms, so we can better understand how subjectivity is formed in our current consumer culture, one which finds much of its exchange value in digital mediational spaces, such as Facebook, YouTube, and Twitter. Around the mid–2000s, many critics thought "social media" was just a buzz word, another phantasmic creation of our thick-headed news media oligarchy. CNN dubbed the 2009 citizen revolt in Iran the "Twitter Revolution," and, yeah, that sort of reactionary technological pigeonholing smacks of buzziness. Eugeny Morokov and others critical of this kind of ignoramus worship of the digital regime are right in that applying value to a platform as opposed to a people misses the point entirely: revolutionary ideations were conceived off-screen, and Twitter merely facilitated their travel from one mind to the other. An organizational tool is not an idea tool. But witnessing younger generations accept social networking as an axiom of everyday existence confirms that, no, social media is not some passing phenomenon. And when people axiomatically engage a platform ("it has always been thus"), there is no moment of critical examination, only reaction and consumption. What, then, does subjectivity consist of in light of this?

We can turn to postmodernism in answer to this question. Yes, that trite word, which nowadays "signifies nothing." It is true that the term *postmodernism* in the popular imagination carries little worth because its overuse means that is has been appropriated by so many movements, agendas, and institutions. This has unmoored postmodernism, as so many important words and ideas have been chiefly through Internet discourse. Antiquated ideas and belief systems which need subverting are appropriately cut down by the Internet, but there is no fault line of good taste or conscientious thinking when people go toe-to-toe on a message board or YouTube comments section; it is survival of the typist, and everybody has a gun. Feminism, culture, race, religiosity—the Internet knows no sacred cows, and game netizens are expert enough to weigh in and debate ceaselessly till all that is left is the husk of an idea that once moved us, helped us make sense of our social and cultural world. Sure, people mused on ideas they had no stake in or clue about before Reddit and 4Chan, but the Internet gives permanence to those haphazard positions so that they can be taken as sacrosanct and then internalized by an unwary (or, worse, wary) reader.

To cut through the haziness of postmodernism, my book adheres to Frederic Jameson's figuration of postmodernity. Unprecedented economic affluence in the 20th century saw American culture redefined by means and as a consequence of commodity culture. Jameson's conception of postmodernism drew directly from this moment in American history, after the 1950s and on. No other Western country could match our ability to convert every art object and free thought into something packaged and sold. From there, culture became "kitsch." What Jameson saw in consumerism was fragmentation, nonessentialism, instability, infinite pastiche, an unrepentant sort of shallowness—what I define in this book as *surface orientation*. This was not the earlier variety of postmodernism, which writers like Lyotard and Borges heralded, experimental creations that played with and subverted the status quo for great social, political, and artistic returns. Jameson's version of post-modernism—what he associates with "late capitalism"—exerts the tenets of postmodernist experimentation for *no redeemable reason* (at most, mere recognition of those tenets). How to make an evaluative reading of postmod-ern surface orientation depends on your vantage point. Decrying essentialism is fundamental to race and gender studies because an "essential self" is where hegemonic patriarchal voices draw much of their power. But to consider the articulation of self, separate from power dynamics except consumerism, is never to do so as a surface-oriented thing. Consumerism by means of the digital regime is not revered by critical theorists even if it does help destabilize an essential selfhood; as a moral imperative, capitalist consumption is and will always be decried. At its best, the self, even the fragmented self, is one of complexity and depth. This is an important distinction for this book. I am not championing oppressive, hegemonic forces in decrying tenets of post-modernism often valued within race and gender studies, but instead defend-ing the human subject as a complex, depth-oriented thing; this is what unchecked consumerism via social media and reality TV siphons from sub-jectivity which has had the effect of *resituating* the subject.

N. Katherine Hayles, whose work is a significant foundation for this book, sees subjectivity in the digital age as emergent, fragmented, and dis-jointed. The self is not "essential" or "born" in any way, but is the emergent product of so many processes. Sherry Turkle, the MIT psychologist, correlates self-referentiality via digital constructive spaces with identity crisis among people not literate enough to distinguish their real experience from virtual ones. In Turkle's view, the inherent "play" (a consecrated postmodern attrib-ute if there ever was one) of virtual spaces is liberating, yes, but can also lead to a dangerous sort of multiplicity which has the effect of crisis in the subject, and, in my view, of surface orientation. So many of the traits people attribute to digital representational platforms adhere nicely with postmodernism. Researching this book, the more I read of new media studies, the more I saw that one-to-one connection between postmodernity and all these digital mediational platforms (see products) which were somehow being anointed as entirely singular in their ability to produce "fluidity" and fragmentation in their users and the culture which they disseminate. Social media, then, is a sort of literal manifestation of postmodern logic in the Jamesonian sense because it allows people to actively submit themselves to postmodernity—this is an act of *mutation* in the subject.

My decision to discuss reality TV in Chapter 1 probably seems puzzling amid all this thinking on social media. This book has a historical trajectory, and, yes, reality TV is now a historical artifact, as it evolves to accommodate new, digitally-informed iterations of television in the 21st century. Underwritten by analog ideological machinations, reality TV is the base of my larger conversation because it projects a mediated subjectivity presented by a top-down hierarchical system: what most of us colloquially refer to as "producers" or just "the producer" of a given show. And, to be clear, "the producer" shares no exclusive blame, just that the term itself is a catch-all for the people and processes shaping reality TV. Through the mass medium of reality TV, we learn about other cultures, personalities, etc. This activity is not so different than what some users acquire via social media, save Facebook and Twitter's democratic provocation. Yes, I am the user! The choice is mine! Reality TV, though, is a consumer platform, and social media, too, is a consumer platform. To interrogate one platform that is universally maligned and distrusted alongside one that is held with higher regard produces some revelatory results, especially in conceiving the content of the emergent subjectivities this book isolates.

And, really, history communicates much of what we should know about social media. In the 1960s, before the consumer Internet was even a blip on some AOL executive's mental radar, media studies godfather Marshall McLuhan thought young consumers' relationship with TV was very democratic and participatory, so much so that it seemed quite dangerous to him such that it might coax young people into an exploitable ideological mode by way of that participation. McLuhan's television consumers are first and foremost *involved*, and demand that involvement from all the other aspects of their lives. TV asks of them, as McLuhan says, "participation and involvement in depth of the whole being," but this can only result in "myopia" as the intensity of the TV experience turns attention back to the individual viewer, continuously (334, 335). McLuhan was concerned about the question of satisfaction, and TV's unified mosaic of undetached ideas and images were deeply satisfying, not dissimilar to the satisfying agency digital consumer tech provides its users. Think of all the choice TV provides: channel surfing alone is akin to sniping a certain colored M&M from a jar of candies, satisfying (but shallow) in its seduction. Conventional television only seems undemocratic nowadays because of DVRs, streaming video, and the like—again, the paradigm of the "consumer led" experience irons over so many of our qualms. "I hate watching videos online because they are inundated with ads!" you say? Well, then just download an ad blocker, then you will be free from the villainous grasp of advertisers! It's not such a stretch to look at the most important and motivation-shaping media platform from the late 20th century with that which reigns supreme today—this makes the most sense, actually. I do not think so much has changed since kids sat in front of the boob tube, trance-like, internalizing advertisements, the hidden themes of some shows, the neatly-produced and easy-to-comprehend worldview of TV. Today, those same machinations are merely cloaked by a prevailing democratic ethos and by a new sort of agency that compels people to delve ever-deeper into their consumer devices. Remember: the customer has won.

Introduction

The discourses among today's various media studies explore technical structures of media dispersal (Jenkins, Ford, and Green's *Spreadable Media*), capitalism's role in the techno-paradigm (Robert W. McChesney's *Digital Disconnect*), and how the brain thinks through and as a consequence of technology (Nicholas Carr's *The Shallows*; Hayles's *How We Think*). But technology and media analysis should not lose sight of the "human," subjective element. The territory assessed by N. Katherine Hayles in *My Mother Was a Computer*, subjectivity's relation to computational mediation, was more than just a theoretical provocation: Hayles was mapping postmodern, human complexity onto a motherboard. This book, not unlike what Hayles vies for, promotes a return to Marshall McLuhan-esque readings of media, which are practically metaphysical in execution; they reflect the humans behind them, and the humans intimately engaging that media. This book maps human complexity, or lack thereof, onto three popular consumer platforms: reality TV, Facebook, and YouTube—this act brings *ontology* back into the media study equation, as consumer behavior has now been relegated to quantitative analysis, talking points, *New York Times* op-eds. This is a humanistic project, part of the public conversation, but also an academic one. Where the two intersect is where the conversation matters. As such, this book advances regard among contemporary media studies for the *consumer as subject*, and examines the historical and cultural processes of that subjectivity.

What Does Postmodernism Mean for This Project?

While it is true that the concept of "postmodernism" emerged from the study of experimental art and culture reacting to World War II, postmodernism, as it has evolved over time, has given way to late 20th century and the current American consumer society. The theoretical backing for this position hinges upon thinkers such as Terry Eagleton and Frederic Jameson; this project is indebted to Jameson's theory of "late capitalism," his compartmentalizing of the artistic and consumer modes that have arisen from postmodernism. Jameson believes "modernism" continued historically through postmodernism's first declaration, and that postmodern work which was created out of post–World War II anxieties was actually "high modernism" (3). In Jameson's reasoning, postmodernism did not arrive until the rampant consumerism of the latter half of the 20th century, a byproduct of America's postwar economic affluence. Jameson's postmodernism is the "cultural logic" of "late capitalism," in which "nature is gone for good," where high and "mass" culture (i.e., pop culture) have degraded into one another, and where culture and art experience a "superficiality in the most literal sense" (ix, 3, 9). Further, this book takes Ihab Hassan's impression of the cultural and spiritual climate of postmodernity as its specific cultural context: "the public world dissolves as fact and fiction blend, history becomes derealized by media into a happening, science takes its own models as the only accessible reality, cybernetics confronts us with the enigma of artificial intelligence, and technologies project our perceptions to the edge of the receding universe or into the ghostly interstices of matter" (7).

The trend Jameson was trying to define with "late capitalism" exists quite literally within reality TV, Facebook, and YouTube. Reality TV especially conveys a contemporary postmodern variant of "kitsch," which Jameson isolates among America's fascination with Elvis. What is more, these three platforms are consumer platforms in the purest sense in that there is no escaping consumer capitalism within their usage because of, among other things, *advertising*. While advertising articulates itself in distinct ways on each platform, an issue explored in individual chapters, it is still ever-present, and alerts the consumer/user as to the platform's status as "product."

Admittedly, there are current movements in the world of criticism which hold postmodernism to be "over," that there has been some definitive paradigm shift in cultural creation and consumption. This book addresses that particular issue again in relation to Facebook in Chapter 2. Pertinent "new" movements include Jeffrey Nealon's "post postmodernism [circa 2012]," a concept which grasps at the same logistical zone as "late capitalism," and Billy Childish and Charles Thomson's "remodernism [circa 2000]," a return to the systems of meaning within modernism. Both of these new cultural forms are impeded by the fact that postmodernism itself signals a dead end for cultural creation; according to postmodernism, paradoxically, there is nothing beyond postmodernism. And "remodernism" is actually included within postmodernism, because postmodernity is composed of "pastiche," or infinite return to previous cultural forms (Jameson 17). To suppose there is culture and art beyond postmodernism nowadays is a misreading. Granted, attempts within Academia and in the public conversation to move criticism away from postmodernism are in keeping with larger trends in technology and consumerism. Consumers embrace democratic, Web. 2.0 technologies via an ethos which exemplifies a desire for meaning disparate from "superficiality in the most literal sense" (Jameson 9). Indeed, the current preoccupation with authenticity in digital media mirrors the anxieties of previous movements (e.g., modernism). However, as articulated in this book's individual chapters, a return to "the authentic" is merely a machine dream. There is a desire for new incarnations of culture beyond late capitalism and/or postmodernism, but desire does not guarantee a tangible result.

To be sure, this project is not *minimizing* the consumer desire for authenticity. It is, in fact, an indelible part of the current media climate. Chapter 3 argues that a large swath of the amateur video on YouTube emanates from this very desire, and at moments achieves its goal of "genuine emotion," what Childish and Thomson seek out in "remodernity." However, these moments are fleeting, can be co-opted by the consumer agenda, and thusly commodified so that they reflect the consumer objects that Frederic Jameson decries. Indeed, this consumer behavior explicates nostalgia for the *substantive* subject.

What Does Subjectivity Mean for This Project?

The cultural desire to move away from postmodernism is an indication that subjectivity weighs on the minds of consumers, viewers, users—people trying to reach out beyond the screen and make "genuine" connections. When amateur YouTube creators and viewers claim that what they acquire on that platform is "more real" or "more authentic" than what reality TV offers, this implies a concern about *depth orientation*. Human depth, in this book's context, means complexity, substance, privileging interiority as opposed to explicit visibility. Before postmodernity, modern and premodern subjectivity was thought to have occurred almost exclusively along the y-axis of human articulation, the vertical stratum of selfhood, typified by intangibility, ambiguity, perception. As contemporary theorists have speculated on the subject, its conception has changed in the academic imagination.

Ostensible "constructions" of subjectivity, then, have shifted subjectivity away from intangibility. Yet the subject is nevertheless still embroiled in ontology, a point Judith Butler negotiates in 1990's *Gender Trouble*. Butler posits that the subject is "culturally enmired," above all else, though she is curiously remiss to wholly denounce discourses that might consider the subject "stable" prior to its cultural interpellation. Instead, Butler asserts that active subjects are at the center of a reflexive relationship with the belief that they are the "agent" or "doer" of their own subjective devising; this is where subjectivity exists in postmodernity (195). Certainly Butler does not contend that such an "inner" or "outer" distinction among people ought to exist; her position is that these are "linguistic terms" which facilitate the mere fantasy of a "stable" and "coherent" subject (182). But even if "inner" and "outer" selves are imaginary, and culture constructs subjects, people still explicitly *doubt* that their interiority is indebted to this process, assuredly why Butler does not say, outright, that "the inner life does not exist." And this is part and parcel to the various consumer modes and ideologies which today's media engages, influences, and constructs; thus, the struggle between depth orientation and surface orientation among contemporary conceptions of subjectivity. As such, there are degrees of depth orientation belonging to the subject. On-screen subjectivity, in this project, refers to the technologically-mediated subject, consumed via screens, while the off-screen subject is the consumer. Off-screen subjectivity is still "culturally enmired," but on-screen subjects are enmired and also *directly* mediated through technology. Both can achieve depth orientation, but this is predicated on fluid terms for both mediation and consumer involvement.

Alternatively, a subject's identity signifies the horizontal, x-axis stratum of human articulation (see Figure 1). As Butler figures, identity is "always already signified," and therefore of a strict surface orientation (196). Especially within the academic conversation regarding technology, there has been a discursive shift away from contemporary theory's emphasis on identity, *mirroring* the shift in the public conversation desirous of more depth-oriented articulations of selfhood. Sherry Turkle's groundbreaking work in social media (e.g., 1995's *Life on the Screen* and 2011's *Alone Together*) has found fault in mediational platforms, such as MUDs (i.e., multi-user domains or chat rooms), which rely on the paradigmatic construction practices constituting "surface" versions of the self (i.e., identity), which she argues are reductions of humanity (*Alone Together* 183–184). In N. Katherine Hayles' schema of human subjectivity, there exist "analog subjects," from the 20th century, and "digital subjects," from today's digital age, which signify *disparate artic-*

ulations of the self, both informed by consumer technology. This book operates at the intersection of these schemes, as postmodernity has splintered subjectivity amid ever more complex consumer modes, amid people's intense involvement in online and digital communication technologies. These modes and fragmentations are inflected by a cultural transition, from *analog* subjectivity (depth-oriented with "mind/soul" correspondence) to *digital* subjectivity (disjunctive and "fragmentary"), which this project isolates (*My Mother Was a Computer* 203).

To further detail this book's conception of subjectivity beyond the interior self, in the simplest formulation of objectivity, a coffee mug does not communicate interiority. There is no question as to its referential value; it has none. In order to exceed its object status, the coffee mug would have to communicate something about itself which *cannot be readily acquired*. In a more complex understanding of objectivity, Tom Cruise is a flesh-and-blood celebrity who transitions from one appearance/acting role to the next, resulting in a fragmentary and also distant personhood, which to his viewers *does not speak to who he is deep down*. Therefore, when it comes to referential value, Tom Cruise is unstable. Identity, then, relates to the object in that identity also does not guarantee an interior life, thus its surface orientation. An identity can be complex, and Chapter 2 argues that identity has seen incredible depth orientation conveyed through social media, but this is a horizontal complexity, not vertical. A parallel is Nicholas Carr's *The Shallows: What the Internet Is Doing to Our Brains*, which argues the Internet (Google, especially) increases the variety of human knowledge, but impairs people's depth-oriented understanding of that knowledge. This book posits that the same is happening to the subject, but in varying manifestations via different platforms, along a historical trajectory.

Figure 1 explicates subjectivity for this project. Notice the location of "emotion" on the axis: it is near center, but down the y-axis enough to convey that "emotion" is still hampered by ambiguity no matter how performed/mediated that trait has become in postmodernity—yet, paradoxically, its contrivance is still palpable. One of the ancillary goals of this book is to consider the perceived authenticity of human emotion as it has been mediated through consumer platforms, something explored at length in chapters 1 and 3.

In Sherry Turkle's *Alone Together*, a major text in Chapter 2, the mistake Turkle's young test subjects make when they embrace Sony's robot dog AIBO as a living thing, capable of complex emotion, is that the idea of "emotion" or "depth" beyond surface-level performance (virtual performance) is some-

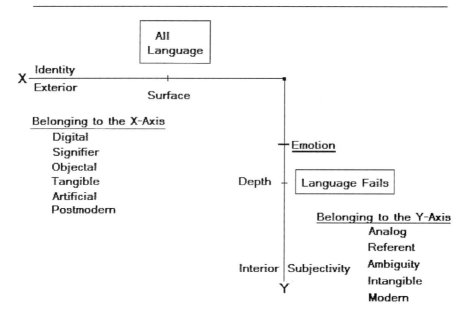

Figure 1. A graphic representation of this book's figuration of subjectivity.

thing that appropriately belongs to the subject. The consequent psychic malady that follows mistaking the object, however potentially convincing that object, for a subject, results in a deep misunderstanding of subjectivity and other people in general. After a series of dark rationalizations from test subject Paree (eight years old), Turkle attempts to explain to Paree how the robot AIBO functions internally, how the machine "projects" emotions rather than feeling them deep down. Indeed, AIBO's functionality only requires *external* stimulation in order to work appropriately; the robot's internal mechanics are completely unrelated to the real world cause-and-effect AIBO reacts to. Instead of accepting what she has been told as proof of AIBO's fraudulence, Paree instead wonders what is so different about what AIBO feels if the external, surface presence of the emotion is still visible. This robot dog, it should be said, can "exhibit" happiness and sadness and pain, among other feelings. In the end, Turkle surmises that, in Paree's view, if "inner states lead to the same outer state" then "inner states cease to matter" (54). Paree's (mis)understanding, an outgrowth of ever more fulfilling technological contrivances, conveys the present articulation of digital subjectivity.

Nowadays, subjectivity must be weighed alongside a historical process of lessening referential value, also associated with the "fragmentation and recombination" attributed to digital technology and the Internet (*My Mother Was a Computer* 212). This process illustrates a distancing effect from substantive and intangible selves to ones that are more closely related to identity, with its surface orientation. As AIBO's "inner state" ceases to matter, so, too, do complexity, interiority—the depth of the subject is mooted by the seduction of surface meaning that has no depth beyond what is readily visible. AIBO whimpers when it is hurt, an irrefutable indication of its pain, whereas non-cybernetic organisms can provide no stable equivalent; the simplicity of surface, then, is quite reassuring. Empathy conceivably convinced Paree of AIBO's actuality, but her ideological disjunction made AIBO *real*.

Why Reality TV, Facebook and YouTube?

ORDINARY PEOPLE

Reality TV, Facebook, and YouTube are the media this book focuses on because they convey the consumption modes of what Deborah Jermyn calls "ordinary people," who are outside the celebrity paradigm, even if their media usage and self-perception is still (directly or indirectly) informed by celebrity status (74). The question of subjectivity is troubled by celebrities in the postmodern era, as *they have breached the subject/object barrier*, according to theorist Chris Rojek. A celebrity's flesh-and-blood actuality makes no difference because audiences admire celebrities from a place of "abstract desire" that results in "psychic damage" because the celebrity remains so far from the fan's (literal or figurative) reach (Rojek 47–48). Even meeting a celebrity in person is no substitute for the already-established perception of their fan—celebrities encompass a mental geography, and layers of mediation, that cannot be destabilized by their flesh, which is why Tom Cruise no matter his humanity is arrested to his surface orientation. However, ordinary people who have not transitioned into "abstraction" still have the potential for depth-oriented subjectivities, either perceived through their own selves or by others; in other words, unlike codified celebrities, ordinary people have not breached the subject/object barrier, even if those people are desirous for that end goal. In light of this ideological circumstance, sometimes their authentic ordinariness can manage to seep through even direct mediation, as was the case in early seasons of MTV's *The Real World*, which is illustrated further in Chapter 1.

A person sitting in front of another, whose reputation carries no reach beyond the mental and physical geography to which the two are constrained, is not abstract: quite the contrary. That other person is fully knowable. This is the "ordinary person." Identification is axiomatic between the two; neither's authenticity is immediately in question. Also, making a distinction between "attributed" celebrity and "achieved" celebrity is helpful in this regard. If people have not spent some portion of their lives being groomed into the celebrity paradigm, then they are not *strictly* celebrities. Susan Boyle, for instance, achieved fame solely as a consequence of appearing on a reality TV show (*Britain's Got Talent*)—this is "attributed" celebrity. Under no other circumstance might this unconventional woman, no matter how talented, have been given worldwide exposure. Internet infamy is also considered attributed celebrity, for which Justin Bieber is example par excellence. This is different from someone like Madonna, who "achieved" her celebrity through complex channels of cultural intermediaries, such as talent agents and others who groomed her into long-lasting and iconic fame. The point, here, is that there are *varying levels of contrivance* to be considered between ordinary people, who perform in their daily lives as a matter of social and cultural circumstance—theirs is a performance of "the everyday self"—and celebrities who perform in a much more exacting/pervasive way.

The Authenticity Problem

Reality TV, YouTube, and Facebook have succumbed to ongoing criticisms about their "authenticity," as is conveyed in their individual chapters. Authenticity's invocation has not necessarily deterred any of these three platforms' consumer engagement; instead viewers/users are having that conversation on top of their normal consumption practices, oftentimes flavoring those practices. The authenticity problem is something illustrated further in this book through specific textual readings, but the notion that authenticity weighs heavily on the minds of America's reality TV viewership is self-evident. Authenticity matters for this project's argument because *subjectivity and authenticity have a symbiotic relationship*. Authenticity is a thing's truthfulness of origin (i.e., referent): this implies that, in order for authenticity's declaration (in the affirmative or otherwise), there must be some process by which the thing in question could possibly have changed. In the case of these three platforms, that particular process is mediation, one which takes various pathways and exists in numerous forms (producorial, technological, etc.) and this mediation, to reemphasize, is of ordinary people. However, the notion of authenticity is contradictory nowadays because authenticity is, in fact, antithetical to postmodernity. Postmodernism is about "lack," "performance," "deconstruction," "play," all ideas which suggest that a truthfulness of origin is an *impossibility* (Hassan, "Toward a Concept of Postmodernism" 6). Yet, viewers and users of these three media persist in their quest for authenticity.

This is not to say that ordinary people have not caught up to contemporary theory, and that they somehow need to be elucidated regarding the "true" inauthenticity of contemporary life. As is argued more fully in the individual chapters, baby boomers and Generation X have already reacted to postmodernism's revelations; at the start of the 21st century, the authenticity demand upon digital media speaks to what has come afterwards—the desire for a *return* to authentic value. This is not to say that such a return is necessarily conceivable, but that desire for it to return exists.

The authenticity problem is by no means unique to 21st-century media. In fact, "authenticity" is a consideration long made by thinkers when postulating on human representation and mediation. This project does not contend that the authenticity problem is somehow a "new" phenomenon, but that it has been exacerbated by digital technologies which lay claim to deeper and deeper degrees of referential value. Actually, the fact that the authenticity problem has a historical backing lessens the exceptional status of troublesome *authentic* platforms such as YouTube. And as is argued more fully later in this book, the technological assertion of authenticity, even amid complex digital mediators, is still highly problematic. Major aspects of this argument are poignantly addressed by historical writings on photography from the 20th century. Chapter 2 draws on Walter Benjamin's "The Work of Art in the Age of Mechanical Reproduction" to establish a foundation for authenticity in 20th-century image world writing. Indeed, as Benjamin states, "the presence of the original is the prerequisite to the concept of authenticity," and photography, with its technological advancement in the "reproduction" of its referent, troubles the necessity for the original's presence (222). The doing away of this necessity, then, mirrors digital mediators such as YouTube and Facebook, whose usage/participation often insinuates the same truth. As example, André Bazin writes in "The Ontology of the Photographic Image," photography "bears away" the "faith" necessary to consume a representation; the representation becomes fact. Bazin continues: "The photographic image is the object itself…. No matter how fuzzy, distorted, or discolored, no matter how lacking, in documentary value the image may be, it shares, by virtue of the very process of its becoming, the being of the model of which it is the reproduction; it is the model" (8). Here, the authenticity problem blossoms from technologies which blur the distinction between representation/referent such that *the question of referential value* no longer weighs on that technology.

Also interesting is how photography ushered in the technological ethos of living "publicly" as opposed to "privately," a very Internet-centric criticism amid the popular conversation. Roland Barthes writes on that subject, "Each photograph is read as the private appearance of its referent: the age of Photography corresponds precisely to the explosion of the private into the public, or rather, into the creation of a new social value, which is the publicity of the private" (98). CCTV, reality TV, and Facebook, among other popular scapegoats, are not the death of privacy; instead, it is useful for this book's overarching argument to accept that privacy either died or ceased to matter in a conventional sense long ago. Privacy and authenticity, to be clear, are not somehow interlinked.

THE VALUE OF ESTABLISHMENT AMONG CONSUMER MEDIA

Also important to this media study and its chosen platforms is one of the lingering issues with contemporary media studies as a whole: obsolescence. Because of the speed of development and endemic ephemerality of media in the 21st century, each new critical text in media studies has a shorter and shorter shelf life. Media critics, then, must find ways to make their writing last longer than the texts and technologies they write about. This project's solution is to focus on *established* media and platforms—meaning, widely and persistently consumed media. A treatise on a hip, new technology has the potential to hit a zeitgeisty wave, propelling it to momentary relevance, but may well be impeded by the shaky promises of *early adoption*. Early media adopters risk much nowadays: a recent (non-academic) example is the optical disc wars of the mid–00s between Toshiba's HD-DVD format and Sony's Blu-ray format. After a few years worth of marketplace quarreling, Blu-ray won out; yet not before many consumers had ventured to buy HD-DVDs and their expensive proprietary playback devices, which have been rendered useless. In conjunction, many analysts predicted the fast-approaching death of Blu-ray in the wake of spiraling physical media sales, as streaming video and cloud storage have basically replaced actual shelf space in people's homes, adding an extra degree of irony to Sony and Toshiba's costly skirmish.

In academic media writing, much consideration was dedicated to 2003's *Second Life*, an online avatar space, which peaked in popularity around the same time Blu-rays entered the public conversation. Sherry Turkle was among many scholars who wrote and researched on *Second Life*. However much that virtual reality space communicated the desires of netizens to indulge in posthumanist virtual role-play, the historical fact is that *Second Life* did not thrive beyond the current onslaught of social media platforms, or engrossing online fantasy games such as *World of Warcraft*, which offers a more structured system of reward for the user. Game theory has focused much time and attention on *World of Warcraft* amid its popularity, though that conversation, too, has begun to wane. This is not to say Turkle's writing on *Second Life* did not transcend that medium, because it has. But as time goes on, her argument will lose merit by proxy as *Second Life* withers into obscurity.

This books approach, however, is not impervious to obsolescence. These arguments will die out as consumer behavior and technologies inevitably change; thus the inherent problem of any writing on popular culture and technology. But considering *volume of usage* betters this project's chances for relevance, especially since a platform such as *Second Life* was considered fringe even during peak usage, due mostly to its stark resemblance to a third-person video game. *Second Life* initially billed itself as an objective-free "virtual world" or "community-driven experience," despite a graphical makeup and esoteric interface that signified the contrary. Non-casual video games tend to alienate older demographics and also require a level of engagement that cannot be replicated easily on a smartphone or other mobile device; most social media platforms are safely and efficiently accessed in subways and night clubs, while *Second Life* requires more prolonged attention and has a greater learning curve. Nowadays, portable technology is privileged among consumers—Facebook is a medium that works well anyplace on any device. Also, Facebook is the most *regularly* accessed social media website in the world and has been so for years after its inception in 2004, though Twitter and (more distantly) Instagram have long been on the heels of Facebook (Alexa). And while YouTube hovers around the third slot in regards to overall Internet popularity, there is no disputing its integral role in contemporary digital consumption modes, which is illustrated at length in Chapter 3. Reality TV's popularity has dwindled since 2000–05, but the inexpensive format has sustained itself in such a way that it still draws solid viewership on basic cable, and has quite literally settled into a zone of "established acceptance" among the television audience, padding out network TV schedules and serving as throwaway entertainment. Chapter 1 considers reality TV as more of a historical document than one which belongs to the immediate zeitgeist.

Looking at *established* media is beneficial, quite obviously, because questioning how an established medium actually garners that status speaks better to cultural milieus and ideologies, far more so than a trendy or fringe medium. Reality TV, Facebook, and YouTube are easily recognizable axioms of the current media climate, and therefore will more likely participate in a recursive dynamic with culture, a principal concern of this project.

Now, a Variety of Consumer Modes: Savvy, Magical, Creative

The awareness (or mere existence) of postmodernity has given way to new consumer modes. The individual chapters explicate three varieties: savvy, magical, and creative. In savvy consumption, the consumer takes pleasure in "not being duped ... they know just how bad things are and just how futile it is to imagine they could be otherwise" (Andrejevic, *Reality TV...* 178). Savvy consumption is the crux of 21st-century reality TV viewership; meaning, "reality" is no longer the dominant issue of reality TV, but rather the knowledge that it fails so fully to represent reality. This impacts the behavior of reality TV on-screen participants in equal measure, who embark on the reality TV enterprise not to affirm their own reality, but instead to become part of that contrivance. And savvy consumers are met by TV producers who take full advantage of the "complacent knowing" involved with savvy consumption, to the extent that those viewers who take pleasure in "not being duped" are, in fact, duped by their ambivalence. These consumers delight in on-screen abjection and the distinct schadenfreude of reality programming. And in expecting no reality and nothing authentic on-screen, savvy consumers are easily coddled by reality TV production that makes no attempt to hide its contrivance. The result is a paradoxical sense of realism and authenticity incurred by the expectation of inauthenticity.

In Chapter 2, this book's second isolated consumer mode emanates from Jean Baudrillard's *magical thinking* of consumers, an idea first posited in his

1977 text *The Consumer Society*. Under "magical thinking," the consumer forgets (or ignores) the ideological and cultural forces by which an object of consumption arrives before them (32). It is a reversal on Marx's alienation of the laborer, in that the consumer, the recipient of the laborer's product, is alienated by the seduction of the object. By way of magical thinking, the consumer is no longer intimately acquainted with the larger context of said object. This kind of consumption occurs amid some digital technology, a point proven by tying magical consumption to N. Katherine Hayles' analysis of contemporary technology which "mystifies" its material reality by signifying complex, emergent operations through simplistic real world signs (*My Mother Was a Computer* 60–61). In the case of Microsoft, they anchor the Windows OS with user-friendly icons such as "the recycling bin" and "folders," rather than invite the consumer into the esoteric, and actual, digital processes by which those signs arrive to them. Through this mystification, the consumer is ignorant of the emergent, unstable digital mechanism supplying their consumption experience; thus, the technology appears magical before a consumer thinking magically.

Creative consumption, a mode discussed primarily in Chapter 3, involves an act which is not dissimilar, but also not indebted to Web 2.0 or the "participatory media" ethos outlined by Henry Jenkins and his contemporaries among New Media scholarship. Creative consumption, according to scholars Jean Burgess and Joshua Green, is meant to communicate both the accelerated potential for "access to culture" and also the ability to "participate as producers" in cultural creation (*YouTube* 14). Those same consumers will engage in what Burgess and Green call "a continuum of cultural participation," which asserts that Web 2.0 creative consumption can vacillate fluidly between *affective* content creation and *profit-driven* content creation, such that the inherent human value of either piece of content has become increasingly indistinguishable (*YouTube* 57). What is more, while creative consumers are imbued with a greater agency than consumers prior to digital technology, those older, 20th-century passive consumption modes have not been left by the wayside; the greater availability of content to consume, via platforms such as YouTube which is a veritable black hole of full motion video, has actually exacerbated passive consumption, and the various economic and producorial hierarchies through which passivity is benefited. The trend nowadays, especially in the public conversation, is to grant the consumer with a style of agency which somehow *trumps* the producer. The discursive goal in Chapter 3 is to challenge that notion through the complexity of creative consumption and the continuum of cultural participation.

Chapter Summaries and Historical Frame of This Book

Chapter 1, "If Only Reality TV Were Not Real: Advertising, Ordinary People and Savvy Consumption," begins by outlining the generational shift in consumers' relationship to televisual media and emphasizing the value of authenticity in burgeoning media forms. After some brief context and historiography on reality television in America, the chapter pinpoints Generation X reality programming, specifically MTV's *The Real World: San Francisco* (1994). The cultural significance of that season, and of reality TV to Gen Xers, conveys a much broader valuation of authenticity/ontology within their shared ethos, which has influenced post-millennium ontology considerations. From there, the chapter transitions into a more recent season of the show, *The Real World: Portland* (2013), to communicate a change in the show's content which reflects a change in off-screen subjectivity, particularly among Generation Y (Millennials). That *mutation* is decidedly postmodern and surface-oriented; as such, this chapter relies heavily on Frederic Jameson's theories regarding late capitalistic postmodernism in order to support the idea that there is a recursive dynamic between reality TV and its off-screen viewership. The chapter supplements textual analysis of more recent episodes of *The Real World* with close readings of other emblematic MTV programming, such as *The Hills*. Once that cultural milieu is established, the chapter defines the content of this surface-oriented subjectivity by reading terse but hyperbolic syndicated program *Maury*, on which hysterical emotions burble amid its densely mediated translation of reality. On-screen subjectivity (and off) develops around those kinds of strictly drawn mediational parameters because, as the chapter proves, reality TV extends beyond its technological boundaries. Lastly, the focus shifts to self-consciously manufactured basic cable reality programming, specifically truTV's *Lizard Lick Towing*, to illustrate the logical conclusion of reality TV subjectivity, entirely surface-oriented, and this is also tied to recent historical and political truths outside the televisual.

Chapter 2, "Ontologies of Facebook: *Catfish* and the Magical Thinking of Consumers," complicates this project's discussion of authenticity to convey how authenticity's prevalence among social media platforms, such as Facebook, has created an environment in which undue *truth value* has been placed upon them by consumers. This, in turn, results in a paradigm through which the subjectivities of their users are deeply susceptible to the interfacial machinations of a given digital medium, not just Facebook, thereby mutating those users. For support, Chapter 2 works with a number of N. Katherine Hayles texts to effectively develop the unstable digital culture Facebook inhabits. The chapter also explicates the history of online social media—from electronic bulletin boards of the 1980s to salacious American Online chat rooms of the 90s—in order to flesh out a consumer ideology which instantiates an *impetus for authenticity*, one that deludes Facebookers into accepting the truth claims of other users at face value. Also included is an interrogation of the cultural phenomenon of "catfish," users faking their online personas on social media, which develops the specifics of how this Facebook authenticity problem manifests itself; close readings of Nev and Ariel Schulman's 2010 documentary *Catfish*, as well as a number of episodes from Nev Schulman's MTV program of the same name, are deployed to further elaborate on these delusions. The chapter's focus is then redirected to the specifics of Facebook users' subjectivities, using MIT psychologist Sherry Turkle as the basis for a discussion of what these subjectivities entail. Indeed, Facebook subjectivity is informed by Turkle's notion of identity/subjectivity conflation among consumers, especially young ones. Facebook identity *appears* complex, as its wealth of identity designations communicate, and this complexity facilitates that conflation. What is more, the platform's general conception of being "closely related" to an off-screen reality, social or otherwise, exacerbates user dupery, which is proven in the chapter using actual Facebook profiles as its textual backing. After giving form to Facebook subjectivity, the chapter argues that consumers' relationship to that platform is part of a historical process, harkening back to mid–20th-century consumer theory by Jean Baudrillard, in that consumers who *ignore* or *purposely forget* the truth of their consumption practices prompt their own submission to the authenticity problem.

Another reason users are convinced of Facebook's truth claims has to do with the democratization of media, part of the Web 2.0 ideology which says, essentially, that the consumer dictates/produces worthwhile media content. Since the Internet's reemergence after the dot com bubble burst at the turn of the millennium, netizens have proudly touted the consumer's victory over corporations and hierarchical production modes—this assuredly enhances democratic media's authenticity quotient, also bolstering its truth value. The power dynamics which keep reality TV participants on the outside of that mediational process, for instance, are supposedly subverted and conquered on democratic media such as Facebook but, more so, YouTube.

While users are comparably more laborious in their consumption on

Web 2.0 platforms, Chapter 3, "How YouTube Subjectivizes: Vlogging, Hauls and Creative Consumption," argues for a more nuanced conception of democratized media; the consumer is not victorious necessarily, but instead engages what Jean Burgess and Joshua Green designate a "continuum of cultural participation" *informed* by hierarchical consumer capitalism (Burgess and Green, *YouTube* 57). YouTube is a perfect showcase for this consumer mode, as users/creators vacillate between affective and capitalist communication. They express themselves into their web cams in order to reach out across space and time to feel alongside and through their viewers/subscribers, but also do so to achieve a YouTube partnership with Google so they might share in the advertising revenue accrued through their personal videos. Chapter 3 illustrates this mode by tracing the brief history of YouTube, isolating a notorious instance in 2006 involving YouTuber LonelyGirl15 who duped viewers into thinking she was a "real" video blogger (vlogger) but was actually a formally trained actress *produced* to seem affective and real to the YouTube audience. This example of outright fakery is followed by a YouTuber entirely outside the traditional production hierarchy, Emily aka paytotheorderofofof2. The chapter juxtaposes her conveyance with LoneyGirl15's in order to isolate their differences technically, aesthetically, and emotionally. From there, the chapter transitions into "haul" videos, in which YouTubers display their recent purchases, to argue that YouTube's affective encounters are tempered by this continuum of cultural participation on the service. As the lines blur between consumer capital and consumer affection, one contaminates the other resulting in a mutation of all subjectivities involved: viewer, creator, and YouTube commenter. The chapter engages all of these consumer types on YouTube to expand that key point of *mutation* expressed throughout. Chapter 3 ends with some close readings of a few ASMR (autonomous sensory meridian response) videos, which feature visual role-play and three-dimensional sound experiments in order to convey the paradoxical consumer, trying to "reclaim" genuine affect amid the schizophrenia of expression on YouTube.

In the conclusion, "Beyond Reality TV, Facebook and YouTube," the book expands its media purview by discussing issues among other popular digital platforms, such as Snapchat and Twitter, to identify the mentality of those whose media literacy, at times, can get in the way or ignore the determiners which mutate subjectivity in the digital age. The conclusion employs Svetlana Boym's theory on nostalgia and nationalism to discuss the power of nostalgia working within the ontology considerations of digital consumption, and tempers the romanticization of hackers and digital transgression—transgressions, it should be said, often executed by those dreaming to be at the top of the hierarchy such as Silicon Valley nobleman Mark Zuckerberg. The conclusion's outcome calls for *critical distance* amongst present day consumption practices.

The specific historical frame of this project is shaped by media from the late 20th century on into the 2010s. So the cultural generations this project encompasses are the baby boomer and Generation X dichotomy (reality TV), discussed in Chapter 1, and also Millennials (Web 2.0 platforms), the generational preoccupation of the other two chapters.[1] Web. 2.0, or democratic media ideology, dispenses an *ideal* of "free and open," bottom-up consumerism. Supposedly pre-democratic media, such as TV, tends to be traditionally hierarchical, with consumers squarely at the bottom. The result of investigating this cultural range is the revelation of Millennials' subjective interiority, as their relation to the digital regime is comparably more intimate (and axiomatic) than previous generations. Millennials are hyperbolized in their depiction both within the academic conversation and the popular one. Some believe Millennials' deep engagement with digital media is to blame for their superficiality and stupidity (Mark Bauerlein), while others are certain their technological literacy will usher in new advances in humanity (Douglas Rushkoff). This project does not attempt to advance either side of this binary, as Millennials' mediation and resulting subjective status, not intellectual status, are its principal concern, though these characterizations flavor all arguments regarding the Millennial generation. This project does accept that Millennials' relation to digital consumer technology is significant and fundamental to the construction of their selfhood. It traces the mediation of self along the "value chain" of the cultural industries, as consumer power positions have shifted. In contemporary consumer culture "author" and "producer" have been overridden by amateur consumer creators, and media consumption has evolved from a "read-only" activity to a "read and write" one (Hartley, *Television Truths* 27). As a result, Millennials' subjectification *relies* on digital technology.

1

If Only Reality TV Were Not Real

Advertising, Ordinary People and Savvy Consumption

Which is why *Real Housewives* reigns as the Grand Poobah of reality series. It is a glitzy window into mainstream values, if not mainstream lifestyle. It offers more insight into American consciousness than most TV scripted dramas. We just have to be willing to see ourselves in it.

—Kareem Abdul-Jabbar, "How *The Real Housewives* Have Made America Better"

PBS' *An American Family* did not start a television trend in 1973. It is the first recognizably exhibitionist, fishbowl-style factual TV program, one in which the conceit is to capture (or manufacture) some real social or professional world. It would be years before its format would be embraced on a wide scale. Part of the issue here was that *An American Family* was met by palpable backlash during its initial run. Many critics were repulsed by the notion of viewing the downfall of the Loud family in full motion; their divorce, their son's coming out of the closet—it was exploitative, critics argued. These were intimate moments, someone else's emotion possessions. The 19th-century bourgeois panic regarding public and private spheres was now invigorated by TV. Worthy of note is that this show was more sober than the reality programs seen on television today, it being PBS, yet the flames of criticism burned anyway. *An American Family* was an exceptional kind of TV experience which evoked an exceptional response. Only the BBC dared to replicate the show, though the BBC's tradition of documentary gave little precedence to a front row glimpse into domesticity. The critical reaction related to the show's breach of familial intimacy was little acknowledged by

27

a viewing public eager to explore ever deeper chasms of invasive reality programming. The question, then, is why *An American Family*'s production process took so long to finds its way into the American television mainstream: costs were cheap, similar to today's reality shows, and drama required little to no prodding, just years of anxious emotional buildup for camera crews to stumble onto (or encourage).

In 1992, Mary-Ellis Bunim and Jonathon Murray's *The Real World*, which was directly influenced by the Louds, premiered on MTV. *The Real World* lacked the sobriety of its PBS forbearer, mostly because the young people featured on the show had little need for restraint—sex, ideology, and squabbles (often a consequence of ideology) were the focal point. These were not the intimate details of a suburban American family. For viewers, *The Real World* was never truly about demeaning some sacred barrier between the public and private, but, rather, the potentiality of a world in which that bourgeois ideology was nonexistent. What followed was a love affair with real people doing comparably real things inside a box in the living room that was not synonymous with reality, and society was left to deal with all the critical problems that arose consequently. Never mind the kitschy talk shows, *The People's Court*, and Fox's *Cops* which had already broadcasted realness into American homes since the 80s; it was *The Real World* that serialized the format, gave reality TV its now-familiar trashy-voyeur flavor. By the new millennium, the reality style championed by Bunim and Murray had not only spawned a variety of offshoots, but was now dominating the airwaves, with CBS' reality competition *Survivor* achieving larger viewership numbers than any reality show prior. By 2001, *Survivor* was averaging 28.8 million viewers on network television; scripted rival *Friends* on NBC could only muster 22.1 (Rice 22). And the 2000s were the apex of nationally-televised reality programs.

In contrast, 2013's network television maxed out at 18–20 million viewers during premier season, not including event TV such as the Super Bowl which always claims more viewers per event but is not even in the same realm of sustained television consumption as *Survivor*. NBC's *The Voice* and Fox's *American Idol*, two singing competition shows, were the most reliably successful network reality programs airing in 2013, but viewership numbers only averaged at or below 15 million. Scripted multi-camera sitcom *The Big Bang Theory* (approximately 19–20 million viewers) and crime procedural *NCIS* (approximately 19–20 million viewers), both airing on CBS, were America's most popular shows of 2013, and topped the Nielson ratings with the premiere of every new episode. In the 2010s, reality TV has found a more comfortable home on basic cable networks, where *The Real World* originated. Generally lower television viewership these days is more a consequence of the Internet than anything else; most Digital Natives, born in the 1990s, scoff at the notion of sitting in front of a TV, and consider DVRs exempt from the TV paradigm.[1] For them, consuming "TV," a distinction that belongs to an earlier media generation, is tied to commercial breaks. What they fail to realize is that the medium of television, commercials and all, shapes the narrative beats of a show, whether they are watching on Blu-ray, streaming video, or DVR. Streaming service Netflix, for instance, premiered an original series in 2013 starring Kevin Spacey called *House of Cards*; individual episodes do not exceed an hour, action rises and falls at a strict pace, and cliffhangers abound. While beats built around commercial breaks and network mandated episode orders artificially intrude on televisual narratives, these beats have become normalized to the extent that streaming shows which do not abide by that standard feel somewhat off. So even freed from the tether of commercial breaks, television shows are inflected by traditional modes of advertising and the need to keep viewers attached to their boxes, whether that box is technically a TV or not. Historically, TV is a mass medium which has configured not just a "particular spectacle" but the potentiality of "all spectacles," even those disseminated by newer technologies (Baudrillard, *The Consumer Society* 123). Indeed, TV's mark on contemporary digital consumer products and platforms is substantial; the direct integration of advertising into Facebook, for instance, is only tolerable because that invasive gesture was already made commonplace by TV production and consumption.

The early 1990s proved to be the most significant generational marker for reality TV's development and later success. This is a matter of cultural circumstance. Frederic Jameson, in 1984, asserted that American subjectivities had yet to evolve alongside all the postmodern consumer goods and art they were creating and becoming intimately involved with. He writes on 80s consumer culture: "there has been a mutation in the object unaccompanied as yet by any equivalent mutation in the subject" (39). From Jameson's critical position, this *lack* of mutation was a positive phenomenon because the subject, then a product of the post–World War II baby boom or their parent, was in a position to feel a kind of *unnerving dissonance* when encountering the distinctly American postmodern objects Jameson opined about, and this would make them keenly aware of late capitalism's fraudulence, inauthenticity, and preoccupation with surface.[2] Jameson was assigning a lexicon to the eerie revelations that followed a trip to Las Vegas, to a contemporary art museum: schizophrenia, pastiche, historical amnesia, pure material signifiers. In Jameson's writings on postmodernity from the 80s, the world of creativity and representation had become a consumer landfill devoid of meaning, but then there were still enough people hip to that notion, savvy baby boomers who felt as uncomfortable as he did.

Yet the offspring of the baby boomer generation—Gen Xers—were a different matter, especially in light of Frederic Jameson's cultural chronology. Taking Jameson's late capitalist model as inviolable here, it is only natural that generations after his own might be interpellated more fully into a system of blind consumption. Born in the early 60s through 1979, Gen X culture was one typified by the AIDS epidemic, grunge music, rampant nihilism, the Gulf War. Theirs was a generation whose cynical reputation preceded them, and it was the perfect kind of ontological void for consumption to fill. Sometimes called the MTV generation, what Generation X lacked, as uncontested consumerism tightened its grip, was the critical distance necessary to ostensibly *understand* late capital motifs. Though Generation X generally enjoyed the idea of social change and were outraged quite a bit, that outrage was not about the things they consumed, but the people in charge—the people most likely profiting (overtly or otherwise) from the consumer goods that gave their life meaning. In 1993, MTV's Rock the Vote, a nonprofit youth voter advocacy group, directly aided passing the National Voter Registration Act, propelling the voice of MTV viewership to the forefront of American political discourse. Here, the significance of its passing has less to do with the content of the Act than Rock the Vote's principal financier: Virgin Records executive Jeff Ayeroff. This is an appropriate metaphor for much of Generation X (and thereafter) consumer ideology. Down with the man, Gen Xers said, but not at the expense of our boom boxes and Macintoshes and cable TV. Gen Xers reversed the idea that civic awareness and material minimalism went hand-in-hand. In turn, they could experience the feverish highs of protest and anti-establishment angst without making any sacrifices to their consumer lifestyle. Hippies they were not.

Though previous generations had been gradually losing themselves to the irresistible magnetism of televisual entertainment, Generation Xers found the TV imbued with meaning-making abilities, elicited by the promise of realism. Marshall McLuhan was fearful kids would practice *depth model* consumption with TV, a medium he considered unsuited to that kind of involvement. For the youngest viewers, McLuhan believed television to have "a dimension almost of sacredness" that "involves us in moving depth, but does not excite, agitate or arouse" (336–37). In *depth model* consumption, television invites children into a mysticism of mediation which does not overtly call them to question it. And by 1992, thirty years after McLuhan's writing, *Sesame Street* (1969-ongoing) was raising Generation X, MTV was interpellating them in their adolescence, and *The Real World* was putting them on display. They were reflecting on being themselves by watching themselves on TV. Generation X scholar Dan Leidl fondly remembers the influential television of his childhood: "*Sesame Street* was accessible…. We were showered with culture and content that had never been accessed so collectively and completely before. From this one program, much of our childhood and adolescence was spun, establishing a blueprint for how we interacted with media throughout much our lives" (xiv). In this circumstance, TV acts as a tool of subjective referentiality, a means by which to understand the mind and self, and thus retains the "sacredness" warned of by McLuhan.

This is all to say that Generation X consumer subjectivities mutated alongside their objects, encouraged by the flickering box in the living room. Television depth was human depth. Jameson's fears had become reality: there was no more dissonance about postmodernity, just outright acceptance. Reality TV was *not* a strictly fictional television narrative about some distant person living a faraway kind of life: these were *their* stories, or at least what MTV wanted Gen Xers to believe their stories to be. And if they disagreed with what they saw on MTV, or found it phoney or cheap, then it was a matter of saying, "Well, I'm more real than that!" And this is a desirable reaction for producers, because the viewership seems to already be questioning their own realness, and the television made them do it. How do they rectify the fraudulence they see on TV? Attend casting calls for reality shows, try for their shot on *The Real World*, then surely everyone will see how real they are. It is in this cyclical pattern that today's digital subjectivity finds its roots: in order to engage the frauds of popular online spaces, users upload response videos to YouTube, post retaliatory memes, and participate in prolonged message board and Twitter scuffles—many of which are flavored by oppositional ideologies. As with Generation X and TV, an internal drive to engage media, especially to correct some ideological or moral "wrong," communicates a McLuhan-esque *depth model* media response. Within this model, the user's depth in consumption, then, coaxes them into believing their exchange was not entirely predicated on that medium's existence. In the case of reality TV, a participant's "realness" is not hinged upon their technological mediation, but somehow, quite falsely, themselves. How this operation works on the mind McLuhan configures as a "subliminal state of Narcissus trance," in which the ego invests in media consumption (15).

But this complements the televisual consumer enterprise. James B. Twitchell argues that "branding, packaging, and even the act of shopping itself are now the central meaning-making acts in our postmodern world" (14). Consumption itself defines individual complexity today, which gives voice to human subjectivity. And when MTV promised *realism* that meant not only could their Generation X viewership, which finds meaning in the consumer products around them, consume real people but they too could be consumed as a real thing. Mediated through reality TV, Gen Xers could be like the consumer object, just as revered, just as meaningful, and that is reality. As such, the hermeneutical act of Gen X reality TV viewers permitted the "objectal form [to be] taken as a clue or a symptom for some vaster reality which replace[d] itself as the ultimate truth" (Jameson 8). More simply, mediated televisual representations of reality encroached on viewers' understanding of reality outside it, and, consequently, their relation to that reality. Hence, the ontological void postmodernism gave way to was being conceivably rectified by new genres of "democratic" TV programming, in which ordinary people dissolved into the televisual diegesis under the guise of consumerism. In view of Jean Baudrillard's critical gaze, the Loud family encouraged him to believe that TV destabilized the distinction between "subject and object," and MTV's Bunim and Murray reaped to great effect the consumptive rewards of that destabilization (*Simulacra & Simulation* 30).

By the time *The Real World* hit the airwaves, television was no longer an alienating spectacle, it was an organic part of subjectivity. As such, being on reality television was and is the submission of ordinary people to a hierarchical consumer system in order to become like the commodities which give their postmodern lives meaning. The specifics of this reside in reality TV's place in the current system of media consumption. Television is distinct from other forms of full motion, visual representation such as theatrical films because it has been dominated by and found its meaning within and around advertising. TV shows that get produced are done so with the hope that advertisers will want to shill their wares during commercial breaks or through product placement. Is this particular show's audience a niche for Life Alert? Does the 18–34 male demographic care about Vanilla Coke? Movies are made with far less collaborative monetary considerations, unless it is a tentpole Disney movie or the newest superhero adventure. In that way, TV has (and still does) exhibit a comparatively high degree of producorial control.[3] Content decisions are made every day at television studios based solely on the support of one or another advertiser. In contrast, for a Hollywood movie, whatever sells, sells, whether Walmart has a stake in it or not. So unlike what consumers might experience on more democratized Internet platforms, the lines between producer and consumer on television *have not* effectively blurred. Television is inextricably linked to old models of consumption that dominated the 20th century in which production was far beyond the consumer's grasp. Even into the 2010s, much of television production is mysterious and top-down, which is why conspiracy theories regarding reality TV run rampant.

For instance, MTV's *Parental Control*, a reality dating show airing from 2005 to 2010, is the subject of a dense, conspiratorial debate online and elsewhere regarding its fakery. The premise of *Parental Control* revolves around a given teenager or young adult whose relationship with their significant other their parents find dissatisfactory, usually to hyperbolic and hilarious effect. The parents, then, are allowed to cherry pick potential alternatives (selected through an open casting call put out by MTV) in the hopes that their teenager will choose one of them over their current partner. The conspiracies around this show peak with extremes such as "It is totally fake." More middling reactions read similarly to "The parents are not even related to the kid. That house shown is not theirs. Everyone is an actor," etc., etc. These conspiracies are typically hinged on the idea that there is an army of writers, actors, editors, and location scouts waiting in the wings to manufacture the *Parental Control* narrative, except that the logistics of these conspiracies are predicated on a fairly large operating budget. The show does have a phony stiffness to it, mostly because the producers are trying to squeeze three separate romantic dates and then an elimination round into twenty-two minutes of air-time; the structure of the show is tighter than its content can maintain. Four of these episodes, it should be said, are meant to round out an afternoon programming block. But MTV is notorious for filling its schedule with low-cost reality fare precisely because they are *not* willing to pay actors and writers and the like. "Pseudo-reality" is the best way to describe shows that are as contrived as *Parental Control*, but make no mistake, professional televisual "acting" is not part of these on-screen participants' repertoire.

A TV show, reality included (if not especially), is a packaged good; it has to be in order to fit whatever mold an advertiser might need, and whatever that need might be is what the show's parent network needs, and these needs weigh on the lower-tier show runners and producers whose creative agency collapses under this top-down configuration. *Parental Control*, in its excessive mediation, functions as a literal translation of this problematic hierarchy. That is not to say that television is incapable of deep, intriguing stories, of capturing enduring narratives, but that those types of shows must first fill some monetary requirement in order to exist.[4] And sometimes packaged goods can be truly affective works of art—whether something's status as "art" is troubled among cultural elitists makes no difference to the ordinary consumers whose socioeconomic/educational backgrounds might not permit such considerations. A seventeen-year-old watching MTV should not be expected to emotionally react only when embraced by the sounds of a philharmonic orchestra; armies of teenagers cry hysterics forever and on in the face of the "lowest" of culture, from One Direction to The Beatles.

Negotiating Mediation on The Real World: San Francisco *(1994)*

Season three of *The Real World*, which aired in the summer of 1994, elevated the show from its meager trash TV status by garnering tangible social relevance; it was zeitgeistian and political, tinged by the anxieties plaguing the generation featured on-camera and consuming the show on their couches. Set in San Francisco, the focal point of the season was twenty-two-year-old cast member Pedro Zamora, a gay Cuban-American whose AIDS diagnosis propelled him to activism on a national scale. Pedro's abjection underscored his every speech act, which flowed through his fellow roommates and irrevocably influenced the narrative of the show. Producorial control landed Pedro in that house, but there was no saying how his roommates might react to him, never mind the stigma that still resided in the American imagination regarding the disease, never mind his homosexuality. Pedro succumbed to AIDS one day after the final episode of season three aired on MTV.

To be sure, season three of *The Real World* was more relevant by design. Bunim and Murray had tried underwriting ideology and generational significance into the show before Pedro Zamora, but never had the corporeal gone along with the ideological in such a severe way; race, sexuality, and religion had been broached prior to season three, but Pedro was dying on-camera, so preceding (and proceeding) seasonal content feels feeble by comparison. In episode eight, Pedro goes to a local clinic to check on lab results; the nurse tells Pedro his T Cell count has dropped to thirty-two, far lower than a healthy person's, very dangerous for someone already so weak. The nurse lets Pedro know he should take extra precaution: "The numbers can't tell you how to feel," the nurse says. "On the other hand, this is a warning sign for you that you need to take really good care of yourself." In the following scene, Pedro is riding a public bus, alone, vacantly staring out the window while wispy, non-diegetic 90s music plays in the background (MTV's massive catalog of licensed music means there is a tune to go along with every narrative beat). Then, the viewer sees Pedro inside his room back at *The Real World* house, taking off his shirt in front of the window. The foreground is darkened, his thinning torso is accentuated. In a following scene, when he tells his roommates of his current condition, there is more than enough deer in the headlights stupor to go around; it is young people watching another young person die, and there is no literal kind of acting when it comes to that emotional response. And the teenagers at home watch Pedro while the roommates watch Pedro.

Pedro's plight and his roommates' empathy is the kind of affective "embodied human encounter" that gives reality TV depth beyond its producorial manipulation; this is emotional authenticity as a consequence—or, more aptly, in spite of—a manufactured circumstance (Biressi and Nunn 98). Season three of *The Real World*'s conceit might be fake, but the emotional response is not. Real human emotion does not end because of mediation, consumerism, or producorial manipulation; accompanied by the TV, these on-screen subjects signify an internal mutation, and not one devoid of complexity. The tears of a rejected contestant on the set of ABC's *The Bachelor* are not deposited there by some mechanical apparatus or set personnel on the sidelines holding a dropper. Quite the contrary: reality TV is a newfound emotional breeding ground, and the emotions that are felt within these manufactured circumstances speak to a high level of comfort with the entire reality TV mediational process. But it is more than comfort, though, as emotional display grants actual, subjective status. The televisual experience of emotion provides its adherents a *reference of self*, which John Corner sees occurring as part of the "selving" process of reality TV consumption and participation—this is when "true selves" emerge from the "routinized performance involved in everyday and occupational relations" (51, 62). In the right circumstances, reality TV production grants subjective interiority and emotional depth through various systems of relation—relations, it should be said, to the mediated on-screen self, to the off-screen viewer, and to the lives informed by these texts. However, not all reality TV should be treated as genuinely affective. This point is elaborated on later in this chapter in relation to truTV programming; similarly to MTV's *Parental Control, degrees* of mediation/producorial intervention should be considered. But if viewers' and participants' subjectivities have undergone a mutation alongside reality TV, then it stands to reason their emotions have as well.[5]

The interesting thing about the initial conflict in season three is that Pedro's sexuality and disease are never the overt fire starters. It is typical for *The Real World* to include young people of varied ideological/socioeconomic/ethnic backgrounds in its narrative,[6] and this almost always leads to eventual roommate tension. Season three is no different. Cast member Rachel Campos, a Catholic Republican, makes it known within the first episode via confessional footage that she finds Pedro's sexuality and disease unnerving, but spends the season worrying more about her love life than anything overtly ideological. However, season three resonates because the inane and the domestic prove to be most important to the internal conflict. And this shading guarantees believability because the perceived realism of many reality TV shows is the endless recitation of the trivial and rote elements of consumer life. At the turn of the millennium, much of the appeal of CBS' *Big Brother*, for instance, was watching people cleaning up after each other, lounging around, brushing their teeth; it was a new kind of TV viewing that had little to do with conventional entertainment value—the "entertainment" was seeing someone else do the banal things the audience does daily, free of any dramatic arc, which brought a degree of validation to their own humdrum lives. The webcam has funneled much of this (anti) entertainment impulse online, uploaded onto YouTube, where it lives on more as a consumer identification activity than an entertainment one.

From early on in season three, Pedro makes it very clear that he is a hygienic person, which can be surmised as having something to do with his AIDS, though he never outrightly states this on-camera. There are scenes of Pedro wiping down the kitchen, sweeping, making his bed. His confessional footage features comments of his regarding the suspect condition of the communal bathroom. Pedro is most repulsed by fellow roommate David "Puck" Rainey, a San Francisco bike messenger who is taped multiple times blowing "snot rockets" onto the streets, whose body odor is the subject of disdain by all his roommates, whose dirt-filled fingernails are a point of interest for the film crew. In episode two, when Pedro is seen snacking on a peanut butter bagel with his back turned in the kitchen, Puck swoops in from behind and takes a dollop from the Jiff jar, quickly sucking it off his dirty finger before walking away. Pedro turns around and demands to know if Puck took some, asking, "Did you put your finger in there?" Puck denies. The footage tells a different story, even though some of the action is left to the imagination. Pedro brings up Puck's filthy thievery at a house meeting later on that day, and everyone quickly gangs up on Puck, who goes on to serve as antagonist par excellence before being asked to leave the house in episode eleven.

The war between the two roommates, Pedro and Puck, is considered by many the catalyst for *The Real World*'s Generation X significance. What speaks in their squabbling is not ideology—that is an undercurrent—but instead inanity. Would Pedro have gotten as upset over the peanut butter if he had not contracted AIDS? Barring any natural fastidiousness, probably not. Yet that fact is never mentioned. And when the house takes pot shots at Puck later, criticizing his aversion to soap and his body odor, the conclusion is never that someone with an impaired immune system lives amongst them, whose exposure to germs literally threatens his life, but that Puck is just lacking social propriety and acts selfishly. There is a distinct content difference here that strictly fictional characters cannot possess; typically, it would be *out of place* for two roommates to argue about peanut butter in a scripted, primetime drama, in terms of that argument functioning as a narrative propellant. Reality TV relies on the inane and the domestic to articulate a different kind of character, more authentic and subjective. Stella Bruzzi, in contrasting documentary film and reality television, finds that there is no "extended ideological message" to extrapolate from reality TV content (139). This is a very purposeful decision, to leave overtly ideological commentary by the wayside. Even though Bunim and Murray seem bent on staging the attendant war of words two ideologically-opposed cast members will inevitably have on their show, petty semantics are instead where the direct conflict finds itself. This reflects the conditions of the viewership, whose daily confrontations will never boil down to pure ideology and will remain on the surface—not doing the dirty dishes substitutes for a feminist treatise, a passive aggressive e-mail to a boss substitutes for a proletariat revolt.

Reality TV owes much of its perceived realism (or lack thereof) to being just as boring and toothless as modern life; its viewership uses this banal realism as the basis for an identification activity already mentioned in this chapter: The idea that because "ordinary" people appear on-screen, then the viewer, too, can be *elevated* to whatever exceptional status a television character holds. "I can be like them," the viewer might say. However, when "realistic" banality is shifted to the forefront, and narrative structure becomes an afterthought, similar to *Big Brother* or amateur YouTube videos, then the experiential shift for viewers is more than just one of entertainment value, but also in how they internalize what they see on the screen. Watching ordinary people brush their teeth on YouTube is about something different than a straight identification activity; rather than being *elevated*, as on reality TV, viewers are *equated* with these amateur, on-screen subjectivities. The result, then, is that the two subjective elements in that televisual consumption exercise—the active subject viewing and the mediated on-screen subjectivity—are indistinguishable; this is not, strictly speaking, an "identification" ("I am like them") as much as it is a *recognition*. What is more, reality TV does not deploy an "ethos" that "inspires a new kind of subjectivity which transforms all consumers into potential authors," because reality TV participants are an exception, lifted high by its hierarchy of production (Henry Jenkins, "What Happened Before YouTube" 116). So the reality TV subject is not viewers' equivalent, but not far from their reach.

Where the ideological does find some direct articulation on reality TV is in the *confessional*. Bunim and Murray pioneered the technique in season two of *The Real World*, and it has since been replicated by any number of reality shows. And the confessional works nearly the same as one in a Catholic church, which held "liberatory" powers, in Michel Foucault's assessment, except that a camera functions as the guilt-inducer instead of a priest, and maybe a more effective one at that.[7] Sometimes confessional footage is just solitary cast members facing the camera, reflecting on a recent occurrence, and other times they are discussing a past event after watching a clip or being reminded of what happened during taping by producers; in the second case, the use of tenses becomes very important for continuity because confessional footage will be edited into the show as if the cast member were commenting live or nearly live on the event, so often no past tense is allowed.[8] The confessional on *The Real World* happens both ways. For non-producer mediated confessional footage, there is a booth or sectioned off room in *The Real World* house with a mounted camera and a switch to turn it off and on. In the heat of the moment, cast members will sometimes barrel into the room and let loose their anger, disgust, or elation with whatever is currently happening in the house; the cast is contractually obligated to spend at least some time in the confessional, but is not required to use it freely—this occurs naturally as show participants become more deeply involved in their own mediation. In some instances, especially when they have been drinking, multiple cast members will use the confessional room at a time.

As tensions climax in season three, Puck gradually withdraws from his fellow roommates, spending copious time outside the house and sparking tedious arguments for the sake of his power position—by the time he is booted from the house, Puck is assuredly a force to be reckoned with, so his power play works but not in his favor. Rachel admits outright that Puck is all she talks about in her confessionals, complaints mostly, as Pedro breaks down in front of his roommates, demanding they pick either himself or Puck to stay for the duration of the season. And it is not a matter of morality or ethics that got Pedro to this point, but instead Puck's repeated breach of the ubiquitous social contract. To be fair, Puck does exhibit some homophobic attributes, making a few gay jokes, and a lack of empathy for Pedro's circumstance. While Pedro gives an AIDS awareness presentation at Stanford with some of the roommates in attendance, Puck does not flinch when asked if he felt bad about not going to see it: "I don't need to be educated by Pedro," Puck says. "I would never go out like Pedro anyway. If I did have AIDS I'd be in, like, the South of France and Switzerland and Nepal and then I'd die." But it is in the confessional where Puck is more than just glib about Pedro. He considers Pedro's public presentation of his sexuality to be a bit conspiratorial and performative.

After Pedro and his boyfriend Sean Sasser, another AIDS activist, announce their engagement in episode nine, the roommates, even conservative Rachel, congratulate them and offer encouragement. While this goes on, Puck is shown washing his face in the bathroom, actively avoiding Pedro. Then, Puck appears in the confessional amidst a self-reflexive moment: he configures Pedro's engagement within a sort of "in your face" or "controversial" context, as if the cameras are influencing/encouraging Pedro's actions. "I question their motives for actually getting engaged," Puck tells the camera, air quoting the word "engagement." This comes after a restaurant scene between Pedro and Sean where they have an intensely sober conversation about Pedro's life expectancy, and Pedro and Sean do end up getting married later on in the season. But to question whether they do so for the cameras says more about Puck's ideological reservations than their marriage. And even if they are performing the marriage as some form of televised activism rather than a genuine emotional event, Puck's answer to their engagement happens in episode ten when he announces his own engagement to Toni, a woman he had literally met just a few days earlier in the park. In the confessional, Puck remarks on this new turn of events: "Boy, they're just gonna be like really stunned at the whole thing, and whatever Pedro's trying to do by announcing, 'Oh, I'm engaged to my lover,' that's what I got, okay? This is by far sicker than that. Way sicker, man. 'Cause I'm sicker than Pedro." Puck shoots devil horns at the camera while communicating his engagement's "sickness."

Puck's hasty engagement could be interpreted as a homophobic reaction to Pedro's forthcoming nuptials, depending on the ideological vantage point of the viewer, but the subtext of noting his own engagement's "sick" quality is not conventionally ideological; instead, Puck is imposing his *own assumptions* regarding the reality TV platform onto Pedro's life choices. In light of Puck's accusation of performance, it is worth noting that the filmed/edited footage of Pedro's wedding announcement does not appear explicitly as showboating. When he and Sean make their wedding announcement to *The Real World* house, Pedro is blushing and coy about the whole proceedings, though Sean indulges some pre-marital gloating.

Puck's engagement reads as an egoistic move. Puck just wants to be the center of attention. He wants to be the controversial one in the house, not Pedro. And who is the "they" Puck seems concerned about? Excluding Pedro, his perceived nemesis, there is a distinct lack of proper nouns in Puck's confession. He could be referring to his roommates, who he has mixed feelings about, but also—and more likely—the viewing audience. If Pedro's motivation to marry Sean is not pure of intent, a show for the cameras, as Puck sees it, his only logical move is to do the same and drop the plausibility entirely. At least Sean and Pedro had known each other for some time prior to filming. In fact, Puck's engagement to Toni is so blatantly provocative that Puck has to deal with immediate backlash from the women of *The Real World* house, who do not take his matrimonial flight of whimsy so lightly. After Puck brags to conservative Rachel about his newfound relationship status, she storms off and tells him outright that his marriage is "sensational," which Puck does not deny.

This ideological moment for Puck is not strictly about social or political ideology, but entertainment, celebrity, exposure—a contradictory mixture that consists of his self-aggrandizing desires and the desires of the viewing audience to capture him, a fact that does not escape his purview. And Puck confesses from within this dynamic. His roommates' displeasure with his behavior emanates less so from Puck, the off-camera human being, and more so from who he self-consciously tries to represent. He repeatedly insists, using the third person, that "The Puck," extreme dirtball bike messenger, is the person his roommates are getting, but this assertion fails to ground his personality and instead enforces a protean sense of who he is. At various points up until episode eleven, Puck is empathetic, even vulnerable, especially during a trip to his grandmother's house in episode four. Yet, when faced with conflict, Puck has moments of reactionary hyperbole, where he plays up the representational version of himself to try and deflect and uphold any challenge to his on-screen self, "The Puck." He cannot be weak because weakness is antithetical to him being "extreme," and this extremity is what Puck lays claim to again and again in the confessional, in the private moments between himself and the camera. This is why Puck refuses to be filmed while his roommates formally request he leave the house because his dismissal signifies defeat; their request to him occurs over speaker phone, as Puck takes shelter in Toni's apartment knowing full well the house has been plotting this action. And this circumstance was a direct result of his representational self "The Puck," undoubtedly. In fact, even though he says he will see the roommates one last time when he comes by the house to remove his things, *The Real World* producers never provide this footage, probably because Puck demanded it not be filmed. Instead, the last glimpse of Puck on season three is of him pedaling his bike up the hilly streets of San Francisco, with voice over from confessional footage laid over it, in which he calls his roommates "casualties."

As experienced through *The Real World*, Puck, by all accounts, is at odds with a reductive representation of himself, who he thinks he is, and who he *really* is (both are imagined); the result is an on-screen character complex, infuriating, and contradictory. Indeed, there are layers of mediation—including the mediation he imposes on himself—which Puck contends with. In a telling moment from season three, Puck criticizes his roommates for watching Fox's *90210* (the teen soap that peaked in popularity in the early 1990s), saying they are all television addicts, brain-washed, that he is a free thinker for not watching television, which Puck considers wholly contrived. The irony that this condemnation goes on in front of television cameras, to be watched on television, does not elude him. Puck is media literate and consequently resistant to the production process to which he has willingly submitted himself. But the social conditions of having seven twenty-something strangers trapped together in a house,[9] especially when they have done little of this kind of living before, creates a tension between Puck's expectation of MTV fakery and fabrication, which he believes he can manipulate, and his off-camera emotions.

Here, *The Real World* explicates a larger paradigm: reality TV occurs at a crossroads between the off-screen social/emotional world and the technological consumer world, and reality TV *thrives* on this. In execution, as was the case with David "Puck" Rainey in 1994, the result is (purposeful) dissonance. It is what N. Katherine Hayles means when extolling digital subjectivity's "disjunction between surface and interior" as envisioned within technology (*My Mother Was a Computer* 203). While Puck might be deluded into thinking that restricting his on-air camera time to a surface-oriented representational version of himself, i.e., "The Puck," is feasible, the fact remains that he cannot escape the mechanical gaze, and so when the facade of his extremity backfires, he has no choice but to retreat. And, truly, this is Bunim and Murray's end game, to capture each of the roommates at this crossroads—the surface version of themselves, for the camera, coming into explosive contact with their off-camera, internal selves. And if not that excitable mixture, then the on-camera subject's interior self breaking through the surface. The guarantor of raw emotion on reality TV are the moments when on-screen characters "lose it" and break down; in conjunction, they are losing control over the "conditions of production" (Biressi and Nunn 30). When the roommates gang up on Puck and demand he be less abrasive or face eviction, he is no longer complicit in the process of his mediation because that attendant vulnerability means he would appear on-camera as his off-camera self. "Audiences ideally expect cameras to capture 'real' reactions to genuine or contrived provocations and circumstances," as Biressi and Nunn assert, and Puck, already convinced TV is a de facto contrivance, cannot bear to feed the camera the reality of his *own* contrivance (19).

Puck's subjectivity struggles before the camera as it locates itself within it. Is he the subject who will appear on-screen? Is he alive and complex outside the TV's operations? Is there anything to himself outside *The Real World* diegesis? These questions flavor the condemnation reality TV participants often express toward their mediation. The stars of MTV's *The Hills*, for instance, have denounced their on-screen depiction ad nauseam since the show ended its run in 2010. But the answer to these questions, however fair the protestation, is an emphatic *no*. This is the new subjectivity, as conveyed through the reality TV lens. N. Katherine Hayles imagines digital subjectivity as the "emergent properties" which appear after "dynamic recombination and fragmentation," and these *emergent* properties are valued over ones that exist exterior to the diegesis of reality TV (*My Mother Was a Computer* 203). Puck's on-camera struggle emanates from actively experiencing the potential confusion between what he allows to emerge for the camera and the interior self he never wanted to be captured on film—the "recombination and fragmentation" of who he is. Further complicating things are the social and cultural codes Puck had carried with him onto *The Real World*, which also informed the conflict he faced as the conditions of production, to his apparent surprise, ended up dictating his on-screen presence. Indeed, Puck's subjective referentiality, here, is contaminated by a swirling mixture of oppositional ideologies for understanding the self. Unlike his roommates who rebuff his critiques of television, Puck struggles before the camera because he is conscious of a conversation regarding TV's meaning-making abilities, and his confusion communicates literacy to the submission they are all willfully making. But Puck's literacy, it turns out, is insufficient.

In an apt scene from season three, amidst the Puck and Pedro battle, the roommates pass a baseball cap around with questions they have written inside it, many worded to provoke debate and unease. Seated on the living room couch, Pedro selects a question from the cap which reads, "If you could change one thing about our new living situation, what would you change?" He hesitates in answering the question, awkwardly scratching his head, snickering. Puck, sitting cross-legged on the floor in front Pedro, shoots him a stony glare. Pedro finally says, "I wish I had better communication with certain people in the house, which I don't." All heads turn to Puck, who then asks, "How?" Pedro replies, "If I knew how, it wouldn't be a problem." Everyone chuckles a bit and shrugs it off. Then, the show cuts to confessional footage of Rachel remembering that moment: "It was really a lot more tense [sic] than what it may have appeared to be." Rather than a straightforward confession regarding their circumstance, again the confessional is a venue for mediating (manipulating) what will eventually appear on-screen. Rachel happens to think that *The Real World* might not be able to accurately portray the emotionality, the significance, of that house meeting, so she retroactively injects some into it. The on-screen truth of the edited scene precedes her confessions. But it is interesting that Rachel seems to think something is missing. The question is whether it is meaning, or some lack of subtext, but her position is influenced by a divergent understanding of television than Puck's, who knows that once the tides turn against him, retreat from the cameras is the only way he can feasibly mediate on-screen meaning.

From a historical standpoint, it is worth noting that *The Real World*, as a show, has seen a distinct change in content as it has continued on into the Millennial generation. Sympathetic and bright, Pedro Zamora was a high point for the show's representation of American youth, and though season three distinguished the series from its trashy-voyeur reputation, it would later revel in that status on later seasons and into the new millennium. Pam Ling from season three is a Harvard graduate and third-year medical student who helps to treat the poor and homeless of San Francisco. She spends much of the season fretting over Pedro's gradually deteriorating condition, paralleling him with patients of her own in confessional footage. Judd Winick is a talented cartoonist who makes the rounds trying to sell his art, clamoring for a spot in a local newspaper to showcase the skill he spends many hours of the day honing; his roommates cite him as "the hardest working" of the bunch. He eventually lands a strip in *The San Francisco Examiner*, while season three is still being filmed. Mohammad Bilal is a rapper and poet whose political, intellectual leanings often lend house debates a prescience they might not possess otherwise. He also is the lead singer of a San Francisco rap rock outfit. While their professional pursuits are arguably bolstered by their relationship with MTV, these young people's goals are not exclusively hinged upon their participation in a reality TV show. In fact, quite the opposite is true, as they continue with their pursuits unabated while cameras roll. More importantly, the cameras found them doing what they do, and did not somehow sanction those interests and/or talents. Pam transitions from one residency to another, a point of stress for her in an episode. Cameras follow Judd as he flies out of San Francisco to pitch a show idea to an animation studio; he calls it a "Generation X version of *The Simpsons*." Mohammad plays gigs with his band. Quite clearly, these young people have professional and social lives that exist outside *The Real World* text, and will continue once their stay has passed. Puck is really the only cast member from season three who genuinely embraces (or rejects) how momentous being on *The Real World* might actually be, an anomalous attribute that raises questions regarding his desires.

There is an innocence to the cast of season three that endears the show to its viewers. Some of this has to do with a lack of media literacy regarding reality TV, Puck being the exception here, as the format had only just begun its ascent into the American popular culture imagination. On season three, it is as if *The Real World*'s promise of twenty-somethings who "stop being polite and start getting real" might not just be a shallow provocation. But the distinct, apparent lack of exposure to the reality TV format, as of 1994, meant that the shape of the culture around it had yet to be affected by it to the extent that it has been today. As evidence, into the 2010s, the dominant problem plaguing reality TV critics such as Mark Andrejevic is whether reality TV helped to create widespread media cynicism regarding realistic representation, and yet at the same time somehow managed to facilitate society's endemic submission to the reality TV paradigm—it is the ontological problem of reality TV scholarship: did reality TV "make" consumers conspicuously contradictory or "find" consumers that way? It is no secret that reality TV has become the subject of relentless scapegoating by popular conservative and liberal media critics alike, part of a cavalcade of low media offerings that have "denigrated" society and, most especially, youth culture. However, the majority of today's young people assert that reality TV is not to be trusted. But that has never stopped them from watching it, or desiring to be involved with it, and maybe that is the real irony. Culture reflects media, as McLuhan writes, "the 'message' of any medium" is the "change of scale or pace or pattern that it introduces into human affairs," and reality TV's epochal significance lies in how it mutated the subjectivities watching, the subjectivities watched, and how the knowledge of their social conditions changed subsequently (8). Later seasons of *The Real World* convey a new reflexivity and awareness about the reality TV format, and consequently a mutation in the mediated subjects appearing on-screen.

Literal Superficiality on The Real World: Portland *(2013)*

Season twenty-eight of *The Real World*, which takes place in Portland, Oregon, features seven strangers of a much different nature than on season three. Anastasia Miller is a self-described fashion model; the cast refer to her as "Barbie Doll." Averey Tressler, an apparent self-reliance advocate, is proud of her job at Hooters, which Tressler is quick to defend whatever the context—only she is allowed to appreciate the irony. Marlon Williams is an NCAA football player from Texas Tech who bombed at the 2010 NFL draft and is now loosely pursuing a rap career. Rather than explaining their professional pursuits or future goals as they detail themselves for the camera in the first episode of the season, the cast members of season twenty-eight confuse leisure activities for what they actually do for a living—partying, tattoos and piercings, sexual habits, nothing is left to the imagination for the sake of the camera. Jordan Wisely, though enrolled at the University of Central Oklahoma, fails to mention he is a marketing major, or that he has a strong interest in business, instead focusing on his recreational wake boarding skills.

In fact, the venue in which Jordan later reveals his interest in business is a roommate squabble in episode two over what economic bracket belongs to the American middle class. Throughout the forty-two minutes of the first episode (double the length of an episode from season three), all viewers know of Jordan is that he has a crippled left hand, a father who inexplicably beat him as a child—everyone has a nice chuckle about the alcoholism and abuse in their families—and that he has a healthy libido.[10] Actually, according to the first episode, the entire cast on season twenty-eight has a healthy libido.

In contrast, on season three of *The Real World*, viewers' introductions to the cast involve cameras going into familial homes, penetrating these twenty-somethings' personal lives, sewn with voice overs that translate a universe of personal belief and aspiration, and all this in half the episodic running time of season twenty-eight. Viewers see Pedro at home in Cuba enjoying time with his eccentric family. Viewers are shown coy and trepidatious Cory Murphy praying with her suburban family in front of home-cooked macaroni and cheese before she hops onto a train with Pedro, someone from an entirely different cultural background than hers. Instead, Portland's cast members are shaded in an ahistorical, context-free light—even their past hardships have a distant feeling, as if they are being read off the side of a cereal box beside nutritional facts. Viewers first meet the cast of season twenty-eight on street corners in Portland, in the backseat of taxis, in self-directed home videos they had submitted to producers for casting consideration; these take place primarily in their home bedrooms, no different than the setting of an amateur YouTube video. Cast members are always isolated in these settings and do not exist in an off-camera social or personal world that is to be even *contemplated* by the film crew. In his submission video, when Jordan exposes his disfigured hand to the camera as he sits on a dingy couch in his apartment, the weight of his physical ailment is lost amid his nonchalance and the quick, purposeful cut that pulls viewers away from his abjection.

The cast of season twenty-eight's time on *The Real World* is not continuous but discrete. They do not arrive in Portland and go about their lives business as usual, still pursuing their ambitions and livelihood; instead, their tenure on the show alone is the fulfillment of ambition and this is their new profession. What the show's viewership gets in return are the misadventures of people painfully aware of the "conditions of production" on reality TV, never mind *The Real World*, and that their time on the show may well yield ever greater fame. Professional or personal goals outside show business, it should be said, do not apply. In a telling scene from episode two, the women of the Portland house lounge around on the back porch, having a casual chat. Where the conversation started is not supplied by the show, but where it picks up is intriguing: Anastasia says, "I think it's cool. I think we have a good mixture on here," meaning there is a nice variety of "types" of people on the show. Interestingly, she does not say "in" here, referring to the house, but "on" here, referring to the TV show they are being filmed for. Does their internal, off-screen experience of the house exist outside the show it will eventually become? Then Anastasia says, "Honestly, I thought there was gonna be a black chick," which is a reference to the typical diversity Bunim and Murray enforce on *The Real World*. The other women chime in: "I thought there was gonna be a gay person." Averey concurs with a laugh, "Oh, I totally thought there was gonna be a gay person." More laughing. This moment of self-reflexivity, which the producers sheepishly try to mask by removing the first part of their conversation, is a clue as to the level of engagement this cast has with the show. Indeed, they are hyper aware of the "conditions of production," to the extent that they are already expecting someone to be gay (Marlon comes out as bisexual, to the roommates' surprise and disappointment), and the end result is a more heightened sense of *blatant* performance by the cast than what viewers experienced in season three.

In the case of *The Real World* nowadays, its literate audience's expectation, as a consequence of all this exposure to reality TV, dictates how the cast represent themselves for the cameras. And this is because, as audience members themselves, they have already fantasized about being on the show, what "type" of character they will be. Bruzzi surmises that any "pretence at 'being oneself'" is inevitably circumscribed by [the reality TV] form" (147). Understanding Bunim and Murray's televisual text as it appears in the 2010s means understanding that *The Real World*'s mediated reality has superimposed itself over the "real world" for its participants (and reflexively for its viewership) even if there was nothing beneath that superimposition to begin with. Not only that, but *The Real World* has now realized reality TV's harshest criticisms. The cast hunger for fame and exposure, are devoid of intellectual aspiration or altruistic intent, id-driven, appealing to what some call "the lowest-common denominator." Whereas domestic conflict is underwritten by ideology in season three, Portland's domestic squabbling is tinged by sexual desire. Jordan and Jessica McCain, who fight over what constitutes the middle class, both conclude, almost immediately after their fight ends, that sexual tension is to blame for their spat. This is titillation over mental stimulation. And it is also reality TV devoid of its original ethos, the same that spurred

Gen Xers to watch *The Real World* in the first place. What season twenty-eight communicates is the completion of a process in which the subjects, these on-screen people plucked from the everyday, literally embody the fictional, regressive stereotypes which predominate on sitcoms and dramatic television shows—the very thing *The Real World* was trying to remedy at its inception, or at the very least, respond to. MTV as well as Bunim and Murray overtly communicated that initial thesis, but even the show's title implies its theoretical positioning: this show is not fictitious, such as other TV shows, but quite literally the "real world." Interestingly, this has now become an effective way to read *The Real World* text, as is the case with Andrejevic's pivotal 2005 book *Reality TV: The Work of Being Watched*. Though, generally, as already mentioned, the idea that *The Real World* might actually be the "real world" proves to be a provocation for its viewership, nothing more.

To further illuminate the point here, Corner's notion of "true selves" emerging from the everyday performed self on reality TV is pertinent to what has occurred historically on *The Real World*. The idea that a "true self" can emerge from a mediation in which the participants are so fully self-aware and complicit in the eventual televised product troubles the potential for that emergence. Seeing a "true self" emerge from televisual mediation requires vulnerability, and sometimes ignorance, the kind Puck expresses as he tries to self-mediate for the camera. In season twenty-eight, what the viewer consumes are on-screen identities masquerading as subjects, which lack depth and are reliant on language, rather than nuanced subjectivities. It is not a coincidence that confession time doubles alongside running time in later seasons of the show: the more time these cast members have to contemplate their circumstance through language—to embark on self-reflexive conflict— the more deliberate and prescribed (i.e., "mediational") their actions become. Nuanced, complex subjects make TV viewing more challenging, so deeply mediational on-screen actions function better for the show they will appear on, and for literate audiences who expect certain criteria be fulfilled. When Anastasia guesses what "types" of people will appear on season twenty-eight, she voices the completion of an internal process in which participants no longer run away from their mediation, such as Puck, but instead run toward it. What made season three more authentic was that it was a comparative *failure* of mediation; it did not succeed in fully packaging its on-screen selves, however desirous those subjects were for that outcome, because season three's cast did not fully submit. In Puck's psychic dissonance, this fact was clearly visible. Indeed, drawing from an earlier point in this chapter, season twenty-eight's cast signifies an end to all "unnerving dissonance," as they outrightly accept and delight in their status within commodified culture.

Theorists such as Frederic Jameson would imagine *The Real World* season twenty-eight's subjective representation and expression as "superficiality in the most literal sense," in line with the products of consumer culture that give postmodern lives meaning (9). Reality stars deflect their "literal superficiality" by arguing they are someone different off-camera (someone better?), but today that is fallacy because on-screen experience is valued over its off-screen adjunct. To temper this circumstance, contemporary reality shows will go one step further, combating superficially truthful content within their own narrative structure, as if to project some hope that "real" reality exists onto the whole contrived reality TV enterprise. After years of MTV viewership questioning the actuality of *The Hills*, the producers decided to give into criticism of the show and end the reality series in 2010 by setting the final filmed scene on a Hollywood set.[11] The two romantically-linked main cast members, Kristin and Brody, are supposedly bidding each other farewell in the series' final moments, in front of the Hollywood sign in Los Angeles. There is a melancholy embrace between them before Kristin hops into her limo, headed for the airport. The show cuts to Kristin inside the limo, reminiscing, with a montage from the previous hundred or so episodes serving as her "memories." Then, Brody is again shown in front of the Hollywood sign, glumly watching Kristen's limo drive away. Soon, the Hollywood sign behind Brody is rolled away, revealed to be a fake backdrop. The camera pulls back. Non-diegetic theme song music begins to play louder. There are set pieces, camera operators, stage hands, and lighting conspicuously left in the shot. Kristin jumps out of the limo, which apparently had not traveled anyplace, and casually hugs Brody, removing any sense of melancholy from their farewell. Credits roll. There is no question now: the whole series was a staged production, because the show is literally communicating that fact. And in post show interviews, the cast sold the final scene as commentary on the fakery of living in Los Angeles rather than the show they were on. Brody told MTV News that the series' ending "was perfect because you still don't know what was real, what was fake, and it's kind of like L.A." (Vena). But, in actuality, this whole narrative move serves as a diversionary tactic, attempting to get the viewer to ignore the larger truth that the two people hugging as the camera pulls back are just as superficially constructed as the ones who were merely characters on a TV show.

The Hills fails to accept the dissonance that once existed between representing the self on camera, and the reality of a person's off-camera and/or interior self, has fallen by the wayside. Puck's struggle is over. So this intensely literal move that *The Hills* makes to save its cast from fakery really does the opposite: by raising doubt as to the sanctity of its content in that final reveal, the show troubles the cast even further. The casual hug between Brody and Kristin does not communicate they are friends off-camera; it says the only way they can be real and not reality TV characters is by displaying it for the camera, the same camera capturing them on their reality show. But the camera does not capture reality, it mediates reality. So the off-camera Brody and Kristin are just as contrived as their on-screen counterparts.

From the reception end, reality TV characters should be understood under the guise that they are "ordinary" people made "extraordinary" as a consequence of their participation and exposure on reality TV (Jermyn 74). The specifics of this "extraordinary" quality vary and are usually less "extraordinary" and more exploitative, but it is a disparate cultural circumstance from ordinary American life, to be sure, if nothing else for the fact so many viewers are looking in on a group of people and so few are looking out. The Internet can only produce these results if there is a police chase or a keyboard playing cat as part of the equation. Celebrities (usually C-list or below) who submit themselves to the reality programming experience do so as a kind of challenge to their "extraordinary" status—to make themselves more accessible, to alter their public persona. "Look at me! I eat bran and get into fights with my siblings just like you do!" Joan Rivers, Ryan Lochte, Kathy Griffin, to name just a few, have given their lives over to the reality TV enterprise to achieve this end. The hope, then, is that their "realness" will result in ever greater celebrity and success—it is a paradoxical means of reversing the celebrity trend only to propagate it. And it worked for The Osbourne family (MTV's *The Osbournes*, 2002), the Kardashians (*Keeping Up with the Kardashians*, 2007 and ongoing), and the late Anna Nicole Smith (*The Anna Nicole Show*, also 2002) whose careers saw major improvement after their reality shows premiered on basic cable. The entitled kids on *The Hills* operate from a comparative middle ground in the sense that they already lived extraordinary lives of wealth and excess before the cameras ever showed up; they are divergent from *The Real World* cast as far as socioeconomic origins go. But, quite clearly, this notion of on-screen "ordinary" people made "extraordinary" has been broken down across the board in Millennial culture precisely because today consumers "embrace the drive to make [themselves] seen" (Andrejevic, *Reality TV...* 189). Whether through the Internet or on some television show, appearing on the screen is not an exceptional exercise any longer: it is literally part of the system by which today's subjects garner "ordinary" status. Off-screen experience is no experience at all, even if it informs the content and rhythm of what appears on-screen, and vice versa. In other words, the screen is privileged.

Traces of this logic have spurred the universal adoption of social networking platforms. One of the aphorisms of Facebook is "If you aren't on Facebook, you're not real," and the "you" in that phrase can be replaced by just about any life event outside death: marriage, birth, travel, etc. Romantic relationships are not tangible until they are "Facebook official," for instance, stamped onto individual profiles like a trophy. This is not an indication of the irrepressible prowess of Mark Zuckerberg's platform (if Facebook ever attempted direct monetization outside advertising, there would be a mass exodus of users) but instead the 21st-century axiom that *divulging* the intimate details of their life helps validate people's existences. And in upcoming generations, this "drive to be seen" is already unconsciously manifesting itself. As Steven Johnson writes, the screen, which is now at the center of human experience, "is a place to work through the story of your life as it unfolds" (29). More simply, the screen is how people literally write the narrative of their lives. An archaic concern about valuing the separation of public and private spheres has been eroded by digital mediation—indeed, the idea that there be such a thing as "public" and "private" assumes there still exists some domestic or personal life which matters off-screen. Again, on-screen experience is privileged over off-screen experience. Just as Generation X learned about each other and themselves by watching *The Real World*, Millennial youth learn the same through social networking, except the question remains whether this exercise is actual *learning* anymore or if it is something more ideological, an idea explored in Chapter 2.

Maury Povich and the Limitations of Reality TV Subjectivity

As such, exposure is integral to digital subjectivity, and reality TV offers it the widest possible venue—again, lots more viewers reliably gazing at the TV medium.[12] The problem is how reality TV deals with the multiplicity of people who do not make it through casting calls, who toil away with their lives unimpeded by camera operators and the obligatory confessional time enforced on primetime reality TV. While they can settle for some online infamy, and the meager pleasures of social media such as Facebook, they will long for exposure on a greater scale. Some of these "lesser" reality participants, not exceptional enough for their own twenty-two minute shows, are divvied out to daytime TV reality fare, such as *Jerry Springer* and *Judge Judy*, where their exposure is limited to the twelve minutes or so between commercial breaks. *Maury*, hosted by ex-news anchor Maury Povich, which has run in syndication in some form or another since 1991, has long banked on these particular people for its success. And it appears there is no dearth of them willing to air their dirty laundry for Povich's show. The variety of individual *Maury* episode themes include topics such as "Who's my baby's daddy?," "Male or female?," and "He abuses me and I like it," not exactly highbrow content, but it is not meant to be. This is the daytime audience demographic; television producers and advertisers decided long ago this demographic had no aspirations to consume programming outside trash TV, a debatable assignment in some cases. Also, ordinary people do not come onto TV to talk about their taxes: television appearances are reserved for the sensational, the ecstatic and inflammatory—and the more intimate, the better.

Confusing *Maury*, as it appears in the 2010s, with talk shows from the 1980s and 90s, such as *Donahue* or *The Sally Jessy Raphael Show*, would be a mistake. The pretense of "talking" on *Maury* is dropped entirely. In fact, nowadays there is more talking on *Jerry Springer*, a wildly more salacious show. So this is not a genre problem; *Maury* is a reality show if there ever was one. The only major difference between *Maury* and a typical fishbowl reality TV show (such as *The Hills* or *The Real World*) is that *Maury* is not trying to tell an overarching narrative with its characters. Instead, the viewer is given micro-encounters anchored by an emotional climax that *The Real World* might take an entire season to work up to—and these happen up to five or six times in a single *Maury* episode. If, as was the case for Puck, viewers need to see emotional breakdowns and a loss of control over "the conditions of production" in order to assess the authenticity of these on-screen characters, then *Maury* grants them that opportunity many times in a terse forty-two minutes (Biressi and Nunn 30). It is a highly concentrated reality TV experience, with none of the filler, and copious amounts of exploitation for viewers to enjoy or abhor.

In a given *Maury* segment, guests will exhibit a full range of emotion, confess their darkest secrets, succumb to the scrutiny of the studio audience while reacting to that scrutiny, and also comment on their own filmed lives while they are still in front of the camera (self-reflexivity). Very often, the friends and family unwittingly asked to go on *Maury* to hear some terrible secret will demand to know why this all needed to happen on national TV. One answer is that going on *Maury* lends complexity to their lived experience. Beneath the potential humiliation of all of America knowing a mother's adult son wears diapers and fantasizes about being back inside the womb, there lies the satisfaction of knowing that this moment is not just that person's own but many people's. The moment is neutered of its significance as a personal experience, but the public and personal are no longer distinct; meaningful events happen out in the open, and are made more meaningful because others have confirmed that they are, in fact, meaningful. And the *Maury* studio audience, not unlike the fiery indignation users spew on popular Internet message boards such as Reddit, react to guest revelations with bloody, condemnatory cries, while viewers at home lap up this fervor largess. Studio audience members will jump up and shout along with *Maury*'s guests after they hear the results of a lie detector test which reads that the denying, loud-mouthed, forty-year-old has-been cheating on his seventeen-year-old bride. Moral rage flows through the entire *Maury* set like some Pavlovian trigger; everyone is salivating in unison. And Povich as host just sits back and soaks it up, as if the thrill of these people's exposed emotional wounds were as banal as the commute home. And maybe that is the host's job, to remind viewers of how tiresome it all really is—it is worth noting that Jerry Springer conducts his show with similar detachedness.

The standards for truth on Maury Povich's show are decidedly less filmic and more corporeal in nature. DNA tests confirm a baby's genealogy—this after guest mothers desperately make the case to Povich and his studio audience that their children are the genetic relation of one or another accused father by pairing a picture of the dad next to his potential offspring. The fathers wait backstage, listening in. Their hyperbolic reactions are filmed. Beside the large screen at the rear of the stage, mothers excitedly point out hairlines on their babies that match their father's. Similar shapes of the nose and mouth. Large ears. The studio audience howls in agreement, and condemns and accuses along with the mother. But they will turn on her without a second's thought if she is wrong. The most gut-wrenching segments are ones when the mother brings along her disabled baby, and the accused father angrily demands, "I could not produce a thing like that." Somehow his sperm is superior. When the offending man enters the stage from the right, everyone is in agreement that he is a cad, a liar, just another dead beat dad. He might raise his arms in disgust, or, worse, revel in his moment of televised emotional infamy, flipping off the camera or laughing like a maniac. The heat on set is palpable. Povich might greet the accused man, might not, but will most assuredly return to his seat, cross his legs politely, and ask his routine questions—if the mother and father are not going at it already. And that is the secret to Povich's show, maybe the secret to all reality TV production: the less prodding needed, the more authentic the product. Povich flies his guests out to Stamford, Connecticut, puts them up in hotels, provides hair and makeup services along with a meager stipend. Under these conditions, the guests are compelled to unload all their emotional energy on stage. Yet there is no denying their emotional efficacy: tears flow unimpeded, spit flies, screams, fists, the full spectrum of physical and emotional reaction is showcased.

Thematic issues plague *Maury*, and it shares this downfall with much of daytime reality programming. For instance, Povich's show has a despicable socioeconomic bias—the free trip to Stamford, Connecticut, as well as gratis DNA and lie detector testing, are a tempting offer for the poor and disenfranchised unable to receive such services elsewhere (lie detection is especially lavish and untrustworthy, but is embraced as the gold standard for truth on *Maury*). The typical guest on his show tells stories tinged by the hallmark struggles that go along with their economic status. Their living conditions are terrible. There is not enough money to pay hospital bills. They have sunk this low because society has given them no other option. They will pass this fate onto their children. Half the dead beat dads on *Maury* are trying to run out on child support, which they could not afford in the first place; this is where Povich's show functions as the courtroom, since, outside his show, the courts failed his downtrodden guests. It is a pageantry of abjection, and Maury Povich can conceivably save his guests from it. This is not to say that the financially rich are exempt from reality TV exploitation, that their wealth somehow saves them from this fate. *The Hills*, even when troubling its own narrative, still managed to exploit its cast, privileged offspring of California's upper crust. Bravo's *The Real Housewives ...* is equally exploitative, but the standards by which the wealthy women on that series are exploited are different in the sense that they are a part of the process; theirs is a willful submission to exploitation, whereas Povich's guests are desperately consenting. And even those who go on *Maury* for fame-seeking reasons (the minority) do so out of an act of desperation, as *Maury* does not reliably attribute celebrity status on its guests. On the surface, reality TV's exploitation value is equal opportunity, but the power dynamics vary from show to show.

Instead of reducing *Maury* to a purely exploitative piece of Americana, which is the common dismissal of most daytime TV, it is more advantageous here to consider the show as a concentrated platform for engaging embodied humanity in a time when embodiment has been shifted to primarily digital spaces. In the 2010s, consumers formulate human complexity largely through the Internet. And though technically consumers receive *Maury* on a digital platform, as television is now universally broadcasted digitally, TV belongs to an older analog media ethos.[13] So when viewers watch television, they are consuming it as analog media even if it is not really and truly analog. When Digital Natives scoff at the notion of watching TV, it has less to do with a conscious choice not to watch TV and more with a physical or mental incapability to do so; their media consumption habits have been defined by digital technology, such as DVRs and smartphones, which gives Digital Natives the illusion of consumer agency, unlike TV which restricts them to a predetermined mode of consumption. As reality TV has gradually settled into its place in the broader media community, it is apparent that the format is more than just a fleeting gimmick. The notion that this style of show will simply die out as network broadcasters (NBC, CBS, ABC, Fox) again embrace scripted shows seems to have dissipated. One of the reasons reality TV endures is because it attempts to "reclaim what seems to be lost after digitalization, to connect with other subjects across time and space" (Biressi and Nunn 32). What viewers receive on *Maury* is the frenzied articulation of this sentiment. The desperation of his guests is more than just an expression of their material conditions, which are, granted, deplorable. They are also clamoring for the corporeal experience (real or imaginary) that digital technology has taken away from them, or, if not taken away, then made obsolete. *Maury's* guests are at once making their interior lives visible, a very Internet-centric activity, but also doing so through an analog medium that captures their body in all its emotional and physical weight.

The set-up for an individual segment on *Maury* is established with titles on the bottom of the screen that point to the core problem being settled on stage. One segment from an episode which aired in February 2013 read, "Stop denying it…. I saw you cheating on video!" Segments usually begin with a close up of the victimized person (or confessor) on stage, sometimes already crying, always with a dead serious expression on their face. Povich will say something such as "Tabitha has a secret. If her husband finds out, it could end their relationship. They've been married nine years. Take a listen." Then, viewers see previously shot footage where the victim (or confessor) details their side of the story. The show cuts back to the front stage. The studio audience reacts accordingly—oohs and ahhs, gasps, screams, etc. The show will then cut to the cameras behind the scenes, watching the guest about to make their entrance onto the stage. If the guest is going to hear a secret, they are in isolation. If they are going to be confronted by a victim or accuser, then they will be listening to stage sound and reacting. Following this, the viewer is shown previously shot footage of that guest's side of the story. Once the entire party is assembled on-stage, viewers watch emotions crescendo. Often, there will be bodyguards present on stage to prevent any real physical harm, and also to heighten the severity of the encounter if there was no threat of harm to begin with. There are multiple cameras both on stage and behind it to capture all the action as it unfolds. There are plenty of close-ups, far shots, and reactions shots from the studio audience. The geography of *Maury*'s set is fully realized, and so are his guests. Every inch is surveilled, from the green room, to the hallways and emergency exits, to, unbelievably, the parking lot. Guests have been known to flee out there when escaping the terror of what is happening to them on-stage. Similar to Puck, they understand mediating on-screen meaning means fleeing the camera's gaze, even if that move is ultimately futile.

Reality TV restores a material fullness that the individual subject loses when represented on many popular online platforms. Under these conditions of exposure, the subject on *Maury* is granted juxtapositional complexity, however short their time on-screen may well be. The viewer is even provided footage of what goes on during commercial breaks, after the guests have achieved their emotional end goal, as they stew in the cathartic (or horrific) aftermath. On Facebook, the digital subject is often relegated to static photography, the occasional quip, comment, or meme identifier. If a Facebook friend expresses too much, their friends will either unfriend them or set their status updates to ignore. Also, the details of their individual achievements and cultural interests serve as tools for embodiment on Facebook, yet in execution these have little to do with their corporeal form. Worse, supplied photographs are the subject of stage-management, wherein users strategically construct their own embodiment. Amateur YouTube videos are traditionally shot from a single angle, from the vantage point of an open laptop or mounted web camera, and are informed by amateur styles of production. One perspective, one shot of the abdomen to the head, reduces the bodily representation of YouTube's on-screen subjectivity—this is where reality TV, and television in general, stands apart: higher production values equate to a better technical environment for physical representation, and a hierarchical power distribution assures that a filmed subject's strategic intervention is limited. So while the Internet dominates current formulations of subjectivity nowadays, television, however consumeristic and doomed to obsolescence, is unique; TV, as a figuratively analog technology, can project an impression of the body that guarantees, similar to Hayles' analog subject, "the meaning of what is deep inside" (Hayles, *My Mother Was a Computer* 203).

But, while physical complexity is present, especially compared to social media, *Maury*'s terse format disables any sense of emotional nuance in favor of an exaggerated version of interior externalization. When participants scream and fight on his set, they do so because this moment, short and well-documented, is their chance to prove they are actualized beings (i.e., "their moment in the sun"). This will not be accomplished with a reserved tongue; the participants are not afforded the passivity of the show's host. For their selves to appear authentic, the High-Definition cameras need to capture the droplets of spit flying from their mouths, the creases in their hands when they make a fist. Povich's guests are embodied, but it is the embodiment of people who know there is an expiration date on their actuality. So they act superficial, as Jameson puts it, "in the most literal sense" in that their on-screen expression is highly reducible, akin to a consumer good. Their feelings are unmistakable—intense anger, joy, despair, the guests' emotions are so loud and clear they are deafening. Again, a reliance on surface-oriented identity is apparent in these mediated selves, though the *Maury* show is even more pervasively reductive when it comes to its on-screen subjects. And these hysterical emotions create a sensory overload in the viewer, resulting in a gradual numbing effect—this, in turn, allows viewers to deny these guests' of their emotional validity. At some point in American history, it would have been inconceivable for the effervescent moral indignation flaunted on *Maury* to be perceived as if it were boring and cheap. But it is. And if *Maury* makes viewers nostalgic for old-fashioned American social propriety, then really those viewers have missed out on an entire generation of social development that has imposed new terms for propriety.

The conditions of Povich's show, which result in "packaged" personalities and emotions, reflect the conditions outside it; these emotions are symptomatic of an emotional milieu inflected by an intimate relationship with easily reducible consumer products. A twelve minute segment on *Maury*'s show is an on-the-nose analogy for Andy Warhol's "death of the world of appearance" postmodern art—his pulpy representations of the Campbell's soup can and

Marilyn Monroe speak to the American fascination with consumer products (Jameson 9). And now that postmodern sensibilities have come full circle, the on-screen subject has become the ultimate fascination, both in relation to other people's subjectivity and also the consumer's own. And, in the case of *Maury*, a fascination which has lost its luster amid televisual saturation; even if talk shows grant complexity to a subject's body, they deny them emotional fullness. This is what Mark Andrejevic means when he posits reality TV "accurately portrays the reality of contrivance in contemporary society" (*Reality TV...* 17). The contemporary system for understanding the self and others has been qualified by a process of manufacturing and packaging. For some people this is illicit and for others it is invigorating—for those it invigorates, to be commodified as a subject who relates to their commodities is 21st-century nirvana and Maury Povich a consumer prophet.

Looking at *Maury* in comparison to *The Real World*, for instance, it is obvious that differing reality show formats affect the quality (or at least the depth) of on-screen subjectivity. It also does not help that there is no such thing as a reality TV ethics. Within documentary film, how one represents subjects before the camera is a serious issue, even if exploitation does still exist within documentary. And documentary taxonomist Bill Nichols rightly challenges "informed consent" as the "ethical litmus test" for realistic representation because informing subjects that they might appear on-screen as malfunctioning, reduced version of themselves does not take into account cultural circumstances that encourage subjects to expose themselves, no matter the cost (53). Consent paperwork people sign prior to filming reality TV (or after as with *Candid Camera*) is about protecting the people behind the camera not in front of it, and is often written as an exploit-at-will kind of creed. In the case of some successful reality TV shows, contracts are redrawn so that participants might enjoy greater affordances regarding how they appear on-screen—something which happened with the cast of MTV's *Jersey Shore*—but this is the exception not the rule. And because television is still very much a top-down enterprise, ruled by a production hierarchy that outwardly disenfranchises the consumer (and future reality TV participants), then on-screen subjects are reduced not just as a consequence of show formats, such as *Maury*'s, but also the relations of power producing these shows. As such, on-screen complexity also varies wildly depending on the intentions of the producers. *Maury* benefits from having no need for telling an extended story about its guests—since each segment is a singular event, the guests represent themselves in all their idiosyncrasies without that representation interfering with a particular narrative expectation. However, subjects on *The Real World* do feel the pressure to fulfill a predetermined role/type (e.g., Anastasia: "Oh, I totally thought there was gonna be a gay person"). This is not an accusation of tampering against the producers, which does exist, but instead the cultural knowledge held by those on-screen that (some) reality TV shows should achieve particular narrative and character criteria. The first season of CBS' *Survivor* would never have achieved the incredible success it had without the help of Richard Hatch, antagonist par excellence who managed to manipulate his fellow survivors out of the million dollar reward. Since then—*Survivor* has surpassed its thirtieth season—the cast, arguably more than the casting decisions, have been informed by Hatch, and not just because they want to win the hefty cash prize, but because their ideological understanding of *Survivor* the TV show is beholden to Hatch's on-screen prowess.

However palpable its current cultural impact and what it says about the Millennial generation's unconscious desires, contemporary reality TV remains highly stigmatized both from a popular perspective and also an academic one. Ideologically, this is not because of its trashiness (the kneejerk view), or its self-consciously reflexive on-screen performers trying to mimic David "Puck" Rainey or Richard Hatch, but because of show formats that really do not aspire to *truth*, never mind *reality*.[14] When *The Real World* premiered in 1992, Bunim and Murray never had a reason to directly fabricate action or narrative particulars because an impetus for authenticity still drove its creators and the people watching. MTV's Gen X consumers, rebellious and usually media literate, could explicitly sense disingenuousness, so there was no deceiving the Gen X audience into believing *The Real World* was some untampered version of reality. Confessional footage shot in those early seasons, for instance, would often be set in staged environments that reflected deep producorial manipulation. Muhammad Bilal of season three appeared outdoors in confessionals, sitting in a La-Z-Boy placed atop a grassy hill, a far cry from the roommates' house in the heart of San Francisco. Clearly, these confessions were not shot anywhere near the dramatic moments Muhammad is seen commenting on. So the idea that all the filmed then edited pieces of *The Real World* conform to some linear temporal trajectory is foregone. In the early 90s, the show was appreciated as a manufactured thing, and, arguably, because there was no illusion that this representation of reality had not been tampered with, the authenticity of what went on in the house *did not* suffer. Indeed, making apparent how/where the confessionals were conducted was more truthful than masking or manipulating how their constructedness appeared on-screen, as is the case with *The Real World* season twenty-eight. The purpose of masking constructedness is such that viewers might be duped into accepting on-screen content as fact, or, worse, viewers might embrace *The Real World*'s contrivance so fully that their pleasure comes from the inability to *ever* convey some authentic version of human representation. Indeed, when reality TV is most dishonest is when it tries to purposefully hide its constructedness, when reality TV takes the notion of "reality" TV literally.[15] Contemporary reality TV, by and large, is marred by the need to produce increasingly "real" TV shows; these are shows that propagate the illusion that they are not TV programs but real reality, even when this is obviously not the case, even when the audience is literate enough to know otherwise.

The Real World of the early 1990s was an exception to the dominant fictive televisual media environment. Now that fact and fiction have effectively blurred, and mediation is embraced, there is a new attitude of consumption to account for. Gen Xers were media literate but they were also open-minded enough to *embrace* the negotiation of reality on their TV screens. Given the kind of media literacy that blossoms online—which is characteristically cynical as is the case with popular message board Reddit—Millennial viewers know that reality is always doomed to be represented on TV, in which *The Real World* lives on as some campy gag. The popular colloquial designation for these cynics is hipsters, a word with quite a history in American culture; its most popular use in the 20th century was in reference to pre–Beat-era jazz aficionados from the 1940s. Admittedly, into the 2010s, "hipster" has become a cliché, and probably will not survive much longer as a way of classifying cultural elitists, but the fact that the term has become so widely used, and in so many different contexts, is worth noting. Many people do not historically trace the 21st-century version of the hipster to the Internet, probably because of the hipster's love of vinyl records and everything antique, but the hipster's refined taste and breadth of cultural knowledge undoubtedly have a one-to-one relation to the existence of Google. Mark Andrejevic, when thinking about the savvy consumption of contemporary reality shows, pinpoints what seems to be the hipster's modus operandi for reality TV viewing: "Savvy subjects [hipsters] derive pleasure from not being fooled by either the elite or the social critics: they know just how bad things are and just how futile it is to imagine they could be otherwise" (*Reality TV...* 178). Andrejevic figures their pleasure in consumption is part of a "complacent knowing" that "gets off on the very cycle of failure that it highlights, exhibiting a certain scorn for the fuzzy hope of the duped: that things might be other than they are" (*Reality TV...* 178–79). Whereas Gen Xers sought out meaning in their consumer goods—TV and elsewhere—the hipster settles at the bottom of the proverbial hole; the hipster's sense of meaning may well be meaning found in the lack thereof. But, more likely, the hipster is reveling in the void of meaninglessness, in the utter failure to ever represent reality (not that this is true, but that it is perceived to be so). And the hipster's ethos supposes that someone out there still manages to get "duped" by the producers of reality TV, but this is not the case. In the 2010s, the term *reality TV* literally invokes fakery and not reality.

But, amidst all this cynicism, there remains continued interest in reality TV, and the pleasures of camp or savvy consumption are not enough to justify its success. However mainstream the Internet has made camp, it is not the dominant form of consumption and will never be because of its inherently "esoteric" quality, as Susan Sontag puts it.[16] Ironic appreciation does not have the monetary benefits of genuine appreciation, as any Hollywood producer can attest. In April 2013, basic cable network A&E achieved record viewership numbers for the season three finale of *Duck Dynasty*, with 9.6 million consistent viewers (Kenneally). Reality TV viewership on network television still manages to garner tens of millions of viewers. As Biressi and Nunn have figured, "despite popular skepticism about the representation of reality evident in debates about fakery in factual programming, there has not been a wide-scale rejection of realist modes of representation by audiences" (34). What happens when someone who watches reality TV watches it despite knowing how much of a failure to represent reality it actually is? This is the paradox of reality TV consumption today, which is where the throng of new, highly-constructed shows, such as those that litter basic cable outlets TLC and truTV, emanate.

The Reality of Contrivance

The knowledge that audiences know how fake reality TV is has emboldened producers to create shows that tickle viewers' authenticity radar, as already alluded to here, but that also do their best to cover up (or redirect) their constructedness. In critiquing reality TV, Stella Bruzzi makes an identical point but goes a step further: "Modern factual entertainment," Bruzzi writes, "does not signal its constructedness, nor does it forefront any serious subtext. It also fails to make a distinction between the 'real' person and the 'performance,' a slippage that troubles critics and prompts accusations of trivialization and 'making human beings into freaks for us to gawp at'" (151). On the surface, outwardly troubling authenticity while also maintaining it seems like a self-defeating proposition for reality TV. In execution, the hipster's expectation that fakery is to follow allows for a new kind of consumption that is not just purely savvy (e.g., what is real and what is not?) but also genuine. If the world outside reality TV is as contrived as reality TV—Adrejevic's "the reality of contrivance in our society"—then there is really no paradox to be had, especially in Millennial consumption habits; real is fake, fake is real. There is no complicating it any further than that because the world outside reality TV has absorbed the superficially truthful attributes of reality TV. To figure viewers cannot get genuine pleasure from things that are contrived, either overtly or deceptively, dismisses the long simmering confluence of postmodern consumption habits which have asserted the contrary.

A popular distribution platform for this new style of consumption is basic cable channel truTV. Established in 1991 under the name Court TV until its rebranding in 2008, the channel showcases some of the most highly contested reality shows in the history of the form. The intention of the channel, prior to the new millennium, was to offer unvarnished, non-stop coverage of court hearings, primarily ones being discussed in national newspapers and tabloids. Court TV, though initially obscure, earned its place in America's pop culture imagination during coverage of the Menendez brothers and OJ Simpson murder trials, respectively. After changing hands a few times over the years, Turner Broadcasting acquired the channel and began pumping it full of cheaply produced trash TV reruns and originals. Along with a lineup aimed squarely at "the lowest-common denominator," Turner added a paradoxical tag line onto the channel that it has yet to live up to: "Not reality. Actuality."

To grasp whatever "Not reality. Actuality." means, viewers would have to be privy to a few things, like, for one, the broader conversation regarding reality TV shows, mainly that the designation "reality" is considered a pejorative. On the truTV website, when they explain their raison d'être in their viewer FAQ, truTV poses a hypothetical, "[Question]: Is truTV a reality network?" No prefacing to that question, the reader just has to assume the context is whether or not the channel is a *reality TV* network. Obviously, it could be construed as something more insidious. And the answer to truTV's hypothetical question is a loaded one: "[Answer]: No. Our focus is on series that feature real-life situations. That is why we're using the theme 'Not Reality. Actuality.' for the network. The goal is to let people know that truTV programming is different from typical reality shows, which often involve contests or other highly staged events." The level of nuance in this reply is astounding, and either speaks to great media literacy or profound ignorance, on both the part of the producer and the consumer. What does truTV mean by "real-life" situations? The shows they feature, such as *Hardcore Pawn* and *Lizard Lick Towing*, focus on real professional worlds, pawn shops and repossession outfits, not unlike the conceit of typical fishbowl-style reality shows. However, these particular professions are predicated on the involvement of random people who are not consenting participants until they engage first with producers; Fox's *Cops*, alternatively, manages to create hours upon hours of content with blurred out and pixilated on-screen subjects. *Lizard Lick Towing* banks on random derelict spenders to flesh out its twenty-two minute episodes, and rarely a blurred or pixilated face is to be seen: the implication, then, is that no on-screen participant is spontaneously running into a camera crew here, despite much of the dramatic tension relying on that very fact, which means the notion that truTV is somehow devoid of programming that features "highly staged events" proves patently false.

TruTV shows are "different from typical reality shows," Turner Broadcasting maintains. The assertion that truTV shows are different is an inducement to watch, nothing more. And any disparity between "reality" and "actuality" exists only in the minds of marketers, producers, and those already speaking the lexicon of reality TV. In truth, depending on the dictionary used, either word will include itself in the other's definition. It is no secret "reality TV" is a misnomer, but what truTV wants the viewer to believe seems to be more a mistake on their part about what actually constitutes reality. And maybe that is the larger mistake made by Millennial culture. If there has ever been a time to be confused about reality, it is right now. "Whence the characteristic hysteria of our time," Baudrillard writes, "that of the production and reproduction of the real" (*Simulation & Simulacra* 23). If a reality TV show forces consumers to consider their relation to reality first and foremost, then that is when consumers have stumbled onto the most self-reflexive and prescribed of its kind.

Repossession shows have been a basic cable staple for a number of years, along with pawn shop shows, with Spike TV and truTV producing the majority of these. TruTV currently airs four repo shows: *All Worked Up, Operation Repo, South Beach Tow* (exec-produced by Jennifer "J.Lo" Lopez), and *Lizard*

Lick Towing. A spin-off of *All Worked Up*, *Lizard Lick* stars boss man Ron Shirley, his body-builder wife Amy, and repo agent Bobby as they traverse the North Carolina countryside seeking out repossessions. It should be said about the show, no one is ever happy to see them. But the level of resistance the Lizard Lick employees encounter, with no police intervention, belongs to redneck mythology. Ron will chalk it up to good old-fashioned Southern living, "nine miles of Talladega ass fought on Alabama Sunday," as he oddly puts it, but the fact that nearly every episode features a gun fight lends the show a level of Schwarzenegger-esque pageantry that could only belong to fiction. This is not to say Ron is not and has never been a professional repo man; the fakery does not happen until truTV producers step in, and the notion that anything existed before the camera arrived is dispensed with entirely. The production style of *Lizard Lick* borrows from cinéma vérité documentary in that camera operators will often be seen on-screen.[17] Mounted cameras in the cabin of vehicles and inside Ron and Amy's office are never hidden. Filming comes off as shaky and amateurish. According to reality TV scholar June Deery, "Unstable hand-held camera footage has long been used to *suggest* deeper intimacy and immediacy" (emphasis added, 41). And though some French new wave documentarians held that this style allowed for truth to come through, those critical of vérité have seen its more nefarious qualities come to fruition on reality TV—in the televisual sense, vérité is a petty affectation. Making apparent the mechanical reality of a (supposedly) non-fiction narrative troubles believability as much as it propagates it, as evidenced by the slew of fictional TV shows and films that employ this style, to various ends.[18]

In season three, episode twelve of *Lizard Lick Towing*, Ron and Bobby pursue a repo down deep in the dirt roads of North Carolina game territory, someplace called Old Johnson's Hunting Grounds. They exchange casual banter over walkie-talkies as the mounted cameras inside both their vehicles capture the conversation; the scene switches between Ron and Bobby's speaking parts. They plan to repo a black Chevy pickup while the owners of the vehicle are distracted by their hunt. In the driver's seat of his tow truck, wearing Oakley shades and a frayed jean vest, Ron sets up some false expectation for the forthcoming repo: "This ought to be easy, with all these boys out scouting and working the land." Ron and Bobby head down Old Quarry road. Bobby drives ahead, incognito in his Dodge 4x4, to avoid the possibility of these hunters getting spooked by Ron's company tow truck. Bobby lets Ron know the coast is clear and verifies the VIN number on the parked Chevy. It is the correct vehicle, so he directs Ron into the dirt clearing so they can slip the tow truck's wheel lift beneath the rear axle of their repo. The viewer sees the Chevy gradually rise behind Ron's tow truck. Then, at the far end of the clearing, a group of four camouflaged hunters come tearing through the trees, guns in hand. Bobby screams out to Ron, "Look out!" The viewer hears gun shots but sees no actual gun fire from any of the approaching hunters. The shots sound distinctly post-production. Ron and Bobby duck beside the tow truck. Camera work starts to get imprecise while edited together scenes become shorter and a less coherent. There are bleeped out expletives aplenty (the show is TV-PG). Somehow the two manage to get back inside their trucks, but how they manage is a thing of mystery for the viewer—the last the viewers sees of Ron and Bobby before the show switches back to interior vehicle cameras is Bobby on the ground beside the black Chevy. That is a huge logistical piece missing from the on-screen action.

Once Ron and Bobby are a distance away from the disgruntled hunters, who tried running after them for a bit, Ron notices something wrong with his tow truck. The non-diegetic background music picks up pace. They drive a little further ahead and over some railroad tracks. Then, Ron stops to get out and inspect the tow truck. He quickly sees the problem and shouts, "They shot a hole in my freakin' tire!" The handheld camera operator zooms in on the hole so the viewer can verify that there is an actual bullet lodged in the tow truck's back tire, akin to what a magician might do to make sure the audience has no illusions about their illusion. While nervously spying the road behind them, Ron and Bobby hurriedly change the tire knowing full well the hunters were already halfway down Old Quarry by the time they were able to stop. The camera stays on Ron as he kneels beside the offending tire, trying to remove the bolts. The driver's side door is open behind him. The viewer hears a blast from off-camera. A hole appears in the driver's side window, and then it shatters. Ron and Bobby are in hysterics at this point. The show switches over to a fixed camera placed on the rear of the tow truck, revealing the hunting party.

Bobby grabs the spare tire and tosses it at the hunters' legs as they run towards him. They stumble onto the dirt head first. Ron gets into his own scuffle with another one of the armed hunters. Beside the road, viewers see the camera operator and other crew, including one who's holding a boom mike, capturing the brawl. They seem to have a lot of faith in Ron and Bobby's fighting ability. Bobby wrestles a gun away from one of the hunters he tripped, then points it at them. Ron gets the gun from the hunter he has been fighting and turns it on him. This all happens within a few seconds of on-screen time. The hunters stop dead in their tracks and back away from Ron and Bobby. "We're good, man. Y'all got the guns," one of them says, hands in the air. The fight is over. The repo is a success. Ron gets back into his tow truck as the hunting party stares on. From inside the cabin, Ron says, "That's the problem with the world: too many freaks, and not enough circuses."

The tables turn so deftly in Ron and Bobby's favor, with so little physical reaction from the camera crew, that accusations of staging cannot be argued down. And the idea that these hunters, if they were truly wronged by this towing company, would consent to have their faces appear on-camera is absurd. *Lizard Lick Towing* and its truTV brethren are fully-manufactured reality programs that tell fictional stories and feature literal not figurative acting (the requisite acting "skill" is debatable). *Lizard Lick's* only relation to a real, external world is that these are not conventionally trained actors and their professional settings are (sometimes) actual, real-life businesses, as is the case with *Lizard Lick* which is an actual towing company. But their real business practices are not part of the narrative of this show. Consequently, the pleasure derived from consuming truTV has nothing to do with a nego-tiation between reality and its mediation, consumer worlds or tangible social ones, but just pure fiction. The most simplistic, reductive critique of reality TV is that "it is not real." But when that actually proves to be true, when reality TV reflects its cheapest readings, then it is worth asking whether the producers are to blame or the critics, amateurs and professionals alike, who have been dismissing the format since its inception. TruTV is the realization of years upon years of snobby dismissal, through which reality TV has been happily whipped into submission. The cultural snobs wanted uncontested fakery. And that is exactly what they got.

This historical shift in content can be traced back to the early 2000s, the apex of nationally-televised reality programs. To compensate for the intense demand, networks and producers were scrambling to find new twists on the usual competition or fishbowl-style reality shows, sometimes merging the two styles. Out of the consequent glut came *Who Wants to Marry a Multi-Millionaire?*, *Temptation Island*, and *The Swan*, among other TV shows, that pushed the boundaries of good taste and common sense because they were solely about exploitation, and the people watching were experiencing schadenfreude, not just entertainment value. Authenticity had been displaced for the sake of shocking content. Fox's *Temptation Island*, for instance, fea-tured romantic couples (married, long-term dating, short-term, etc.) whose relationships would be put to the test, as they were segregated from each other and "tempted" by hired models. Proof of infidelity would be shown to their partner after the fact, in some incredible video reveals that were equal parts gut-wrenching and laughable. This format guaranteed wild breakdowns, and managed to terminate a marriage or two. The first season logged exceptional ratings numbers. And out of the success of shows like *Temptation Island* came copycats from near and far. What reality TV consumers receive now and into the future are the mature, more perverse versions of these exploitative shows. The cultural catalyst, in the early years of this new millennium, was arguably less a matter of economics and more of an American historical moment.

Indeed, the near universal reaction to 9/11 was that it was like "something out a movie." And it was true. Advanced technology, never directly intended to spur death, colliding with thousands of otherwise safe and protected souls was something only a paranoid Hollywood screenwriter might conceive, and a CGI-addicted director like James Cameron might execute. Jean Baudrillard figured this reaction to 9/11 stemmed from the collision of America's lack of reality with the Jihadists' excess of reality. "But does reality really prevail over fiction?" he writes in the aftermath of 9/11. "If it seems so, it is because reality has absorbed the energy of fiction, and become fiction itself." Baudrillard does not even afford Americans the benefit of a traumatic moment, neutering what could have been the "violence of the real" by emphasizing that reality, even in great terror, is "jealous of the image" (*The Spirit of Terrorism* 28). Because there was no genuine "resurrection of history" after the attack— Baudrillard means a *resurrection of authenticity*—does not mean America was not changed. The emotional reaction manifested itself in reality shows that, out of necessity to viewers, were becoming more and more contrived, because that was America's truth.

2

Ontologies of Facebook

Catfish *and the Magical Thinking of Consumers*

> The fundamental metaphorical message of the computer, in short, is that we are machines—thinking machines, to be sure, but machines nonetheless.... [The computer] subordinates the claims of our nature, our biology, our emotions, our spirituality. The computer claims sovereignty over the whole range of human experience, and supports its claims by showing it "thinks" better than we can.
> —Neil Postman, *Technopoly: The Surrender of Culture to Technology* 111

The desire for authenticity among digital culture is apparent in how some users of Facebook engage that social media platform. This is not to say that, somehow, all Facebook subjects are entrenched in a negotiation of authenticity through the service, but that there is a *burgeoning* cultural ethos which instantiates a drive for ontological stability in social media, an "impetus for authenticity." In these cases, the axiomatic acceptance (or preoccupation) with a stable referent is the basis for a particular mode of usage, ensnaring users into a system of thinking antithetical to postmodernity and digital culture already elaborated within this project. The result, then, is dissonance: emotional, spiritual, and sometimes corporeal in form, which is illustrated in this chapter. This "impetus for authenticity" found on Facebook has equivalents throughout modern consumer technology. Facebook serves as the explicator for a progressive consumerism, in a way reality TV and YouTube do not because their usage often carries attributes of 20th-century consumption, some of which may not be long for this world. In light of those media, Facebook manufactures a distinct variety of consumer mutation, one shaped by digital logic not explicitly analog logic, though using analog logic as a reference is still helpful because, again, analog media "guarantees the meaning of what is deep inside," thus its relation to a referent is comparably higher than digital media's (Hayles, *My Mother Was a Computer* 203). And this depth-oriented meaning is what authenticity-driven Facebookers are grasping at. But as *modernism* "grounded the self" through authenticity, *postmodernism* often rejects desires for authentic selfhood, resulting in ostensibly postmodern subjectivities through the digital medium of Facebook (Deresiewicz 308). As stated elsewhere, in accordance with N. Katherine Hayles' writing, digital subjectivizing is marked by fragmentation, disjunction, and instability. What is more, Hayles' "computational regime," to which Facebook is beholden, states that ever-deepening emergent digital properties can "simulate" the "most complex phenomena on Earth," except that complexity is still a simulation, and is only, in her words, "envisioned" as something more than that (*My Mother Was a Computer* 18, 19). This is a succinct means by which to encapsulate the larger Facebook authenticity problem.

The subject/object (human/thing) barrier is key to the authenticity considerations made through Facebook. The technology which enables Facebook mediation (its "black box")[1] is computer technology: the personal computer, the mobile phone or tablet, set-top boxes and smart televisions, for instance. Basically, Facebook can be run through any digital consumer product capable of running independent applications or a web browser—Facebook only requires some form of operating system in order for its most basic functionality to begin. As such, Facebook differs from reality TV and YouTube in that both those media are not entirely predicated on the digital; quite the contrary is true, as full motion video is, in its artistic conceptualization, an analog enterprise, especially in terms of reception. YouTube's genealogy, though thematically different, can be located in domestic (analog) home video production. Facebook is a testament to purely digital formulations of the self, due in part to a very-recent historical trajectory which is elaborated on below, but mostly because its reception and interaction have *always* been foregrounded by digital computers. With this in mind, subjective referentiality should be understood differently when applied to Facebook because the potential subject explicitly mediates through a digital object, reliant on emergent complexity, as a means of subjectivizing. In the Facebook subjectivizing experience, it is the assumptions of the user that matter most. Profiles of ordinary people on-screen are explicitly *mediations* arriving to users by means of a digital space, one grounded by an idiosyncratic interface, its own set of cultural cues, and consumerist impulses. And users are evaluating people's authenticity through those Facebook profiles.

Before proceeding, there should be some preface regarding authenticity and forthcoming terms. While authenticity weighs heavily on this book's other chapters, here it is the crux of the analysis. As such, it is important to consider *degrees* of authenticity; here stated, the type of relationship an attributed thing has to its referent, or its *ontological value*. Such considerations are by no means revolutionary, nor are they being stated here as such. Semiotics and Structuralism, for instance, are fixated by ontology and authenticity. In contemporary theory, which Jameson posits as distinctly postmodern,[2] Derridian deconstruction was the precursor to a wealth of unstable signifiers, "decentered" from their originary locale, through which Michel Foucault and Judith Butler challenged various power structures. The value in assessing these characteristics in Facebook is not to assert that they are new, but, even more importantly, that they are historically endemic to postmodern culture and consumerism; indeed, their stark appearance within Facebook emphasizes its postmodern qualities. Past cultural forms continually affect present ones, and this action is itself postmodernist. Furthermore, and this point is elaborated on elsewhere in this book, a critical response to this sort of positioning might argue, "But postmodernism denies ontology; this is also foundational to postmodernism." Turning to Brian McHale's concept of postmodernism in 1987's *Postmodernist Fiction*, it is not oxymoronic or self-contradictory to consider ontology in relation to postmodernism because its outward denial of ontology merely exacerbates that very concept—thus, the insistence upon authenticity espoused by many consumers living in postmodernity. Ontology's valuation within postmodernism is a paradox, not an oxymoron. Also, the goal here is not to signal a referent by pointing out an ontological problem on Facebook, because "to *do* ontology in this perspective is not necessarily to seek some grounding for *our* universe"; indeed, this project is not an attempt to "center" Facebook, YouTube, reality TV, or their mediational subjectivities, just to say that long-standing authenticity issues play out amidst these media as well (McHale 27).

Where this project locates the authenticity problem is as an outgrowth of image world discourse because the mechanically reproduced image best conveys the degrees of relation that occur under the guise of digital mediation, especially of the kind written about in this book. A useful theoretical starting point is Walter Benjamin's 1936 piece "The Work of Art in the Age of Mechanical Reproduction," in which Benjamin establishes a historical shift in a representational thing's relationship to the thing it is meant to represent, beginning with the Greeks and on into full motion film. Gradually, as technology becomes more invasive/prevalent, these reproductions lose their essential "aura" of authenticity. Benjamin posits that "the presence of the original is the prerequisite to the concept of authenticity," which is similar to the issue a percentage of Facebookers have when assessing other user profiles through the service; their assessment *does not* begin with the question of a referent ("the original"), but instead the existence of that profile (a mediational interface output) serves as proof of the referent (222). But, considering that technology has advanced exponentially since Benjamin's era, it behooves this argument to select a more contemporary term than "aura."

More recently than the 1930s, studies in documentary film have also been impacted by the authenticity problem. Bill Nichols, in considering what he calls the "indexical quality" of documentary film, explicates that indexicality is the "uncanny sense of a *document*, or *image* that bears a strict correspondence to what it refers to" (emphasis added, 34). On Facebook, a combination of "document," the text-based profile information, and "image," the shared profile pictures and (to a lesser extent) audio and video, work to shape varying degrees of Facebook indexicality. The more users share on Facebook, the denser their timelines and photo libraries, the greater the sense of indexicality, as evidence of their real world existence increases. Indeed, we tend to believe a person's Facebook profile is who (or what) they say they are when their updates are frequent, personable, and idiosyncratic—and when the associated profile and images have a close relation to the person they actually are in real life. A Facebook user, for instance, who chronicles their daily experiences, whose timeline will reveal explicit ties to an off-screen life, is made (more) authentic through that means, at least from the reception end. Some of my Facebook friends, for instance, have more than a decade worth of content to asses in order that I might discover how they have lived their lives; a multitude of photographs and "status updates" can assemble a convincing record of humanity, even if strategically. Some older aged users I know, such as distant relatives of mine, will upload photographs from their childhood, share anecdotes from their past, by way of this digital recall even their maturation can be accessed through Facebook. Experiencing ordinary people by this means is not somehow an *equivalent* to directly experiencing other people offline, though neither should be privileged, but that conflation can happen if the ideological underpinning fits.

On Facebook, the result of all its off-screen content is an uncanny resemblance to a real world referent, even though this resemblance ascribes to Facebook's idiosyncratic terms of mediation. This resemblance is predicated on a user's knowledge of that other person in real life, the very crux of Facebook's social networking popularity. While it is common for users to friend people whom they have never met, this is actually an aberration and deviates from Facebook's exceptional status in contemporary culture. As Mimi Marinucci of Eastern Washington University asserts, "Usually, our Facebook friends are people with whom we already have (or have had) offline relationships. This feature of the Facebook environment also tempers the characteristic *invisibility* of online communication" (71). Facebook, then, differs from the "characteristic invisibility" of archetypal online socialization, instead favoring what some commentators call "persistent identity" between real world selves and virtual ones. So when a user accepts friend requests from other users they do not know outside Facebook, they are defying Facebook's ideological understanding of itself, at the very least from a corporate standpoint. There is a reason Facebook, Inc., as of January 2013, asks, "Do you know this person outside Facebook? Yes or No" every time users accept a new friend request. Users who receive a reply of "no" twice in one day are penalized, resulting in a ban from sending friend requests for a set period of time, one week to a month depending on their disciplinary status within Facebook's community of moderators. As such, Facebook is literally enforcing an ideology of actuality through its interface—a paradigm which helps to instantiate an axiom of authenticity within some of its userbase.

Assuming an assessing user is already Facebook friends with a profile they are questioning in order to bypass the requisite privacy settings, and that profile contains a wealth of biographical information as is typical on the service, the assessing user probably knows where that person was born, currently lives, went to school, who their relatives are. The typical Facebooker also supplies what Christine Rosen designates as social networks' "metaphors of the person," hobbies and consumer interests solidified through presses of the "share" and "like" buttons, ways of uncovering a user's surface identity (182). Additionally, beneath a profile's "basic information," users can supply terse biographical and ideological information about themselves. On Facebook, the "metaphors of the person" serve a twofold purpose: identity boundaries for the mediated person and their Facebook friends (or future friends) and also data for Facebook advertising partners so that profiles might be targeted appropriately by consumer capitalists. And, of course, a convincing profile has at least some photographs to convey an embodied self, however strategically. Ordinary Facebookers will upload audio or video, but not with any reliable frequency; lengthy audio or video tends to be antithetical to Facebook consumption. Generally, the News Feed containing a user's friends' activities is skimmed, so much of that content is easily digestible text, digital photo, or static image. Life-affirming memes (e.g., image macros, Vines, or .gifs) are also very popular on Facebook; these memes are either an uplifting short video clip or photograph accompanied by an emotional quote such as "Time Heals Everything." My aunt shares them often. Now, to surmise that with all this information there might be any question as to who (or what) might be controlling a Facebook profile is fallacious. Surely the Facebook profile conveys a markedly high degree of indexicality. But many users still make mistakes in their assessments, and it is because, generally, they have an ideological misunderstanding of Facebook and the Internet in general.

For some users, the Facebook profile affirms a self-contradictory impetus for authenticity online. This impetus is "self-contradictory" because the Internet, in its formative years as a consumer platform, had basically no indexical value and had no need for it. Its various manifestations over the years have actually *challenged* the very idea of the Internet as a place for authentic subjective expression. The first successful corporate project to sell 'time-shares' of online space to consumers was through CompuServe in 1978, and similar to MS-DOS or BASIC, it was aesthetically computational in that it spoke to the *vacuum* of digital meaning: black screens, blinking cursors, and command-lines. Digital audio and images had yet to penetrate the philosophical system of Internet space because of the limitations of computer hardware and communication infrastructure. Before graphic user interfaces (GUIs), all meaning *explicitly* emerged from the interface; none of it came front-loaded such as with the newest image-driven iterations of Windows. The first functional GUI for personal computers did not arrive to store shelves until 1984, installed on Apple's Macintosh. But Apple's early operating system was too clunky to carry anything even resembling the first popular web browsers, such as Netscape Navigator or Internet Explorer (Ryan 53). Indeed, ARPANET, the Internet's direct forbearer, was a military endeavor to pool American intellectual resources, what the Department of Defense in 1968 called a "resource sharing computer network," free of any indexical value (Ryan 29). Just as YouTube began as "Your Digital Video Repository," so, too, was the Internet formatively an *information* repository; indexicality, or even authenticity, did not figure into ARPANET's ethos of usage. And while information must take into account stake holding and credibility, information certainly lacks the ontological complexity of the subject. After communications infrastructures improved and offered greater potential for consumer interaction, the subject found its way onto what would become the Internet because democratic consumer participation *guarantees* that eventual outcome, as evidenced by both reality TV and YouTube. And when information and subjecthood co-mingle, the byproduct is problematic.

Breaking away from its status as an information repository, as academics and hackers co-opted the Internet from military interests, a social media platform called The Whole Earth 'Lectronic Link (The WELL), founded by techies Stewart Brand and Larry Brilliant in 1985, served as the proto-Facebook, excluding photos/images. By requiring a subscription fee, users of that social platform dialed into message boards called "conferences," and created intimate connections with people through cultural interests rather than proximity, a very Facebookian sense of community. Assuredly, someone's geographic location does not impede social media. What is more, all WELL users had to be highly literate in computational technology as PC interfaces for online interaction were still too esoteric for mass consumption. By coupling computational literacy with a monetary bias, authenticity found its way onto an online social space, and amazingly without images or any other conceivable way to measure indexical value; the chaotic freedom of digital anonymity was stifled by Brand and Brilliant, who demanded The WELL be an "intimacy" experiment between people (Ryan 84). And while this experiment was fruitful, as the Internet grew and personal computing became more consumer accessible, free popular message boards appeared, many of which thrived on the copious instability and anonymity the Internet offers *axiomatically* as a fragmentary, unstable digital space (Hayles, *My Mother Was a Computer* 203). This is the "characteristic invisibility" to which Marinucci refers, as the Internet—in the popular imagination—would retain that character along its historical development. What netizens were discovering was that *authenticity*, in fact, hindered the Internet's most valuable and revolutionary attribute: to "unconstrain" ideas and data from the shackles of "hierarchy and categorization" (Ryan 106). Quite literally, this lack of constraint could decenter human digital output from its real world (off-screen) referent. The same is true of some users who were engaging the platform as a venue for subjectivity.

Indeed, by 1990, the Internet was where some users unshackled themselves from the "prison" of human embodiment constructed in a societal context, which is steeped in presumption, stereotyping, malady, pain; for these users, the Internet was the material body's respite, and also, paradoxically, a fertile ground for subjectivity. Techno-optimist Douglas Rushkoff remembers this historical moment fondly: "There was a whole new space out there [the Internet], unlimited by the constraints of time and space, appearance and prejudice, gender and power" (118). There was no saying who (or what) was on the other side of the screen then, and for cyberfuturists this was liberatory not stifling; it was a technological push for the distinctly postmodern notion of protean identity play. "The first phase of web culture, one must admit," Alexander R. Galloway writes of 90s-era Internet, "carried a revolutionary impulse" (2). The same "anonymity-as-liberator" flavor of Internet activity still thrives online today, though this activity is often relegated to the perceived "dark corners" of the Internet. For instance, high traffic message boards such as Reddit and 4Chan, the supposed home of infamous hacktivism group "Anonymous," have been the subject of repeated popular and academic denouncements, as much of the anonymity these message boards celebrate has lead to systematically regressive racial, gender, and sexual discourse, often enabling endless ideological flame wars and real world crime.[3] Reddit and 4Chan, then, stand in opposition to Facebook's now mainstreamed claim to authentic online mediations of humanity.

The argument here, it should be said, is not meant to stigmatize digital anonymity, as that does not forward the premise of this chapter, but that the authenticity and high indexicality upheld by many Facebookers must be considered juxtapositional—and equal—to the instability and anonymity of message boards and other popular online social spaces. 4Chan and Reddit are demonized in the same way early Internet detractors demonized The Whole Earth 'Lectronic Link (The WELL), America Online (AOL) chat rooms from the 1990s, open source e-mail platforms, or the Amazon.com customer review system. An antiquated way of criticizing the Internet is considering its potential, first and foremost, for the *abuse* of anonymity because that criticism has been left by the wayside, especially when held alongside the thick regressive discourse(s) on YouTube and occurring elsewhere online. Just as "trolls and haters" are normalized within YouTube, anonymity's abuses are normalized within the Internet ethos (Burgess and Green, *YouTube* 96). In Web 2.0 contexts, it is commonplace for Internet users to anonymously deceive, adopt new (oppositional) virtual personas, harass, bully, and abuse.

In Sherry Turkle's 1995 book about multi-user domains (MUDs), *Life on the Screen*, she posits that "[users] *insist* that a certain amount of shape-shifting is *part* of the online game" (emphasis added, 228). She made this observation in 1995. Therefore, the abuses of anonymity should no longer engender fiery zeal, or then there is the risk of impeding progressive thought about the Internet. Users can anonymously say whatever they want online without consequence to their real, material selves—this actually says more about lived reality than its digital mediation. When users turn to the Internet to indulge abusive behavior, the result enforces how psychically arrested these users are to the material world. Indeed, to enact anonymous abuses alerts other anonymous users to the personality failings and insecurities of its perpetrators because all involved know how *easily* digital anonymity facilitates that behavior; to anonymously transgress against others is the height of material impotence. What is more, abusive anonymity is now being punished by others within the very system that encourages it: Michael Brutsch, a computer programmer from Texas, was a longtime anonymous contributor to some of Reddit's most flagrantly offensive message boards—ones which contained deep-seated racism, sexism, and illicit pictures of underage women. Brutsch had garnered Internet infamy in his heavy usage and atypical offensiveness as Reddit user "Violentacrez." Brutsh moderated and helped to grow a subculture of Redditors who freely disseminated photos of underage women, using categorical tags such as "Creepshots," "Chokeabitch," and "Deadjailbait," which was a tag attributed to photos of dead children. Brutsch notoriously defended his group's actions in various arguments conducted throughout Reddit, and later blamed Reddit for encouraging his usage; at one point, in fact, Reddit mailed him an actual trophy for his well-trafficked "jailbait" board, a golden statuette of the web site's mascot Brutsch showed off during his infamous CNN interview. In October 2012, his off-screen identity was discovered by some shrewd fellow users who reported the information to gossip blog Gawker, who then divulged that information in a public blog posting. Brutsch subsequently lost his real world job and made the national news, with CNN personality Anderson Cooper calling him out explicitly, in an act of digital public shaming (vigilantism?) that has also become integral to a new conception of digital conduct (Holpuch). Similar to what has happened on YouTube, there is some degree of ethical fluidity on Reddit's message boards; users have become less tolerant of intolerance, and their act of punishment is to reach out into the material world, breaking the contract of anonymity. This reaction to Brutsch's breach of a prescribed moral order, one which was valued prior to and exterior from the Internet, conveys the significance of the real world to the digital, anonymous one.[4]

Defining Facebook

To be sure, Reddit is about the Internet, and its reliance on anonymity communicates that fact. Facebook, similar to The WELL, is about people;

people mediating their real world selves online, to whatever end. Facebook signifies a fundamental shift in thinking about online mediations: the dangers of anonymity, Facebook implicitly states, live elsewhere on the Internet. On Facebook, users are accountable for their online behavior because generally their profile represents, in varying degrees, who users are in real life, off-screen. No Internet sleuthing, such that happens within the Reddit community, has to be performed so that some moral order can be upheld. But all the trappings of anonymity—the lack of tactile materiality, for instance—are still attributes of Facebook. Anonymous users on Reddit who post hateful comments do so because they *believe* they will never see any consequence to their actual, physical self. And, in moderation, these users can get away with their hate, unlike Michael Brutsch whose transgressions were too visible in a community which prides itself on insularity. Granted, this also has to do with the culture of Reddit, the same which dedicates message boards to "speculum porn," "upskirt shots," and "rape jokes." Transgression on Reddit is not exceptional, and neither is it within the broader scope of the Internet. Also, these transgressions are a consequence of the technological reality of online communication at-large, that "characteristic invisibility" which ideologically *encourages* transgressions. Online anonymity is enabled by digital computational technology, a thickly designed mediator for the self. Every textual speech act transmitted on Facebook, for instance, must pass through a keyboard or smaller input device, an operating system, a browser or application, and then the mercurial Facebook interface in order to arrive to its recipient, never mind the off-screen social dynamics of the communicator. And Facebook employs computational technology just as Reddit does. As the Internet has evolved along a trajectory of increasing indexicality, and some users adopt an impetus for authenticity, it is important to remember the Internet's unstable, protean attributes because Facebook's service encourages authenticity through that very same source. As McLuhan figured, "no medium has its meaning or existence alone, but only in constant interplay with other media," as is true of Facebook (162).

Despite the popularity of Facebook among Millennials, the social networking platform is not singular in its functionality; it is just a conceivable breakthrough that has been advanced upon by other alternative platforms in various respects, though none has achieved the cultural significance or popularity of Facebook.[5] According to Facebook user metrics, a source with some troublesome stakes, nearly forty percent of *all* Americans use the service on a daily basis. Into the 2010s, the consensus outside Facebook's own figures has hovered around fifty percent of all American Internet users, a more reasonable figure, though Twitter and other social media services have lured some of that userbase away. While the number of registered users and their time spent on the service is significant in order to effectively gauge the popularity of Facebook, also valuable is its disdain: nothing on the Internet is so widely maligned and yet also still manages to be so prevalent. If everyone in the U.S. (and possibly planet Earth) can identify a medium and agree on their mutual hatred for it, then it is undoubtedly popular—Facebook is also the second most popular website in the world, one above YouTube, one below Google (Alexa). The common dismissal of Facebook among the young is that it is no longer "cool" because older people have begun to use it since its peak hipness, toward the end of the 2000s. According to a 2013 Pew Research Poll, those same teens have also refused to shut down their Facebook accounts, thereby shifting Facebook's status into a social "utility" rather than a zeitgeisty, hip digital service such as Instagram, Twitter, or Snapchat (Matyszczyk). As such, Facebook is an established platform, with a userbase that includes an incredible diversity of real world people—the critique that digital culture excludes those of the lower economic strata, in fact, has proven more and more irrelevant as digital communication technology has become cheap and incredibly user-friendly. If anything, the great bias of the Internet and Facebook is one of cultural geography; if a person is not born in the West, then odds are their relationship to the Internet has suffered consequently.[6]

The key components of Facebook for consumers are accruing and organizing "friends," other users on the service, and sharing personal, informational, or political communications (consisting of text/image/audio/video) with these friends. Out of a sample of a 125 users, all well-educated and middle to upper income, the majority described their usage as purely social in nature, or "staying in touch with family and friends." Of the same group, they were least inclined to use the service as a political platform (Zúñiga and Valenzuela xxxvii). "Reconnection" of real life people with one another from years gone by is a common emotional theme of Facebook usage, and as a consequence of the platform's wide adoption in the U.S., especially among Millennials, a theme fully-realized by its userbase. Some Facebook "profiles," especially those associated with Hollywood actors[7] and politicians, share posts publicly, but most ordinary Facebookers utilize some amount of privacy setting, blocking any curious non-friends (or public) from viewing their personal information. Facebook now offers a number of tutorials to assist the process of activating privacy settings and other of its identity-shielding features, ensuring its billion or so users know how to get the most privacy from its service.

While social media has largely helped to reinforce the sense that privacy has been devalued in 21st-century consumer culture, Facebook certainly offers a wide variety of ways for users to keep their posts private, though not private, of course, to Facebook, Inc. or its advertising partners. As of the 2010s, most Facebookers know better than to share personal phone numbers or home addresses, to name a couple of personal items that have become taboo on the service. Facebook also functions as a way of transmitting factual and emotional information about its users for potential real life employers, friends, and lovers, in a (deeply) controlled setting. More broadly, teens nowadays are embroiled in a scapegoating enterprise which characterizes them as "public creatures" with little regard for privacy due to their heavy social media involvement; my own tendency is to view them in this way. But researchers like danah boyd conceptualize new standards of privacy emerging from the social media menagerie of everyday teen usage—privacy articulates itself via shifting manners per platform. Teens might engage Instagram on a public scale, for instance, sharing family photos and innocent pictures with friends. Yet they will reserve certain utterances for cellular text messaging or other social media they have set to higher privacy settings. "When [teens] think something might be sensitive," boyd writes, "they often switch to a different medium, turning to text messages or chat to communicate with smaller audiences directly" (62). Privacy, then, can be viewed as a qualified experience for teen subjectivity, an extension of the mediated selfhood prevailing today.

Returning to Facebook specifically, subjects are afforded a high degree of "stage-management" by self-mediating through Zuckerberg's service. While this should be considered parallel to the performance of the ordinary self in the everyday, Facebook is exceptional in that the fragility and unpredictability of material, real world performances of the self are disrupted by its operations. Indeed, a static photograph and text-reliant interface such as Facebook's offers a comparably objective platform for the subject, contrasted by that objectivity which full motion video takes away from the subject. Reality TV and YouTube video convey in their mediation of ordinary people, at their core, an *imposition* upon their on-screen subjects. On reality TV, the subject/participant is imposed upon by the production hierarchy and the technological embodiment that full motion supplies; the reality TV subject's only conceivable escape, as was the case with Puck on *The Real World* in 1994, is to try and sabotage that mediation—this struggle, paradoxically, better serves on-screen complexity. The same is true of YouTube: no matter how much YouTube vloggers edit their videos before uploading, full motion video's indexicality works against their attempts at unmitigated agency. A conspiracy regarding popular YouTubers the Fowler sisters' nose job(s) is an example, as their haul videos are heavily edited/produced, with ample post-production filtering and other effects. A Facebook profile, then, is akin to a hermetically-sealed version of the subject, with photographs carefully selected which *they believe* best communicate their interiority or physical appearance. A cultural trend since social media's burgeoning mass popularity in the mid 2000s, the "MySpace Angle" is a social media profile photo taken from a strategic angle which hides the subject's full embodiment such that only the face is captured (Sessions). These photos tend to be taken from an elevated vantage point, above the forehead. A MySpace Angle can also be an extreme close-up of a person's face which leaves definition and bone structure out of the frame. In contrast, social media users would not be afforded that level of "stage management" on reality TV. Here, the problem is whether mediated subjective complexity has to do with the subject's *lack* of agency in that mediation, certainly a defeating proposition in the age of Web 2.0 participation. So while agency is increased in the Facebook mediation exercise, it seems the complexity Facebookers convey is part and parcel to the degree of forethought in that engagement.

Historically, as a social medium, The WELL was anomalous in that it attracted subscribers already entrenched in the cyber ethos—to figure that it was a consumer platform in scope is problematic, despite its attendant fees. Also, The WELL was closely moderated by its users and developers to impede abuses in representations of the self, antithetical to what goes on today. Also discussed in Chapter 3, "light-touch" governance is the mantra of (successful) Web 2.0 moderation. Facebook's consumer trajectory instead begins with subscription MUDs from the 1990s, when the indexical values were low but subjectivities still engaged online spaces—the authenticity of its users' self-mediation, also, was of no consequence to the service providers. CompuServe and America Online (AOL), dial-up ISPs that also serve as proto-social networks, provided similar functionality to Facebook, allowing members to easily organize their social groups (AOL refers to "friends" as "buddies"), and efficiently maintain long strings of text communication between one user and another, as well as facilitating multiple, simultaneous communications in the form of instant messaging.

These primitive social MUDs should be considered transient "delivery systems" that still prove to have viable media traits, but face inevitable substitution by newer technology (Jenkins, *Convergence Culture* 13). There is a distinct interfacial difference between 1990s dial-up platforms and what Facebook offers, but many core features persist: for instance, the interface of Facebook also provides for instant messaging, and uses similar colloquial terminology (e.g., "like" and "friend") to create greater relatability for less computer literate users. In order to make their interfaces functional for a wide consumer base, it was a necessity for CompuServe and AOL to "dumb things down." Drawing a parallel here, between the old and the new, is meant to lessen the rarity some ascribe to Facebook, so that its infractions in authenticity might not be so perplexing. It should also be said that AOL and CompuServe were notorious for their abuses of anonymity—Sherry Turkle interrogates American Online chat rooms in *Life on the Screen* to point out the "identity crisis" arising out of unstable online spaces. A lack of literacy regarding MUDs in those days resulted in explicit off-screen *dissonance* in her interview subjects, leading Turkle to conclude, "We must understand the dynamics of virtual experience both to foresee who might be in danger and to put these experiences to best use. Without a deep understanding of the many selves [e.g., online protean identity play] that we express in the virtual, *we cannot use our experiences there to enrich the real*" (emphasis added, 269). Indeed, to play in these digital spaces can, in fact, "enrich" the subject's off-screen sense of self, but when play is mistaken for sincerity, then Turkle's fears for the digital subject become reality.

Millennials, to their credit, are digitally literate, having grown up alongside thriving consumer MUDs. And it is true that every year since Facebook's inception in 2004, increasingly "older" people have been creating profiles, with around thirty percent of its total userbase over thirty years of age, according to Facebook's metrics. As example, my eighty-four-year-old grandmother is on Facebook, as well as many of her friends. Her computer and cell phone have never been so easy to use, thus spurring her current embrace of social media. Hers is a generation that missed out on MUDs, AOL instant messaging, message boards, and the like—she does not understand that there is some negotiation of truth value going on within social media in the first place. As far as my grandmother knows, everyone on Facebook is exactly as they are in reality, not because she is not socially intelligent, but because she lacks the savviness and media literacy to suspect otherwise. The trouble is that Facebook not only "reconnects" real world people but its service also permits users to friend those they do not know in real life, even if that usage is considered aberrant by Facebook, Inc. After repeated charges by her colleagues, when Sherry Turkle finally relented and created a Facebook profile sometime from 2008 to 2010,[8] she went through a two-week period of accepting only friend requests from people whom she knew in real life, what she calls "plan A," that she adhered to as a means of utilizing the service exactly as her teenage (Millennial) research subjects did. After those two weeks, Turkle began accepting friend requests from Facebook profiles—fans—she did not know in real life, "flattered" by their appreciation of her work. After doing so, she asked herself, "But now that I had invited strangers into my life, would I invite myself into the lives of strangers?" a deep question that captures all the pertinent anxieties that *should* be felt as users mix anonymity and actuality, oil and water, in the social cauldron that is Facebook (*Alone Together* 182).

Yet Turkle understands Facebook truth value. Turkle has no illusions about her fans, now Facebook friends; they are "strangers," and she is giving them access to her "life." The subtext of "stranger" invigorates a sense of uneasiness and abjection. And this is not just another digital mediation of Turkle's life; her Facebook mediation is, as she figures, *actually* her life. Facebook profiles can carry similar weight (or reflect) the intrinsic value of lived reality, not that they are truly equivalents, but that they are *perceived to be so* by some users. The impetus for authenticity online has established a greater sense of self-relevance to digital social spaces. Self-relevance is the degree of internal human value virtual spaces hold for its users, according to Jim Blascovich and Jeremy Bailenson's studies in virtual reality. In Blascovich and Bailenson's estimation, the degree of self-relevance a person has with a given digital platform depends on what amount of their real world self that space asks for: a game of *Pac-Man* engages the user physically, but requires no real world credentials for its use and has less corporeal immediacy than something like an online dating profile on OkCupid (80–81). An artificial intelligence could be playing *Pac-Man* and the game would not somehow change or retain any greater value. *Pac-Man* carries a low degree of self-relevance, and Facebook carries a high degree of self-relevance because of its *characteristic visibility* for the mediated subject, in contrast to Mimi Marinucci's characteristic invisibility online. People generally strive for some relation to their real world self in their Facebook profiles. Arguably, self-relevance on Facebook is so high that the large percentage of subjective worth accrued through its means, especially for the young, must be measured alongside the fraud and abuses that also exist on Facebook.

Authenticity's Delusion: The Digital Culture of Catfish

The 2010 documentary *Catfish*, directed by Ariel Schulman and starring his brother Nev, chronicles Nev's long-distance Facebook romance with a stranger, a young woman named "Megan Faccio." The structure of the film's narrative establishes their union, the tender Facebook messages exchanged between Nev and "Megan," all the assumptions Nev was embracing about this person in spite of the outright fraudulence he had already discovered before traveling from New York to rural Michigan to meet "Megan." In traveling to her home, Nev and his filmmaker brother were holding "Megan" accountable for the lies the Internet (to which Facebook is beholden) made so easy for her to tell, despite their attempts to appear non-combative. And, of course, in a distinctly Hollywood plot contrivance, the revelation of middle-aged Angela Wesselman in place of "Megan Faccio" functions as a perfect moment of pathos, so, despite Nev's unique sense of victimhood that the film builds up, there were victims all around. *Catfish* has been called out for its suspect actuality by other documentary filmmakers, namely Morgan Spurlock who told the filmmakers, "It was the best fake documentary I have ever seen." The Schulmans replied in earnest that the film is "100% real," though they basically did not respond to the film's tidiness and problematic chronology (Brodie). Whatever its truth status, this documentary, now adapted as an equally suspect and fascinating weekly TV show on MTV hosted by Nev Schulman, is endemic of a larger societal trend to hold netizens to a standard of authenticity, but that ethos forgets that the Internet is not a platform suited for authenticity. A widely reported 2012 incident involving a Notre Dame linebacker, Monti Te'o, and his fraudulent online girlfriend catapulted the term "catfish" into the popular conversation, and it is now used commonly as a verb; akin to *googling* something, or *facebooking* someone, *catfishing* is meant to signify any online fraud that involves one person believing in the real world actuality of another based solely on their online representation.

Similar to the majority of Facebook catfish, both Monti Te'o's fake girlfriend, who was discovered to be a man Te'o had known from high school, and Angela Wesselman used pictures and biographical information they had acquired elsewhere on the Internet in order to enact their fraud. Curiously, though, both used their actual voice on the phone with their respective victim, which on the surface says that the human voice is pliable enough to fool people. Instead, this strange fact actually acknowledges the undue value today's culture places upon images to represent the world, probably because "through being photographed," Susan Sontag writes in *On Photography*, "something becomes part of a system of information" (156). And information in the 21st century has been elevated to "metaphysical" status, according to Neil Postman's observations from his book *Technopoly: The Surrender of Culture to Technology* (1993). What is more, the image's indexical value is artificially heightened by its prevalence throughout social media culture—indeed, the ideology to which Schulman and Te'o ascribe disavows the physical legitimacy of human voice *in favor* of the digital image. In the *Catfish* documentary, the scene in which Schulman confesses his love for "Megan Faccio" slyly rests on her photograph, not recordings of her voice. Schulman calls his digital lover—the photograph Wesselman stole—"beautiful" and "sexy" repeatedly throughout the film. The pitch and tone of her voice, which might have alerted him (or the viewer) to her fraud earlier, are of little import to their interaction, despite "Megan Faccio" claiming to be a singer/songwriter in their exchanged Internet messages and more immediate phone conversations.

Nev Schulman and Monti Te'o are both American Millennials with an admittedly high degree of digital literacy, and yet the two were duped by their respective catfishes. Their generation grew alongside evolving technology which was broad in its accessibility and bountiful in its prospects for digital socialization. Prior to Facebook, the failed social networking venture MySpace, which has seen attempted reboots on three separate occasions since its multiple acquisitions over the last few years, started the social networking craze in 2003. MySpace was not necessarily foregrounded by an impetus for authenticity, but enough people online were willing to submit their real selves to its highly-customizable interface. Representing who a user actually was in real life appeared feasible on the flexible MySpace interface; the service freed users from the restrictions of tethered, dial-up platforms such as AOL, which offered low-customizability for the sake of accessibility. In light of older text-based MUDs, MySpace was rapturously indexical: individual MySpace profile pages were a kaleidoscope of pictures and sound, many of which were too data heavy to be accessed by Internet service provider customers with no broadband service, a technological advantage that had yet to universally breach urban and high-income borders. Despite its technical advances in mediation, MySpace upheld no gatekeeping mechanisms to ensure any relation to a real world, and the (mostly young) people authentically using the service suffered the rampant abuses of anonymous MySpace users. For the sake of inclusivity and user volume, MySpace sealed its eventual fate. Successful social media, as has now been proven by Facebook, must exert some referential standard in order that the off-screen self can effectively locate itself on-screen.

The intellectual journey of Facebook founder Mark Zuckerberg's development of this incredibly successful platform has been explored, analyzed, and narrativized ad nauseum,[9] so there is no point in diving deep into the variety of decisions Zuckerberg made when initially designing the platform. Zuckerberg's most important decision, for this argument, was to tie users to an actual, functioning university e-mail address—more specifically, e-mail addresses exclusively from Harvard. The circumstance that would call for an Ivy League institution to issue a fraudulent or arbitrary e-mail address is practically nonexistent, barring the mischievous tampering of a hacker. Smartly, by doing this, Zuckerberg could rely on the admissions office and registrar at Harvard to moderate his userbase, thereby removing the need for him to assess Facebook truth claims. And without having to explicitly say so—the Harvard e-mail requirement functioned similarly to the "high school cafeteria table" Facebook metaphor Turkle[10] is fond of—this gatekeeping measure helped to ensure that a profile would match their real world operator, or at the very least, guaranteed that they were actual students, employees, or faculty at Harvard, thus amplifying Facebook's potential for self-relevance. Logging onto Facebook with a Harvard e-mail address, then, was something primitive Facebookers accepted as an incitement for realness, because their university e-mail was issued by Harvard, and their registration with the school was as their real world self. Plus, there was no reason for Harvard Facebookers to be ashamed or in denial of their enrollment at Harvard in the first place; they were proud of it, hence Facebook's near immediate on-campus popularity. It should come as no surprise that as the service grew in usage among Harvard's student body, peers naturally began gatekeeping each other on Facebook (called "The Facebook" at the time). Not just anyone could go to Harvard, and not just anyone could belong to its premier social network. Similar to how The WELL maintained its emotional intimacy, authenticity on 2004-era Facebook was enforced through exclusion.

Gradually, Facebook spread to other college campuses across the U.S., also with gatekeeping measures that relied on authenticated university e-mail addresses. Then by 2005, a high school version of the website was published, followed by a business version. In September of 2006, Facebook opened its service to anyone thirteen years of age or older asking in return only a *valid*

85

e-mail address, meaning any open e-mail platform would suffice to verify a given profile. By the late 2000s, it was clear that Zuckerberg and his steadily growing social network operation were less concerned about exclusivity and authentic representation and more concerned with getting as many people registered as possible. A Facebook blog post from September 2006 assured already-enrolled users they could always "change their privacy settings" to prevent people from finding them in searches or otherwise communicating with them. Facebook staffers also made sure the users knew they had "built a bunch of tools that [would] help verify new users and prevent spammers" from abusing the service (Abram). Quite infamously, Facebook has infringed its own standards of practice by employing advertising and distributing personal information to various corporations and government interests, something they had initially promised never to do as part of Zuckerberg's (tacky) altruistic anti-profit, pro-privacy agenda. Facebook, Inc. still advertises these values even after going public on the NYSE and manipulating its terms of service numerous times.[11] While using Facebook in an inauthentic way might be considered contemptible by company moderators and a large percentage of its userbase, Nev Schulman and Monti Teʻo communicate in their misrecognition of Facebook the *historical* truth of its ability to maintain an environment of authenticity; this ability was predicated on Facebook remaining exclusive and parochial, but the end goal of consumer technology, no matter its ethical stance, is greater rates of adoption for that added consumer capital.

The impetus for authenticity online is rooted in human desire, not an actual ability for digital technology to truly achieve this end. This desire blossoms from the proliferation and prevalence of digital technology, part of a historical process of lessening referential value which crescendoed in conjunction with 20th-century consumer electronics. As Katherine N. Hayles considers it, which is also stated in Chapter 1, one of the key properties of the 21st-century "digital subject" is a "disjunction between surface and interior that is *instantiated by and envisioned within the digital technologies of computational culture*" (emphasis added, *My Mother Was a Computer* 203). Hayles' implication here is that digital technology at its core has a dysfunctional relationship with its surface output (a Facebook profile) and the internal thing (its real world operator) it is meant to convey. Digital technology is literally the thing consumers have turned to cure them of the lack of referential value *it has fostered*. Facebook is the mechanical articulation of Derrida's "decentered subject." But despite the pervasiveness of catfish, Facebook, for some users, still manages to promote a relationship between the representational and the actual; when it inevitably fails on this front, these users have mediated their subjective worth through a decentered and unstable platform, and will continue to do so even after knowing its potential for fraud. This is of course detrimental for any subjective value users might invest in or accrue from the platform, and not because postmodern play has no worth. The ideal byproduct of protean identity play on MUDs, Turkle rightfully asserts, is "a more fluid sense of self [that] allows a greater capacity for acknowledging diversity" (*Life on the Screen* 261). But when users sincerely engage a medium to represent their authentic, off-screen selves, then play, even "serious play," is left by the wayside. Earnest people who lay claim to their true selves on Facebook, given its real world weight, achieve a *revelation of self*, something that leaves them exposed and vulnerable. And this is dangerous because if Facebook's interface can result in a destabilization of the self, then that will also occur off-screen, in the real, ordinary people who trust it.

Similar to the gun, which carries an ideological bias of use as death technology, for many users, Facebook is a tool with a bias of use for authentic representation: it is just that this bias only has a *historical* referent. As McLuhan writes, "For any medium has the power of imposing its own assumptions on the unwary" (15). My Facebooking grandmother is McLuhan's "unwary." But Nev Schulman and Monti Te'o willfully submitted to a system they already knew could fail their real world selves. And when they chose to accept or ignore this fact, they were (un)consciously enacting a "complacent knowing" that "takes pleasures in not having any illusions about society," an incredibly postmodern ideology (Andrejevic, *Reality TV...* 178). Schulman and Te'o were (at face value) astonished by their catfish victimhood. Surely they knew about online chat rooms and the abuse of anonymity; there is no doubt about that. Indeed, these two young men, on an ideological level, wanted to believe Facebook could do away with the broader societal lack of authenticity. One of the telling narrative aspects of the documentary *Catfish* is that it focuses on the lies Angela Wesselman told, not on the gullible nature of Nev Schulman, who only acknowledges his dupery *once* throughout the film. And in forcing viewers to focus on Wesselman, the film locks itself into an archaic critique of digital human representation. Again, it is *axiomatic* that users lie and abuse online, and if the Internet is the 21st century's mediational space for authenticity, then that circumstance should be elaborated on further.

Turning back to the notion of *indexicality* can lend some much needed substance to the considerations to be made when comparing one online mediational platform versus another. YouTube and Facebook, for instance, prove to be nicely juxtaposed in this regard. The anchoring representational mode on YouTube is not its social network of commentators, who are actually secondary to its system of meaning, but the full motion video on which their discourse is reliant. When subjects approach YouTube, they are asked to pro vide full motion video or consume it, but when they do neither, then their participation with the service is inconsequential or aberrant. In his writing on indexicality, Bill Nichols draws a clear theoretical difference between x-ray scans and documentary film; an x-ray is judged simply by its "fidelity to the original" while the documentary is judged by the "pleasure it offers, the value of insight it provides, and the quality of perspective it instills" (13). In Nichols' frame, the x-ray is a "reproduction" of reality, and documentary film is a "representation." Though users bring the expectation of both reproduction and representation to either mediational platform, YouTube holds a greater *reproductive* value than Facebook in that its bias of full motion video insinuates a greater degree of material and emotional embodiment. Facebook's social interaction, to this day, tends to be text-based in nature, with the only arguable indexical requisite on the service being a profile picture, which is not even asked for until the fourth step of the new user registration process and *can be skipped*. Indeed, as Jeremy Sarachan writes, "Considering the predominance of text, the profile picture offers the major means of [Facebook] visual expression" (61). And even if a user does provide a profile picture, that image is not strictly policed nor does it have to relay a real world person—many Facebookers, in fact, will choose "avatars" or other images (tropical landscapes are popular) to convey their off-screen corporeal form, resulting in a ostensible disjunction between reality and the digital. To repeat an earlier point, not including some photographic evidence of a user's real life self onto a given Facebook profile will impede its prospect for friend requests, but will not stifle it use entirely.

In addition, a Facebook page is not like an ID card or x-ray; it is very much in a "distanced" representational mode—for one thing, text does not hold the indexical value of video or even the photographic image. Since text proves to be the predominant mode of social expression on Facebook, then that is problematic for its engaged subjectivities. While users might suspect a potential Facebook friend who does not feature an image of their real world self as their profile picture, their name stands in for the denominator of trust.

On my Facebook account, I am currently friends with two people's profiles that have no identifying profile picture, which instead feature Facebook's default profile image that only suggests the possible gender of its operator. What is lacking in this usage is the modernist guarantor of the subject: photography. A photo asserts a mimetic relation to off-screen reality; digital text is instead grounded by the interface. Sontag writes that photography is "the inventory of mortality," and when Facebookers deprive their profiles of that mortality, they straddle the subject/object barrier, becoming fragmentary in their mediation (70). At its peak popularity, AOL was plagued by "bots," automated communication programs that randomly instant messaged users in chat rooms, usually trying to con them out of personal information, not dissimilar to the automated e-mail spam delivery of today. Indeed, bots were synonymous with AOL due to the fact that they were actually quite successful in scamming users out of their personal information: the most common bot requests would be for bank account information or social security numbers, asked for under the pretext that the user was speaking with an America Online employee. Bot language was filled with convincing slang and colloquialisms; their text strands were written by humans first, then deployed by the bot program in real time to simulate the immediacy of chat speak, ensuring greater authenticity. The same scam has been mirrored on multiple Internet platforms, including Facebook. Text does not guarantee subjective interiority, nor does it fully deprive subjects of their complexity, thus their subjective status is fragmented. In real life I have a familiarity with and know the names of the people attached to the two picture-deprived profiles I am friends with on Facebook. And because I know someone's name in real life, then I accept that given Facebook friend under the premise that somehow, in the 21st century, a person's name is a reliable signifier.

AOL never explicitly made the mistake of letting their users stride into the fragmentary chaos of the Internet with their real world names prominent—in its registration instructions, America Online asked users to spend time thinking of a "screen name" to go by, such as "swimmingaddict187," to function in lieu of their real world name. The screen name often alluded to some real, off-screen attribute of the user, or sometimes intentionally led others astray as a means of disguise. As AOL achieved great popularity by the mid to late 1990s, the screen name selection process grew quite lengthy, as its early users had acquisitioned the most obvious screen names, thereby forcing late adopters of the service to add numerical suffixes to the most popular choices. This interfacial consequence led to the cultural ubiquity of username suffixes online today, even when those suffixes are unnecessary. And it is worth noting that YouTubers register usernames with their service under the same guidelines of anonymity.[12] This encourages subjects to consider the Internet as *representational* and not necessarily *reproductive*, keeping their critical distance and savvy reception skills intact. If a user on AOL chose to adopt a username that included actual biographical information (a screen name such as "JimmyBilson," based on a real person's name, for instance), then it was either because the user was ignorant of the dangers of the Internet or they were not planning on using digital social services as a means of protean identity play or transgression. When signing up for Facebook, the service does not ask for any sort of disguising username at all, but users' actual, real world name (first and last), and substitutes their validated e-mail address as the service's log-in credentials. This does not mean users are *required* to provide their real world name. Because the burgeoning impetus for authenticity online has normalized the process of putting real world names onto the Internet, firstly not secondly, this proves to be a mechanism by which social media users put *false* trust in language to provide knowable accuracy for understanding other human beings.

Largely, Facebook figures that words—*simply words*—transmitted through a keyboard or read through a menagerie of liquid crystals constitutes subjective complexity. Indeed, Facebook's indexicality is merely perceived to be high, yet proves to be quite low in execution, especially in consideration of catfish. When humans are co-opted into the Symbolic Order as children, they are invited into a reality of lies, imitation, and duplicity. It is the material systems of psychological recognition, then, that Facebook deprives its users of: what a handshake communicates, what a twitch of the eyebrow says, why the way a person positions their arms has meaning. But this is a tired critique of digital cultural. What is *new* is that catfish victims have somehow, from an ideological perspective, accepted Facebook as uncontested truth, even with glaring evidence to the contrary. This has much to do with Zuckerberg's decision to attach Facebook to social realities that exist off-screen, such as Harvard's real world clique of academic elites. Even if a user is compiling a list of "friends" from the ground up on Facebook, odds are their real life association with them has some geographical or otherwise sensible pattern of relation with others—others they will inevitably friend on Facebook because the service is so prevalent. Thus, Facebook's institution of "group" pages on its platform; these often have a real world parallel to groups, intentional or not, that exist offline.

On Facebook, I currently belong to the English department group page from my alma mater, which when I visit the page and see all the familiar names and faces, invigorates a sense of the physical place not just the digital aesthetic in which it exists. What happens, then, is that I coordinate the *cognitive map* of my physical, social experiences onto Facebook, so the two share the same space. With its graphical limitations and disguising screen names, AOL proved to be more of a social abstraction for users' minds. But the authenticity Facebook forcibly prompts means the service can at once impose itself over users' physical social experiences, and also compliment them, vacillating naturally between the two distinctions. This mental process is what N. Katherine Hayles calls a "feedback loop," in which users "connect *culturally potent [digital] metaphors* with *social constructions of reality*, resulting in formulations that imaginatively invest computation [for this argument, Facebook] with world-making power, even if it *does not* properly possess this power itself" (emphasis added, *My Mother Was a Computer* 20). Facebook is not allowing users to compile and organize other "users" on its service; these are "friends," a meaningful signifier which tugs at similar (but not exactly equivalent) off-screen values. What is occurring is a feedback loop between the user's lived reality and the Facebook profile they also occupy, all hinged upon an impetus for authenticity. So when users deploy the Facebookian lexicon to describe off-screen reality—for instance, casually referring to their "relationship status" when outside Facebook, whether they "like" something or not—they are further blurring the disparity between what goes on inside Facebook and what goes on outside of it. The same holds true of other social media, such as Twitter, as users deploy its ubiquitous "hashtag" as a grammatical flourish in their everyday speech.

And while Hayles poignantly makes the correlation between interface metaphors, like "buddy" and "friend," and how users relate to them in relation to their off-screen experiences, Hayles is remiss to give computation all the power of embodied social reality, which she admits might not "properly possess" world-making power on its own. Indeed, users have imbued Facebook with all its meaning. Users have lent digitally-transmitted words all the power they possess on social media. And this is not to make users at fault exclusively—the Facebook medium has certainly impressed its assumptions upon those users—but that their socialization has only been *made* digital. It was not created that way, nor does it garner social value in a digital vacuum. Facebook lessens the importance of materiality, embodiment, in its social equation, but as Hayles posits in *How We Became Posthuman*, "The body is the net result of thousands of years of sedimented evolutionary history, and it is naive to think that this history does not affect human behavior at every level of thought and action" (284). And when Facebook troubles users' conception of material reality and the digital, then they forget the history of humanity, an ahistorical postmodern configuration. This is language as simulacrum, and within social media it exemplifies Frederic Jameson's endemic ahistoricicism within postmodernity: "This approach to the present by way of the art language of the simulacrum ... endows present reality and the openness of present history with the spell and distance of a glossy mirage" (21). The body, then, fails as a reliable referent for the self online, appearing as a "glossy" and distant "mirage." But participation in Facebook, similar to the anonymous hate speech on Reddit, paradoxically *reinforces* embodiment, if not solely because it points to the user's lack, but because it fails on so many fronts to capture the intangibles of socialization, including the common sense cues that might otherwise alert its users to fraud, disingenuity, or sarcasm. In execution, denying embodiment is only a tangential cure for actuality, so the body remains.

Intangibility and MTV's Catfish: The TV Show

On the television version of *Catfish*, Nev Schulman and filmographer Max Joseph answer e-mails from distressed romantics looking to quiet their anxiety about the people they are in love with on the Internet, most of whom they have met through Facebook. The elusive catfish Schulman and Joseph investigate intentionally keep their real world identities hidden for a number of reasons, as it turns out, mostly having to do with insecurity about their physical appearance, or some other aspect of their real world self they would like to keep invisible—a catfish will commonly lie about having children, for instance. It is axiomatic that the complex lies these catfish tell speak volumes about the Internet and very little about the liars themselves, but Schulman and Joseph think otherwise. Very often, when confronting the catfish—similar to the documentary film on which the TV show is based, the two men literally fly cross country to chase catfish down—Schulman and Joseph will spend at least some amount of time chastising their catfish as "selfish" and "mean-spirited," with never a word spoken about the digital paradigms that facilitate the catfish's lies. And this is partly because Schulman and Joseph's primary means of research in catching a catfish also happens to be social networking; the two are so deeply entrenched and reliant upon social networks and digital spaces that there is no visibility beyond social media's purview. And Schulman and Joseph's judgment of their catfish is only partly founded. It is selfish to lie to others, especially those to which someone has professed their love, but a lie must be predicated on some referential basis of truth; no one catfish can be held responsible for all of Western society's induction into the superficially truthful dynamics of digital social spaces.

Catfish: The TV Show rarely has a happy ending, which makes episode four of season two such a captivating window into the assumptions of its creators' and 21st-century society's interactions with social networking. It is the first episode of sixteen prior, including the entirety of the first season, in which a suspected catfish actually turns out to be the real, unvarnished person he represents himself to be online. The episode's plot revolves around Derek and Lauren, a white heterosexual couple who met on MySpace eight years prior to filming, who continued digital interactions after migrating their online mediations elsewhere. Even after eight years, they had never met outside digital spaces mostly due to their being in separate, real life romantic relationships of their own, as well as impossible geographic and economic constraints, though nevertheless both had a very intimate entrée into the other's life. Over time, as Derek and Lauren's real world romances dwindled, their chance to connect outside the Internet became feasible. When the episode begins, co-host Max Joseph, who plays the show's skeptic, listens to Schulman reading the e-mail single mother Lauren had sent to the show, a bold emotional plea, and balks at the idea that Derek has never engaged in a video chat with Lauren, despite her numerous requests for him to do so.

According to *Catfish: The TV Show*, the most egregious sign of the catfish is their unwillingness to submit their bodies to full motion video, no matter the sentiments, no matter the time the two lovers have known each other. The greater indexicality of full motion video cuts through the fraud perpetuated on text-driven platforms such as Facebook; hence, catfish avoid video as a means of emotional survival. Max Joseph says knowingly, "[Derek's] ready to take care of her kid, but he's not ready to video chat with her?" Yet again, the problem, as the show and its producers see it, is not digital technology, but the actions of the catfish, when, in fact, the elimination of the larger cultural paradigm of social media would do away with the digital veneer the show is trying to unravel. Indeed, Schulman and Joseph chase red herrings, not catfish. It is important, also, that Lauren did not send that e-mail asking the *Catfish* producers to discover the off-screen identity of Derek, but instead to help the two meet across the U.S. (from Texas to Maryland), a gratis supplement for participants willing to risk the show's potentially embarrassing outcome. The majority of catfish victims from *Catfish: The TV Show* are at least somewhat suspicious something is awry by the time they contact the show; Lauren defies that trend.

When Schulman and Joseph embark on their investigation of Derek, a process of basic Google searches filmed and edited with dramatic tension, they discover only one piece of evidence against him: Derek's cell phone number is registered to what is revealed to be an elderly African American man named "R. LeVourne." The two rummage through LeVourne's Facebook profile devising a variety of wild theories, and report the information to Lauren who does not care to accept any of what they say. Lauren tells them, "It's not going to be LeVourne. I know that face. I know that voice. It's Derek," which is in line with her insistence upon the *intangibility* of the relationship she shares with Derek; it is the very thing about Derek she is most convinced of. Notice, here, Lauren rests some of her authenticity assumption on the voice of Derek, and not strictly his image, which the producers could neither confirm nor deny belonged to Derek; this is contrasted by Nev Schulman's authenticity emphasis on the image of "Megan Faccio" in the *Catfish* documentary. Intangibility is the element Lauren presents repeatedly as rebuttal to Joseph and Schulman's doubts from the outset of the episode, but they are unmoved by her protestations. When Lauren and Derek do finally meet, and no one has lied about any of the facts of their true selves (the faulty cell phone registration was due to a clerical error with the phone company), then Schulman and Joseph finally accept their mistake in judgment. This is not to say their doubts were unreasonable. The previous sixteen episodes of digital deceit serve as valid proof of those doubts.

Intangibility is the thing Lauren values most in what she and Derek share, and the thing social media devalues. What is more, social media, by means of its digital fragmentation, fosters a *selective subjectivity*, which denies the off-screen wholeness that intangibility implies. Nev Schulman and Max Joseph are not interested in the intangible when they embark on their investigations; in fact, their investigations *only* consider tangible items, such as whether a cell phone is registered to the individual who possesses it, physical addresses, whether a profile picture matches its operator or if the image can be found elsewhere on the Internet.[13] The content of the romantic exchanges between the catfish and their victim become like window dressing in the ideology of *Catfish: The TV Show*: however deep the sentiment, it is always marred by their falsified digital conveyance. Once catfish have been caught, one of their common defensive pleas is that their Facebook profile might be a lie, but *their internal feelings are real and legitimate*—and a person's feelings, even a catfish's, are very much off-screen and intangible. The betrayal of a fake Facebook account often proves to be the ultimate determiner for most catfish victims, though, who will rarely value their catfish's pleas. So what room is there on Facebook for intangibility? The self-contradictory impetus for authenticity makes an enemy out of human intangibles, emotional attributes such as love—a profile's Facebook "relationship status" is only the document of its user's love, not the content of it. And if the feedback loop some users of Facebook experience imposes its values onto their off-screen lives, then might that not also make their internal experience of love less content-based and more document-oriented? It is the idea that the mere recognition of love is what is important, not the associated emotion. And trapped within an interface of overt "stage management" for subjectivity, how those intangibles are expressed is selectively reduced. Turkle notices her teenage interviewees use communication technology in such a way that "feelings are not fully experienced until they are communicated," and, without the necessity of embodiment, it stands to reason that this technological impulse also means feelings will often be communicated and never felt (*Alone Together* 175). And this is what the catfish's victim intrinsically reacts to; they become privy to a limitless potential for deceit, even some deceit that has not been committed.

The emotional vacuum some users experience/utilize through Facebook's text-reliant interface can also be understood within the context of Slavoj Žižek's term *interpassivity*. When a digital medium offers its users an interpassive emotional relay, it allows them to literally "externalize" internal emotion. And, distinct from human interiority, emotions no longer have to be "felt" but only "expressed." As Sara Louise Muhr and Michael Pederson write, "Our Facebook profile is interpassive in that it relieves us of the burden of actually feeling emotions *directly* ourselves ... this improved version of our self also defers our emotional responses from the person we are off-line onto a online self, who undergoes these things for us" (emphasis added, 266). Also because of Facebook's feedback loop to users' off-screen reality, these interpassive emotions are no less "true," even if those emotions are not really felt internally; in the same way that emotions on reality TV are "true," except must be juxtaposed by all the various dynamics which weigh on that televisual mediation.

In light of this, it is interesting to consider the assumptions of the catfish, still laying claim to their internal feelings even after the revelation of their deceit. "All of it was me, just not me, y'know what I mean?" catfish Melissa tells Schulman and Jacob in episode five of season one of *Catfish: The TV Show*. "Everything. All of the emotions, y'know … just a different face, I suppose." Melissa is dejected and apologetic once caught, but being the catfish free to deceive is a meaning-infused (therapeutic) exercise of liberation. When explaining why she catfished people, Melissa says, "I had so many self-esteem issues. I used to cut myself…. I had to figure out something to make me happy…. I got so much out of [catfishing]." Catfish take *advantage* of the impetus for authenticity because, on whatever level, they understand the impossibility of that machine dream, so they adopt the protean style of anonymous Internet usage in order to transgress against the off-screen world that has subjugated them; more broadly, catfish commit an act of transgression against modern society with their considerable digital literacy. According to *Catfish: The TV Show*, Facebook catfish tend to be socially abject in some way, not fitting into conventional physical or social milieus, so enacting the role of the catfish allows catfish the social wealth they are deprived of in their off-screen lives. Angela Wesselman, from the *Catfish* documentary, catfished as a means of escaping a depressing reality, in which Wesselman was the disaffected caretaker of her severely handicapped twin stepchildren. Wesselman was operating a total of fourteen individual Facebook accounts at the height of her catfishing career, before shutting them down once she was exposed by the Schulman brothers. Angela Wesselman even went so far as purchasing a second cell phone to help perpetrate her deceit. And since Facebook has a high degree of relation to the off-screen world, then these catfish can feel as valued as they might in more material circumstances, when, such as Wesselman, their real lives actually do suffer from some lack. In their actions, the catfish calls attention to the inability of digital spaces to mediate human beings with unconditional accuracy, but also the freedom and viability social media can offer: it is what happens when Douglas Rushkoff's utopian idea of the Internet as a place of protean identity play "unlimited by the constraints of time and space, appearance and prejudice, gender and power" comes into direct contact with those very real world conventions (118).

Catfish also communicate that intention and literacy are key to Facebook's most effective use, because, for one thing, Facebook does much to manifest postmodern identity. For instance, in criticizing Facebook, Sherry Turkle remarks that Facebook primarily bases its modes of representation within "markers" or "tokens" of identity (e.g., Rosen's "metaphors of the person") and this inevitably leads to a "reduction" of the self (*Alone Together* 183–84). Assuredly, building the content of subjecthood through identity markers is a reduction. So while it is true that depth-oriented formulations of human subjectivity might find a better outlet elsewhere online, Facebook's interface, and its priorities of organization, lend practical sensibility to consumer habits and identity markers that might otherwise hover abstractly around Facebook users, or lay dormant beneath their social practices. A click on the "About" section of one of my friends proves to be a revelatory exercise in identity discovery, especially a Facebook friend who has spent some amount of time genuinely engaging the service; the byproduct of such usage can reveal deep metaphors of the self: an old high school friend whose political views he calls "Noncommittal" also happens to have liked both Bob Dylan and Neil Young's artist Facebook pages at some point. What this says is that while he might desire his political views to read vaguely, my cultural knowledge of Bob Dylan and Neil Young tell me that this friend's social positions are probably more liberal and less conservative. A second cousin of mine from St. Louis, a Millennial but born in the late 1980s, lists her favorite music as Frankie Valli, the Jackson Five, Henry Mancini, among other less contemporary artists. This is music neither she nor I grew up with, which tells me that she might keep close friends with her parents or coworkers from an older peer group. Scanning her friends list proves pointless—she has over 500 of them, too many for me assess with any clarity, and just as many old friends as young—but a peek at her timeline and activity shows me that, in fact, her most consistent online interactions are with some older members of her family and an older boss from the dance company where she teaches. My cousin also had a rousing debate about gay marriage a couple months before with another Facebooker in which she used Britney Spears as evidence for why marriage in modern society is a "mockery," surely evidence as to her ideological vantage point.

But in my analysis of these people through their Facebook profiles, it is abundantly clear I can only hope to acquire some *surface* understanding of who they are. A preoccupation with surface does speak to a postmodern articulation of the self, but the victims of catfish bring a deeper expectation to their usage—catfish have a modernistic view of Facebook, an intrinsically postmodern platform.[14] In negatively citing the Facebook profile as "reducible," this is the question Sherry Turkle raises: are subjects truly the things that litter their bedrooms and kitchens, their cultural identifiers, the consumer objects they purchase, the things subjects "like" on Facebook? Turkle does not seem to want to believe it; her book *Alone Together* has a cautious, critical tone, and the teenage Facebookers in its contents never feasibly elevate the platform to fit their emotional need for depth-oriented articulations of the self. Given the feedback loop users of Facebook experience, it should be said that the depth orientation referred to here is depth in their mediation, and also depth in their lived reality outside of Facebook.

Problematics of Facebook Identity Play

Reality TV asserts that on-screen subjects are ultimately postmodern and surface-oriented, with complicity by consumers through many societal and cultural facets. Yet the impetus for authenticity online, especially on social media, teases the notion that society *at large* might really be desirous for a return to pre-consumerism, pre-postmodern human representation and life. Not that this is an achievable end. As stated elsewhere in this book, postmodernity for Frederic Jameson and other postmodern theorists signals a cultural and spiritual dead end, never to return, never to proceed. But the antithetical desire for complex, modernistic formulations of the self remains. In the art world, several movements to eradicate postmodernism, including "remodernism," which purports to "discard and replace" postmodernism "because of its failure to answer or address any important issues of being a human being" is one of a number of bids to "return" to the meaning and depth existing prior to postmodernity (Childish and Thomson). Postmodernism, though, includes any return to previous modes of thought or representation within its ideology, included under the umbrella of "pastiche." Other progressive scholars have codified artistic systems to come after postmodernism—post-postmodernism, or metamodernism. But postmodernism is the literal end of stylistic change, and is unstable enough to include shifting notions of what it might constitute. On that note, Frederic Jameson states: "Postmodernism is not something we can settle on once and for all and then use with a clear conscience" (xxii). These newfound cultural movements are mere *attempts* at doing away with postmodernism; none signify its conceivable end. While contemporary reality TV says that all people are their surface selves, a message perpetuated by a hierarchy of ideologically complacent televisual production and consumption, Facebook, similar to YouTube, is a democratic, Web 2.0 platform. And how Facebook is utilized by individual users, given their ability to manipulate the platform, offers a glimpse into their very real desire for alternatives to surface-oriented ways of being.

One way to explicate this desire is to further consider Sherry Turkle's notion of "markers" or "tokens" of identity on social media. Turkle uses an observation offered by one of her teenage subjects to ascertain how these markers function for their reader: these markers are "'short smoke signals' that are easy to read" (*Alone Together* 184). Turkle's teenage interview subject implies here that it *should not* be easy to read another human being. And Turkle endorses this position. An "identity" is a surface-oriented proposition, comprised of culturally relevant bullet points which create an assemblage that amounts to a person. In contrast, subjectivity is about interiority, ambiguity, ontological value, among other depth-oriented considerations. When Turkle posits that social media asks "us to represent ourselves in simple ways," she means that it reduces users to strictly an identity and not a subjective human being (*Alone Together* 185). Via this reasoning, identity serves as a mask inadequate to communicating interiority. Smartly, Turkle is careful not to express the central thesis of her critique of social networks with this kind of suggestive language because to delve further into human representation than the notion of identity means that there is something *more* than identity to human beings, and breaching this philosophical ground troubles any kind of scientific or medical basis to her argument. And it is true: a person's interior being cannot be treated with medication (excluding holistic medicines), or understood under the guise of contemporary scientific study, or graphed on a chalk board with any accuracy. It is intangible, unquantifiable, etc.

Yet the democracy of Facebook (and other social media) has given users an open canvas to play with identity, in such a way that identity *appears* subjectively depth-oriented. When I go into my "About" section of my Facebook profile to change my identity markers, the interface allows me to type whatever information I please, so I could potentially invent a new religion when inputting my religious views, or maybe a new political stance. And because Facebook functions as a practical off-screen document, that religion will hold more weight on Facebook than if I would have told someone face-to-face about my newly-concocted beliefs. My cousin, for instance, calls her religious affiliation on Facebook "Pastafarian," something I thought she had made up at first. But once I followed its Wikipedia hyperlink, I found out Pastafarianism, which has garnered 765,352 likes on Facebook as of this writing, is an anti-religious protest group created to decry the teaching of creationism in public schools and uphold rational thought; their parodic "deity" is a "flying spaghetti monster." The novelty of this religion is one uniquely Facebookian—only on Facebook could so many people agree on earnestly citing their religion as something so outwardly absurd, in a very public act of satire. However, my cousin and all the other Pastafarians on Facebook have the backing of three quarters of a million other people on the service. In other words, Pastafarianism is not strictly a humorous, whimsical play for individuality on my cousin's part, oddity for oddity's sake; she has a massive confluence of Facebookers, some with an impetus for authenticity, giving their stamp of approval. As a result, my cousin's social networking identity play does not occur in a trivial vacuum, such that occurs on an anonymous message board (e.g., Reddit or 4Chan), but out in the real world, too. After scrolling through the established religions on Facebook, I counted 1,104 individual religious views, ranging from "Jedi," to "Dudeism," to "Chuck Norris."[15]

One consequence of Facebook's rampant individuality is, paradoxically, the signaling of its end. The promises of postmodernity include the death of the individual, according to Jameson, and the interface of Facebook often imposes (counter-intuitively) a submission to homogenous group-thought. While my cousin citing her religious views as Pastafarian has the sheen of novelty, something unique, the explicit approval of 765,352 people questions that novelty. In all likelihood, she attempted to type in some common religious configuration for herself, such as Atheism or Agnosticism, and was suggested Pastafarianism by Facebook once she began typing, as was I when I began trying to decide what my religious views might read like on Facebook; ultimately, I chose none, because by the time I had sifted through all the various religions, I was exhausted with the whole enterprise. Facebook offers such a wide array of choices for users to construct their identities such that they are compelled to go with its algorithmic suggestions rather than their imaginations. Could I have topped the satirical bite of Pastafarianism? Unlikely. And in the context of Facebook's billion or so global userbase, 1,104 religious views actually seems constrained. Maybe this communicates something about religion and not Facebook, but surely there are enough free thinkers of those billion or so people that they can come up with more than 1,104. Digital social networks, going back to MySpace, have been plagued by the inability of its userbase to effectively set each other apart, partly because users are trying so desperately to do so, which makes for an individuality *glut*. The problem here is not that individuality is dead outside social networking, but that users are taking in a dense variety of people in such a condensed fashion, *a technical impossibility* outside social media and computational technology.

Furthermore, the identity traits assigned to a Facebook profile are used for targeted advertising, similar to YouTube. While users who devise their own traits do transgress Facebook's ability to efficiently taxonomize them for advertising purposes, their usage and friends list will betray that transgression. So a Facebook profile's real world value must also be considered alongside its consumer value. While this is congruent with consumers' subjective formation in postmodernity, especially for savvy consumers, it conflicts with the modernistic impulse of truth value some users bring to social media. Indeed, Facebookers with an impetus for authenticity must contend with its advertising: the News Feed can transmit affective communications about the death of a loved one, about a local kid gone missing, about a national tragedy. Just below that communication is an advertisement for AXE Body Spray, rendering an affective moment impotent. Here, Burgess and Green's "continuum of cultural participation" on YouTube locates itself on Facebook, as Facebookers will themselves indulge in self-advertising through their network of friends. My uncle, for instance, pushed all his relatives to "like" his fledgling Houston-based telecommunications company; by means of my large extended family, the company's Facebook page reflected some steep activity, but it was specious activity as familial obligation served as the stimulus for his page's copious "likes." This relates to one of the broader points discussed in Chapter 3: the more democratic media is commercialized, the lesser its value of subjective exchange.

Indeed, Facebook is so successful at taxonomizing its users' vast array of identity markers that the service makes it too easy to insulate users' own ideological views, thereby artificially reinforcing their belief systems as opposed to challenging them, or, at the very least, holding those beliefs up to scrutiny. The same is true of Web 2.0, participatory media in general, and is a long-standing critique of digital culture,[16] but for a medium which incites a greater relation to its real world referent, this feature is doubly problematic. In off-screen reality, beliefs have no choice but to withstand their alternatives (or opposites) because mediating real life is dependent on community formation. It is not unusual, for instance, for many academics to insulate themselves from ideological views which do not align with their own because they can design social communities within and around their institution of employment/enrollment, or the larger academic cultural space. However, without fault, their students will trouble that space. Even the professional academic's position of authority does little to deter the oppositional ideologies teeming within a classroom, a singular truism of the University. The classroom, then, is an "unintentional community," for there is no predicting what view will come to the fore and challenge the pedagogical exercise (Wittkower xxv). Part of the complexity of lived reality is negotiating these divergent views, views that cannot be irrefutably silenced. Alternatively, Facebook, as an engine for socialization, offers users a wealth of avenues by which to intentionally silence, privilege, and exclude others. I have silenced a number of my Facebook friends from my News Feed, as their posts were too frequent, or aggressively political, or abrasive for my taste. Once removed from the News Feed, I would have to go into my friends list, then select those individual profiles in order to see their postings. And this is more of an interaction than is feasible for me in my Facebook usage; once silenced from my News Feed, my Facebook friends are silenced forever.

Marshall McLuhan contemplates media as it *extends* the physical and mental abilities of human beings (McLuhan's "the extensions of man"), and social media is no different. Thanks to Facebook, users can now manage their social life in the same way they manage a spice rack. But to extend social abilities is to also accept the damaging consequences of this adopted technology, as McLuhan is never reticent to point out, and social networking can extend users' social abilities beyond their human worth—very much in accordance with Sherry Turkle's position that social networks are a *reduction* of the self. When I look at my friends list, I see people from all walks of life, of different beliefs, different racial and ethnic backgrounds, with entirely disparate real world selves from my own. Surely they are individuals; never would I dream of seeing these people in real life and imagine that their understanding of reality is not unique from my own and, frankly, everybody else's. But relegated to my Facebook friends list, these people deceptively appear knowable, an assured reduction of their humanity. I can scan fifteen different profiles and gather specific information about who their real world operators are in a matter of minutes. Accomplishing the same feat outside social media would take days, and much physical geography to travel, even doing the same by phone would take exponentially longer. And as consequence of how efficiently accessing other human beings has become, social media users have (falsely) coaxed themselves into an indifference about the uniqueness of others. In thinking about the billions of readily-accessed people on social media, Christine Rosen writes that social media coveys a "dull sea of monotonous uniqueness, of conventional individuality, of distinctive sameness," because users experience so much from so many people as a result of social media's technological feats (184). Facebook, in so many ways, has helped to immunize users to the wild difference all around them.

In conjunction with the perceived complexity social media lends identity, the surface self appears quite depth-oriented nowadays. But this is only a surface kind of depth orientation. Just because users have real world signifiers for thousands of new varieties of sexual articulation thanks to Facebook, they should not *confuse* identity for subjectivity. In fact, the malicious stereotyping of others—for their style of dress, or particular belief—is part and parcel to this very confusion; the errors of human judgment that emanate from mistaking identity with subjectivity are plentiful. When I interrogate a Facebook profile and imagine that it constitutes a unique, living person, I make the same mistake. Users should, then, similar to the catfish, bring to the Facebook assessment exercise the same savviness and digital literacy that users of anonymous message boards like Reddit do. Generally, Redditors consider their online mediations similar to a video game avatar, which are highly-fluid, protean, and subject to (severe) scrutiny if any authenticity or truth value is claimed. Michael Brutsch, in his defensive interview with CNN, referred to his avid Reddit posting habit as a "game" to "push people's buttons" (Griffin). Redditors also bring to their anonymous usage that same liberatory flavor the catfish bring to their fraudulent Facebook accounts, the kind of Internet usage Douglas Rushkoff is nostalgic for. In Turkle's studies on teenage gamers, the video game avatar serves as a statement "not only about who you are but who you want to be," a seemingly contradictory function for its users (*Alone Together* 180). Instead of reading Turkle's statement as definitional of an avatar, it should read as an explanation of identity. Off-screen, people act out who they *want* to be in adopting new identity markers. And, very often, these same people will eventually drop their new identity markers because they felt that the change was somehow a betrayal of who they were *deep down*. What constitutes *deep down*? It is intangible; what matters is that they made an overture to this figurative location, however real or imagined. A video game avatar, however, is interpassive such that these identity markers can be ascribed virtually but not have to be so off-screen, not dissimilar to social media in many respects. And a concern over an internal existence may well be tied to an archaic emotional affection, but the idea that people still remain concerned about it speaks volumes. Now, these people's overture to a *deep down* might actually indicate a desire to be "unburdened" of such an intangible sense of self, as social media interpassivity illustrates, but that logical step is not ostensibly declared in their overture—indeed, the vagueness of a betrayed sense of self is meaningful *because* it is vague, not because its psychoanalysis reveals a longing to be surface-oriented. Instead, their overture to an internal existence is provoked by the digital consumer technology they are choosing and also being *forced* to relate with, confide in, and trust.

Magical Thinking and Consumer Electronics

Consumerism has imparted on 21st-century society the insatiable drive to buy newer, better, and faster electronics. This is self-evident. The smartphone, for instance, has incurred a wild buying frenzy under the guise of moderately better advancements in technology every six months or so. The iPhone business model, and its unparalleled success, depends on this artificially frequent buying cycle. Infamously, in 2012, the iPhone 5 was touted by Apple for only one significant mechanical change: a newly-placed headphone jack, from the top of the phone to the bottom. Consumers, then, have imbued modern electronics with ever greater worth as electronics have become more transitory and ephemeral, resulting in a self-defeating phenomenon that traps consumers in a fatalistic consumption exercise because they are never sated. The smartphone's prevalence, similar to Facebook, is also made more valuable by its relation to real, off-screen social realities, the major difference being that cellular telephones are "hardware" and Facebook is "software," at most. Without its relation to consumers' real lives, the cellular phone would still be perceived like the abject and esoteric personal computers that hosted The Whole Earth 'Lectronic Link (The WELL), back when Silicon Valley was trying to establish itself. Even the easy to use tactile interfaces on modern smartphones would nary induce a reaction without their real world, social element.

So the ideological bias that has sparked the epochal significance of Facebook—the service and users' practical valuation of the real, off-screen world—is the very thing helping to perpetuate the success of modern consumer electronics. This bias is so effective, in fact, that consumers seem to have deluded themselves into believing these electronics have no relation to the abject computational machines of old, with their vacuum tubes and Teletype terminals. This is due in part to Apple's sexy, minimalist consumer products, which are only a handful of new digital tech that could be placed on the mantel, beside affecting pictures of the family. And a machine is a machine, whether it is texting profound sentiments to a lover, or receiving heart-warming photos from a relative, or playing architect to some sexual confluence of human and machine; even then, that object is still very much a machine, a *mediator* for subjectivity. And the real world tactility of contemporary touch devices has also helped to convince consumers that computational tech is somehow neutered and benign, but not to the extent that Apple or Microsoft might believe. Mark Bauerlein rightfully posits that "the flood of digital tools was and is mighty, but adults and youths generally behave as if it has always been thus. Calmly and expertly, they wield devices and form habits that were inconceivable ten or twenty years ago" ("Introduction" ix). *How* consumers consider the computer axiomatic to their social existence, then, must be explored in greater detail because Facebook's seduction is also dependent on that axiom.

In Hayles' assessment of users interior relatability to virtual creatures, such as those found in laboratory programs, children's toys, or video games, she considers there to be an operation of human psychological mysticism involved. Taking the idea that consumer software has appropriated recognizable artifacts from the real, material world—for instance, "friends" on Facebook, the "recycle bin" and "folders" on Microsoft Windows—in order to *mystify* its computational operations such that a multitude of users might interact with this software, especially with lower literacy rates, digital technology has the power to "produce the conditions, ideologies, assumptions, and practices that help constitute what we call reality," thereby imposing computation onto consumers' "real conditions of existence" (*My Mother Was a Computer* 60–61). What this means is that user-friendliness, as is also mentioned in Chapter 3, has created an environment by which users of these products forget that the consumer content on computers, smartphones, and the like are really just the emergent byproduct of a series of electrical currents. The mystification of how consumer electronics has worked in today's society is akin to how *the cargo myth* worked on Melanesian natives in Jean Baudrillard's *The Consumer Society*; whites landed in their territory, and the Melanesians experienced their technological advancements along with their imperial malice. After the white man's retreat from Melanesia, when the cargo planes delivering Western aid hung over them however many years later, they looked to the sky as if these were a "blessing from nature" and not tied to a blood debt unwittingly forged with their white oppressors (32). The Melanesians enjoyed their aid, the fruit of the white man, free of the history of what they were receiving, very literal ahistoricism. The power of illusion, here, was not located in the intellect of the white man, but in the seduction of their objects, in the act of consumption the cargo planes' supplies incurred. Baudrillard thinks the cargo myth is indicative of the *magical thinking* the West experiences toward consumption, perpetually tinged by this poignant ahistoricism. When consumers buy a marginally improved iPhone after buying the previous model only a few weeks before, they are seduced by the same mysterious thinking. Under this circumstance, a newly-assigned headphone jack on the iPhone, for instance, is considered "innovative" for its umpteenth iteration. When the computer is no longer a static machine, vacuum tubes and motherboards, but instead a friendly enabler, this is not because the thing has actually changed, but because consumerism has co-opted it into its paradigm of mysticism.

It is no wonder that Facebook and digital communication technology have easily invaded consumers' social spaces; thanks to consumerism's mystification of computational technology, consumers were never digitally literate enough to suspect anything otherwise. So what disparity lies between human interaction with Facebook and a person's interior relatability with a simulated organic creature, such as Sony's robot dog AIBO? Here, similar to the larger Facebook assessment exercise, it is pertinent to consider again the assumptions of the consumer and not the object of their fascination. In a simulated digital creature, people's acceptance of it as subjective is reliant upon an *emergent* conception of its subjective status; its artificial-intelligence would have to be convincing enough that they understand it retains something intangibly human, uncanny or not. Among off-screen reality, and a person's real world embodiment, there is no reason to challenge subjectivity unless a person's behavior somehow provoked that suspicion. But never mind artificial-intelligence: more important are the cultural circumstances that permit the acceptance of virtual creatures as subjective. Turkle, amidst the prevalence of social networking, notices that on social media "we are together, but so lessened are our expectations of each other that we can feel utterly alone" (*Alone Together* 154). Indeed, the social responsibilities of Facebook do not readily match what goes on outside it—for instance, the "unintentional communities" of everyday life—and this is due to the foundational importance Facebook has placed on an unstable format of human mediation better suited for anonymity.

Indeed, despite its encroachment into the real social world, socialization on Facebook does not function as it might off-screen; in fact, as has already been stated, its social practices owe more to the anonymous style of Internet usage than it does to everyday, real life interactions. Facebook's invocation of "friend," for instance, does not have a one-to-one relation to the friendships users hold offline. Indeed, my own friends list is populated by people I would not necessarily consider a "friend" in real life, and yet they are attached to that signifier on my Facebook profile. On Facebook, the "friend" *should be* considered of much lesser value than real life friends because these digital lists are compiled based on a system of recognition, not necessarily the degree to which users intimately know these other people off-screen; for instance, it is typical for users to be Facebook friends with bosses, distant relatives, "frenemies," acquaintances from long ago. The real world relation to a Facebook friend is more nuanced than just the singular designation of "friend." But social media would be less efficient if users were given the option of accepting "acquaintance" requests, or "long lost high school buddy" requests. The only kind of organizing users can do in this regard is retroactive; the system for accepting others into the friends list must be simple or else fail the consumer efficiency test. An off-screen friend retains that status through some degree of intimacy, not necessarily recognition—recognition is a cursory concern of a person's intellectual understanding of a real life friend, one which is often implied through that intimacy. I recognized an old classmate of mine on Facebook, so I sent them a friend request, which they accepted. I did not somehow accrue intimacy directly through that action on social media, but only *confirmed* my recognition. So when users experience the feedback loop of Facebook, as their material reality is shaped by their Facebook use, then recognition *supersedes* intimacy. And this is similar to what happens for a catfish's victim: the victim believes the mere recognition of an embodied human opens the flood gates of intimacy. Facebook, in this regard, has impacted material reality more than material reality has impacted it, at least for some users. And also, amid the blur of Facebook and reality, these users can count Facebook friends among their real world ones, thereby devaluing the tangible sign "friend."

Considering the social expectation for friends has lessened in this regard, and that Facebook instantiates a disparate kind of socialization to its real world counterpart, it is not a stretch to imagine that however much consumers might get out of a friendship with a virtual creature might be enough to fulfill their social needs. Turkle, in her study of people's interactions with Sony's sociable robot dog AIBO, notices that only her adult subjects were willing to resist the potential for subjectivity in the machine, due in part to their knowledge that the thing was not actually a flesh-and-blood animal; these were, undoubtedly, ontological concerns. But the question of ontology for her younger subjects—many from the generation following Millennials— is safely dropped; they could have cared less if the machine came from "God or an egg," and those children who accepted that the machine was manmade continued designating it with subjective value anyway. And "in this dismissal of origins," Turkle writes, "we see the new pragmatism" (*Alone Together* 57). This "new pragmatism" is one in which all that ever matters are the desires of the consumer, not the validity of the objects which they consume. Consumers are pragmatic because they are no longer particular about how those desires are sated.

What occurs with these small children and their robotic dog is a "complex system of co-adaptation," in which people "humanize" virtual creatures and they "computationalize" them back (Hayles, *My Mother Was a Computer* 100). Future generations are "suturing" together the "analog subjects" they still are with the "digital subjects" they are becoming, so the notion that a young child might subjectivize a robotic dog will no longer seem exceptional—on the contrary, it will be commonplace (Hayles, *My Mother Was a Computer* 204). So it behooves users to remember that Facebook sits atop a tenuous, unstable foundation; and even if users weigh Facebook as if it were material reality, it is merely a testament to who they *want* to be, not who they *actually* are. And the idea that Facebook can be both real and artificial should alert users to its exceptional status. When Facebook becomes commonplace, then consumers suture together lies with the truth.

3

How YouTube Subjectivizes
Vlogging, Hauls and Creative Consumption

> The increasing technologization of the media has not caused an impoverishment in subjective interiority; on the contrary, it has generated a greater variety of self-referentialities.
> —Jörg Dünne and Christian Moser, *Automedialität: Subjektkonstitution in Schrift, Bild und neuen Medien* 14 [Auto-Mediacy: Constitution of the Subject in Text, Image and New Media]

On June 16, 2006, user account Lonelygirl15, who calls herself Bree, uploaded her first video blog (vlog) to YouTube, titled "First Blog / Dorkiness Prevails," establishing some minute biographical information, accompanied by a montage segment of her trying on dresses and making ugly faces for the web camera situated atop her computer monitor. The video's inanity was typical of teen content popular then, the most viewed of which, such as the infamous "Hey clip" of August 2005, featured teenage women dancing and lip-syncing catchy songs in their bedrooms; their virality was of no surprise to scholars familiar with the dominant reception community on the Internet because today's *digital gaze* is overrun by the isolated masculine viewer. In "First Blog / Dorkiness Prevails," Bree claims to be sixteen years old, to live in a small town the name of which is not worth mentioning, and proclaims her effervescent "dorkiness," using as evidence the copious time she spends on her personal computer. Bree makes shout-outs to some other prominent YouTubers in the video, including user paytotheorderofofof2 who still uploads today, bringing herself into conversation with a community that preceded her vlogging and facilitated her acceptance in the larger cultural space of

109

YouTube. Additionally, Bree was live on (then-popular) social networking site MySpace, replied to comments in the YouTube comments section, and created video responses spurred by individual user critiques, all adding an undeniable richness to her online persona.

Bree's first upload quickly became the most commented on video on YouTube (circa 2006). This was due in part to Bree's attractiveness, as anonymous users fawned over her, but also as a consequence of her behavior in the video, which to many users familiar with the YouTube medium appeared a little too slick, condensed, and calculated, although the userbase readily subscribed to her YouTube channel, undeterred by their misgivings. As of March 2014, Lonelygirl15's channel has accrued 126,290 subscribers and 287,111,611 individual views despite halting video uploads in 2009. And Lonelygirl15's videos are indeed "fake" in the sense that they were professionally produced, antithetical to the popular YouTubian ethos of amateur production. Web 2.0 models of production in digital spaces stress an altruistic "architecture of participation," maintained by the consumer, in which they create and distribute content conceivably free of hierarchical sway, a reversal on conventional television production (Jenkins, Ford, and Green 55). Digital platforms ascribing to this model, such as YouTube, defer the majority of their content volume to consumer creators. Facebook and other strictly *social* media outlets are example par excellence of content platforms nearly monopolized by their userbase. Web 2.0, as a concept, proved to be the corporate signifier the Internet needed in order to rescue itself from terminal status after the dot com bubble burst in 2000. The concept has been widely deployed since 2004, with numerous thinkers and Silicon Valley angel investors venturing to guess at what might constitute Web 3.0, 4.0, etc. (O'Reilly 218). Overtime, however, Web 2.0 ideology and its adherents have faced a more complex problem than enabling the consumer, especially when that consumer content engages, and sometimes replicates, corporate content.

To elaborate further, amateur, Web 2.0 democracy is just the *ideal* of the YouTube platform, and a negotiable one at that. YouTube's function as a service, as a business, is to provide a "low-barriers," low functionality video uploading venue for anyone—including media copyright holders and other corporations—to use, not just the amateur population of users who helped propel YouTube's cultural value (Burgess and Green, "The Entrepreneurial Blogger" 103). User-friendliness enables a corporate content distributor as much as it does a creative teenager. Lonelygirl15 garnered a wide following in close proximity to a pivotal historical moment in YouTube's history. In

October 2006, Google acquired YouTube for 1.65 billion in Google's own stock, making YouTube's progenitors—Chad Hurley, Steve Chen, and Jawed Karim—three very rich Internet entrepreneurs (Reuters). Chad and Steve, to announce the acquisition, posted a minute and a half video on YouTube, clearly trying to modulate fears from its fierce community of creative laborers fearful of corporate interference: "We wouldn't be close to where we are without the help of the community," says Chen in "A Message from Chad and Steve." Even though the two are bouncing around in the frame, egos boosted as only a billion dollars can, their message is reverential to the user, the "You" in YouTube; this was a smart move on their part as their millions upon millions of views then owed much to the word-of-mouth credibility of YouTube, which has mostly dissipated nowadays. Instead, YouTube into the 2010s is an established presence, as other video uploading services have overtaken it in terms of hipness but not in volume, both in number of views and videos— no similarly functioning service comes close.[1] Even free of the hip factor, YouTube persistently ranks around third among the most accessed websites worldwide, behind Facebook and Google (Alexa).

Part of YouTube's mythology of amateur production, Lonelygirl15 functioned as a kind of metaphor for what was to come for the service: a much greater corporate presence that would cut into amateur space. Users were right to be wary when Google bought the service. Amateurs now have to fight for viewership alongside Universal Music Group and the Sony Corporation. To make matters worse, YouTube has struck up deals with a select few professional content providers, such as Time-Warner, and some popular amateur uploaders, to restrict access to their YouTube channels, requiring subscription fees, mirroring other services such as Hulu and Netflix that offer a repository of streaming professional content for a monthly contribution by the consumer. For their part, YouTube promises the platform will still remain free excluding these particular channels (Nakaso).[2] Also important to note, professional "music videos" which "dominate categories such as 'most popular' and 'most viewed,'" despite being "marginal" to YouTube's overall content percentages, pale in comparison to the "long tail" of amateur content which is often "most discussed" on the site (Snickars and Vonderau, "Introduction" 11). But if YouTube can manage a higher degree of economic return through these pay channels, then the whole platform will naturally follow suit. And how will amateurs and YouTube's social networking community be dealt with in an on-demand viewing environment? They will not. All the old top-down mechanisms that control television production and distribution—what many netizens believe YouTube was conceivably a response to—will govern YouTube.

Doomsday prophesying aside, Internet users are astute enough to migrate elsewhere if worse comes to worse, but YouTube still stands apart because it is free to use, has "light touch" governance, and because the standards of quality for amateur YouTube videos are divergent, if not exceptional, from professional content. And this was exactly why users cried foul when Lonelygirl15 started uploading content. Some of the hallmark attributes of YouTube amateur vlogging are the stumbled phrase, the unedited sneeze, the moments when actuality comes seeping through, and not for the sake of it but because editing these slippages out would be too much effort, and there is only so much unpaid creative labor an average user will dedicate to editing. One of the great pleasures of YouTube is soaking up what Jon Dovey calls the "spectacle of actuality," a spectacle removed from traditional narrative story-telling and logic of any kind beyond "the thing before me is real" (Jermyn 74). Alternatively, when a person's sneeze is conveyed on top-down reality TV, it is upheld within the narrative either for humorous effect, as in A&E's *Duck Dynasty*, or because some important exchange occurred in conjunction with that intrusion of a real human bodily function. "First Blog / Dorkiness Prevails" features nary a slippage, and Bree's address to the camera is, by and large, tight and well-spoken, even though some lines feel disingenuous. In the comments section from that video, archived from June 2006, user klebdman asks Bree, "are you ACTING ??? you sound like you are ... are your eyebrows real ???" Bree replies: "I don't really know what you mean.... I turn on the camera and I talk and then my friend helps me edit...." Maybe her ellipses were a hint to her fraud. But because the visual form of a vlog is upheld in her video, not all users were effectively clued in to the manipulation. And even more convincingly, Bree holds conversations in the comments section of her videos with intrigued users on topics ranging from Santa Monica to science author Simon Singh.

Vlogging did not originate on YouTube,[3] nor is it the only place online to find it. Yet Jean Burgess and Joshua Green figure that vlogging has become "an emblematic form of YouTube participation" (*YouTube* 53). Arguably, it is *the* emblematic form of YouTube participation, replicated and satirized throughout popular culture. The only technical necessities for vlogging are a webcam, and today that probably means one fixed to a laptop, tablet, or smartphone, and basic editing skills. The filmic form of a vlog typically involves persistent direct address to the camera (usually full eye contact), at least some embodiment (be it torso or floating head), and a major theme of discussion indicated in the video's title or description, though digressions are not uncommon. A vlog is not strictly associated with the habitual genre of a diary or journal, in the sense that the day's events are detailed, but tend to focus on exceptional encounters, or some interesting anomaly occurring in a person's life, or the expression of a particular opinion or skill. And sometimes vlogs are just completely vacuous, as evidenced by the rash of mundane dancing videos uploaded to the service. In their unvarnished form, vlogs should be thought of as op-eds with the personal tinge of a diary. While a large amount of amateur video on YouTube is informed by the older cultural practice of home movies, capturing the domestic pleasure of laughing babies and dog tricks, the vlog is an outgrowth of exhibitionism on talk shows and reality TV confessionals. Burgess and Green also see these dual practices sharing space on YouTube: "Amateur video on YouTube has just as much to do with the social history of the home movie—used to document the lives of ordinary citizens—as it has to do with exhibitionist consumers appearing on talk shows or being made over on 'ordinary television,' and now racing to broadcast themselves" (*YouTube* 25). To be clear, rarely did home movies from the 20th century feature adult men confessing their love for the children's TV program *My Little Pony* directly into their cameras, which is why vlogging assuredly stands apart as something tied to new millennium digital culture.

As the Lonelygirl15 account continued posting videos, Bree gradually built a narrative of repression, loneliness, and the occult. The YouTube community sensed something problematic in her mediation when she announced she was homeschooled in her first video; user bradleykavin asks in the comments section, "hey I was wondering, why is it your parents seem to be so protective over you? why are you homeschooled if you don tmind me asking." There was no reply from Bree—that would spoil the fictional story. And Bree does not explicitly state her parents are strict in her first video, either; this is an assumption made by the user. On July 4, 2006, she posted the video "My Parents Suck..." directly after she had been told she could not go on a date with Daniel, username Danielbeast, her local crush and the person supposedly editing her videos.[4] Bree says to the camera: "I understand we [our family] have certain beliefs and that means that I can't do the same things as other kids all the time." The *hidden truth* that she is caught up in some violent pagan religion slowly unfolds, as Daniel ventures to save her from her strict and apparently deranged parents, while subjected to their nefarious rituals and ho-hum diet practices. In January of 2007, Bree revealed on camera that her parents were not her biological parents, as confessed by her father before his death, another tidbit included within Lonelygirl15's dense plot. "Season one" of Lonelygirl15 consists of 152 individual videos running at about two to five minutes in length. Over the course of fourteen months, Lonelygirl15 kept the YouTube community intrigued with its gradual revelation of detail, but this is a fictional narrative practice, one tied to the novel, film, and fiction television, not vlogging. Generally, amateur vlogs are a burst in time, short and expository, with no personal detail left to reveal for later videos; they stand on their own merit, almost unrelated to videos past. YouTube is traditionally devoid of serialization, except that which naturally comes with off-screen temporal progression (non-manufactured). Everything comes out all at once—if there is something to say, vloggers do not wait to do so.

Once it was exposed as a professional production, Lonelygirl15 incensed users because it deployed the values of authentic self-expression on YouTube (those associated with vlogging) to sell a fabricated storyline. But the issue was more complex than that, especially from a production standpoint. Lonelygirl15's production team, Ramesh Flinders and Miles Beckett, two unemployed filmmakers, capitalized on a digital community which paid no heed to their honed skills (Heffernan and Zeller). Flinders and Beckett were professionals, near the top of the production hierarchy, who benefitted economically from a userbase with zero expectation for traditional film quality, something YouTubers dismiss based on an implicit contract of *judgment free* amateur complicity. This complicity enables amateur uploaders to contribute without fear that they might be criticized by the community for their production capabilities—the same complicity that emboldened user geriatric1927, retired Englishman Peter Oakley otherwise known as "The Internet Granddad," to post his first vlog in 2006. While Oakley uploaded with some trepidation, as evidenced by his apologies in his first video, that did not stop him from ultimately doing so. Over four hundred uploads later, Oakley has created an eight year deep archive of his retired life, sewn together by strands of nostalgia and wisdom, effectively decimating any preconceived notions about full motion video distribution or demographics, with over nine million views attributed to his account as of March 2014. Flinders and Beckett, though heralded as savvy and ingenious at the time of Lonelygirl15's outing, garnered attention as filmmakers with none of the gatekeeping of their profession— that was the *real* betrayal. The sacred YouTubian professional/amateur dichotomy had been breached, to exhausting effect, and this was not an isolated event. Lonelygirl15 inspired numerous copycat channels and accounts on YouTube, also serialized and many elusive about their actuality. These are more congruent with conventional televisual media dynamics than Web 2.0 ones because they *self-consciously* engage the savvy/duped discourse prevailing among reality producers such as those working for truTV. When vloggers genuinely engage the YouTube medium, for instance, their participation is not predicated on their "realness" or whatever selfhood remains after their digital mediation. Since they dictate the terms of their mediation, they believe, then, that the product is reflective of their actual self. While this conclusion is more ideological than fact-based, and has some similarities to Facebook's problematic mediational exercise, it still communicates something acutely distinct from reality TV reception and participation.

The crux of the issue resides in the postmodern cultural dynamics that play out through the YouTube platform. Supposedly, especially among its mainstream critics, the core problematic of YouTube is its duality: the YouTube occurring inside conventional media practice and the one occurring exterior to it. In the minds of reactionary amateur users decrying Lonely-girl15, there was their version of YouTube, the one its current slogan "Broadcast Yourself" is intended for, and in the minds of professional content producers and copyright holders, there was the other YouTube, the one its original slogan "Your Digital Video Repository" was meant. Indeed, per media scholar Burcu S. Bakioğlu, LonelyGirl15 "exposed the *inherent tension* between YouTube's democratizing goals and its economic potential" (emphasis added, 3). The amateur's thinking embraces the altruistic Web 2.0 promise of pure, non-commercially oriented democracy online, an ideology to which many Internet activists still attest. Douglas Rushkoff, in recollecting the Internet's "2,400 band, ASCII text era," its foundational years, points out that "until 1991, you had to sign an agreement promising not to conduct business online just to get access to the Internet! Imagine that. It was a business free zone" (117). Rushkoff wrote this in the wake of the dot com bubble's collapse, while Wall Street investors were still reeling from their massive losses at the turn of the millennium. The dot com bubble was, in his reasoning, a learning moment. Rushkoff was rationalizing the value of making the Internet valueless to the NASDAQ—remove the money makers from the Internet and return its users to the prelapsarian "public project" web space Al Gore extolled, he argued. Theoretically, this was the Internet rejecting capitalist consumption. However, Rushkoff was reading the collapse through an altruistic Web 2.0 lens, a lens media theorists such as Henry Jenkins have proven faulty (2013's *Spreadable Media*). In practice, the dot com bubble had more to do with separating the wheat from the chaff so investors could make greater economic returns, as evidenced by Amazon.com's survival through the ordeal, a company which has gone on to completely reformat the publishing/book-selling industry.

Whether amateur creatives on YouTube and other ordinary people on (strictly) social media such as Facebook find an expressive voice through it or not, the Internet, as understood in the 2010s, also has many monetary considerations—YouTube is not an exception, but proves the rule time and time again. The service kowtows to content holders in such a way that network television sometimes appears democratic in comparison. Constantly shifting advertising agreements with various corporations means YouTube's terms of service are in flux on a near weekly basis. Amateur YouTube upload-ers who produce movie reviews, or stream video games, or read sections of books are having their videos removed, reposted, and removed again as a consequence of the shaky ground copyrighted material stands on within YouTube, never mind the long tradition of high traffic YouTube postmodern mash-ups that splice together flicks such as *Beaches* (1988) and *Fight Club* (1999) with hilarious results. And this is, undoubtedly, the work of amateurs treading on the domain of the professional producer, and often extends beyond simple parody. In its original conception, one key attribute that Web 2.0 ideology did not account for was Internet users' desire to redistribute content, specifically content which they did not produce themselves, much of which is embroiled in copyright laws. Thus, the discourse surrounding Internet media content now frequently rests on evaluative designations such as "piracy." Jenkins, Ford, and Green posit that the discursive attention pointed at Internet pirates is an outgrowth of a burgeoning "moral economy" online, which is slowly but surely trying to modify the current digital ethos so amateurs and professionals alike can successfully monetize their creative property (48). However, morality and economics are incompatible principles, most especially when envisioned via unstable digital spaces. Indeed, a "moral economy" online troubles its mediated subjects. Before they were exposed, users decried the authenticity of Lonelygirl15's videos because of the qualities already mentioned which defraud Bree's representation—she was called out as an "actor" by some users on that very first video, even if the majority were still duped. The actress who played Bree, Jessica Rose, is a New Zealand native and was trained in her profession at the New York Film Academy. Flinders and Beckett, the Lonelygirl15 producers, would later admit they were hoping for a movie deal as a consequence of their web stunt (Heffernan and Zeller). The lesson, then, is that many YouTubers can sense the disparity when deliberate monetary considerations are made, when the subject is so fully commodified as with Bree, the lonely girl.

In accordance with N. Katherine Hayles' figuration of digital spaces—that they are fragmentary, fluid, unstable—the Internet should be conceptualized oppositional to a "moral economy," instead within a paradigm of "moral disorder," as Andrew Keen puts it. "The Judeo-Christian ethic of respecting others' property that has been central to our society since [America's] founding," Keen writes, "is being tossed into the delete file on our computer desktops" (*The Cult of the Amateur* 142). In light of the questionable economics of Internet monetization, which as Jenkins, Ford, and Green imply *requires* stability, Keen figures that Web 2.0 technology "confuses the very concept of ownership," but he supplies no ready solution to this conundrum, just that the Internet is the "death" of intellectual property (*The Cult of the Amateur* 143). And it is true that piracy will always have a place online because the supposedly transgressive idea of "hacking" is so foundational to the online enterprise: copy-and-paste, remixing, and mash-ups are all euphemisms for "stealing," according to Andrew Keen (*The Cult of the Amateur* 142). For profit-oriented Web 2.0 creators, Keen's assessment is negative, negating the Internet's potential for capital gain, but a "moral disorder" of online economics results in a purer space for subjective expression. What occurs on reality TV is that the on-screen subjects are gradually co-opted by the production hierarchy as the consumer capitalist impulse is indulged further and further: this is what happened on over twenty years' worth of *The Real World*. The monetary desire of the show and its producers co-opted its on-screen subjects, so that they, too, were as commodifiable as the show itself, however complicit the subjects were with that process. If content monetization online functions less successfully than it does, for instance, on television, then that implies that mediated subjects can be feasibly "more authentic" there than on TV, as the *degree* of mediation is comparably less. Thus, YouTube has the *potential* to produce subjects, on and off screen, conceivably distinct from consumer capitalist influence.

So rather than pigeonhole the YouTube conversation within the producer/consumer dichotomy, it is more useful to understand YouTube as part of a historical trajectory of postmodern consumption. To destabilize the producer/consumer dichotomy—and Alvin Toffler's overused term "prosumer" is not the solution, at least not on YouTube—we should consider YouTube "in terms of a continuum of cultural participation" (Burgess and Green, *YouTube* 57). To clarify, amateurs who garner large viewing numbers and loyal subscribers are often invited by Google to become "YouTube partners," sharing in advertising revenue divvied out based on views, channel subscriptions, and community engagement. This means that the unsullied amateur has the *potential* to become part of the economic machine helping to drive YouTube, so the idea that economics somehow distinguishes the amateur from the professional proves problematic—many amateurs upload to YouTube for the sole purpose of making cash, while others with no intention of monetary gain are co-opted into this system. Smosh, one of the top ten most subscribed YouTube channels, was the brainchild of two teenagers, Ian Hecox and Anthony Padilla, who uploaded a grainy video of themselves in 2005 lip-synching the Pokémon cartoon theme song; the video inexplicably drew 24.7 million views (Heffernan). This was before such things as "YouTube partner" or "viral video" existed. However, Hecox and Padilla were amateur video "humorists" not personal vloggers. And watching Smosh's present day lineup of videos, they bear the mark of professional film production, with purposeful lighting, advanced editing techniques, location shooting, and extras, among other distinct differences, including high-definition camera work. It is apparent, though, that Hecox and Padilla shifted from perceived amateurs on YouTube, conceivably free of ulterior motives, to professionals, who are profit-oriented and possess a technical flare for conventional filmmaking.

Cultural participation on YouTube vacillates fluidly between commercialism and more affectively rich forms of engagement because, as TV theorist John Hartley figures, "culture emerges not in structured opposition to economics (as cultural critics hold) but as part of the same coordinated network" (Hartley 135). Burgess and Green's "continuum" of cultural participation is lined by monetary waypoints, in other words, but the subject still survives despite its commercial coexistence. There is room for the money makers and also "The Internet Granddad" on YouTube, though the money makers achieve more dedicated viewership; consumers still prefer commercial products, as evidenced by the "most viewed" videos on YouTube: professional music videos. Even so, the fact remains that many users are actively seeking out YouTube videos which are purely expressive of the self, and this speaks volumes about current postmodern consumption habits. If reality TV is the submission of ordinary people to a hierarchical consumer system in order to become like the commodities which give their postmodern lives meaning, then YouTube is what happens after that submission. The consumer is so deeply entrenched, interpellated, spellbound by consumption that their masters now trust them with the means of their interpellation.

The Authentic Amateur

Bree of Lonelygirl15, in trying to "authenticate" her vlogging, verbally associates herself with vlogger paytotheorderofofof2, Emily, whose videos contain the enticing "spectacle of actuality" fabricated in Bree's. Emily's vlogs are mundane, consisting of everyday moments in her life she deems worth sharing, and they are also ephemeral, in that they generally do not entice viewership beyond a single watch. But the details that escape Emily's creative concern, the pieces of her life and personality that come through without her knowledge, guarantee a kind of depth orientation only an amateur can convey, even if beyond her will; it is the truth of her actuality no actor can replicate. In Emily's first vlog from 2006 ("Blog 1"), she sits at her computer desk, nervously bobbing up and down, attempting to stick to the scrip she had conceived for herself before filming. She tries to maintain eye contact with the webcam atop her computer monitor while speaking, but to no avail, as it seems there is something keeping her from locking eyes with the mechanical gaze—some natural aversion missing from Bree's delivery. The backdrop of Emily's video goes against the aesthetic set conventions of vlogging that have caught on over time, such as minimalistic backgrounds with dim colors.[5] The ruby red sheets on Emily's bed are only slightly made up and oddly match the wall's paint color; there is a flattened cardboard box lying against her bookcase. She does not have to tell viewers she wants to go to art school, even though she does say it, because viewers can clearly see the assortment of paintings in the back of the room. This is what Katherine Peters and Andrea Seier mean when they define the unintended supplementary aspects of the amateur YouTube video as its "aesthetic surplus," and this appropriately calls attention to the subjectivity of the video's creator (193).

The aesthetics of amateur production speak to the viewer on an *analog* level, in that they "guarantee the meaning of what is deep inside" because their aesthetic parameters eschew efficiency and conventional pleasure (Hayles, *My Mother Was a Computer* 203). The complexity of on-screen subjects within amateur production does not "emerge," but is instead self-evident. When Hollywood films try to imitate amateur production styles, such as in the popular fiction horror series *Paranormal Activity* or its progenitor *The Blair Witch Project*, they are attempting to produce this effect in the viewer; and this aesthetic fulfillment, in turn, relieves the producers of some percentage of narrative obligation, especially in the development of one or another character. *The Real World* producers Bunim and Murray invite their participants to come and live in a well-furnished house, one that is quite chic. *The Real World* cast is reliably in awe of their pristine living accommodations. After a few episodes, the house will look quite different, as the participants affix their "surplus" to the beds, the kitchen, the bathroom—indeed, the actuality of *The Real World* starts coming into focus the mornings after drunken nights-outs, when broken beer bottles litter open living spaces, when bed sheets rest haphazardly over naked mattresses. In YouTube amateur production, such as vlogger paytotheorderofofof2's, the *process* of acquiring this aesthetic actuality is foregone: the surplus arrives immediately.

In contrast to Emily's aesthetic surplus, Bree of Lonelygirl15's bedroom is minimalistic, with only a few miscellaneous items hanging around, such as her feathered pink boa and stuffed purple monkey, both of which are featured extensively as props in Bree's bedroom vlogging. The shots of her bedroom are taken with a web camera that is situated farther away from the door than Emily's, so the viewer is afforded a greater sense of geography to buy into the Lonelygirl15 saga. Bree's room is painted a single color, white, which does not interfere with the speaking subject and allows the other items about the room to stand out but not clutter YouTube's smallish viewing window. Indeed, the interfacial appearance of YouTube—that constrained video box drifting amid a wealth of paratext—is greatly considered by its production community. In the video "Proving Science Wrong … with Lonelybeast and Danielgirl15," a reversal of Daniel and Bree's usernames, Daniel wears the pink boa, chatting aimlessly about science, while sitting cross-legged at Bree's computer desk; he is poking fun at Bree's style of vlogging. Daniel's on-screen behavior reflects a self-awareness that would be lost on an amateur YouTuber, but not out of place on reality TV. When vlogging is not being faked or satirized, it serves as a discovery of self and is not purposefully meant to entangle the uploader in a web of reductive self-referentiality. There is an "inauthentic authenticity" to Bree's depiction that, when held up to Emily's, becomes startlingly apparent, but this observation is of course predicated on some literacy regarding the form (Burgess and Green, *YouTube* 28).

A vlogger's motivation for uploading is also key in considering their actuality. In her first video, paytotheorderofofof2's Emily confesses emphatically, "I've been watching video blogs for a while on YouTube, and, uh, it's been pretty interesting, and I've been tempted to make my own just to see what happens." Emily is incited to film herself based on the desire she had seen in others to do the same; this is at the heart of idealized YouTube amateur participation, a recursive dynamic between the desire to watch and the desire to be watched, but never because the producer explicitly manipulates uploaders and the YouTube community into doing so. This creative move is encouraged, often passively, by another ordinary person, in true bottom-up fashion. Within this mode of amateur video creation, the product of which Patricia G. Lange calls "videos of affinity," there is an "attempt to maintain feelings of connection with potential others who identify or interpellate themselves as intended viewers of the video" (71). What is more, these videos "may or may not contain much 'content' or artistic aesthetics defined in traditional ways" (Lange 77). When Lonelygirl15 embarks on narrative contrivance, and continuity forms around the larger trajectory of her content, she consequently removes herself from amateur "affinity" and reflects commerce. Emily makes no great move toward continuity, or even staging, and thus denies the conventional means the viewer deploys to assess full motion video, especially in a televisual context. In videos of affinity, then, the aesthetics and desire to create are disparate than in the consumer products that imitate it. This is not to say that Emily does not "perform" or do "stage management" of her own for her videos, but that hers are different than what goes on in professional YouTube production, such as Lonelygirl15. If anything, Emily's visual performance is closer to the everyday performed self.

In its formative years (2005–06), YouTube quickly adopted its popularized amateur value set. Oddly, amid all its promotion of consumer liberation, the existence of YouTube alone was not enough to encourage its use. Though this dynamic has changed, as YouTube now produces some of its own videos, content providers were originally a necessity in order to expand YouTube's library, so the service's creators had to spark the inertia: YouTube co-founder Jawed Karim's "Me at the Zoo" from April 23, 2005, the platform's first upload, features Karim at the San Diego Zoo, standing in front of an elephant habitat. He is wearing a blue t-shirt and an unzipped red and black jacket, which hangs loosely off his shoulders. Karim addresses the camera as small children chirp in the background: "The cool thing about these guys," he says about the elephants, "is that they have really, really, really long trunks, and that's, that's cool." This was clever marketing, no doubt, because Karim appeared not to be overtly "pitching" YouTube, but instead encapsulated the mundane, everydayness which would become typical of its content, evidenced by his trivial twenty second video and its dry aesthetics. And there is nothing extraordinary about Karim in "Me at the Zoo"; his voice is monotone, his words simple, his style of dress practical. He is ordinary. When Chad Hurley and Steve Chen turned the camera on themselves after the Google acquisition in 2006, they were both wearing smart suits and were steeped in a community discourse that informed their every speech act—a far cry from the whimsical nonsense of "Me at the Zoo," but still decidedly spontaneous and mundane. Jawed Karim, now Silicon Valley royalty, could not escape the visual everydayness of YouTube in "Me at the Zoo"; he did not even try. The platform is what was extraordinary, not the content, and that was the thesis that would go on to inform many amateur creators, including YouTube's vlogging community. When professionals and corporations upload onto YouTube, their videos can feel antagonistic to the amateur community, especially when they siphon amateur viewership, but, in truth, the consequent tension between the two functions on the amateur's behalf.

If the intention of professional content providers is to make ad revenue, or use YouTube as free advertising for their work, then their videos tend to express a detachedness that does not engage the viewer, or the active YouTube community, as an equal agent of production and consumption. Appropriately, when commercialism gets involved, then the dismissive, conspiratorial reception associated with reality TV relocates itself on YouTube—user klebdman's almost immediate accusation of "acting" on Lonelygirl15 Bree's part serves as an apt example. To reiterate, there are attributes to an unvarnished amateur vlog that cannot be co-opted, and those distinguish it from professional content. But rather than solely distinguish, *subjectively authentic* vlogging, such as user paytotheorderofofof2's, can work to subvert hierarchical consumption, especially when paired side-by-side with the commercial videos on YouTube.

Universal Music Group (UMG) has had and still does have a particularly large presence on YouTube. Distributing music videos through Google's free, click-on-demand video platform means UMG does not have to deal with a television intermediary such as Viacom's MTV that might integrate another company's content into UMG's for the sake of advertising interests beyond the initial content provider's. On YouTube as opposed to TV, UMG is granted greater agency in how its content is used to accrue revenue and can retain a larger percentage of ad revenue as a result. Under the joint music video venture "Vevo," Universal, Sony, Abu Dhabi Media, and EMI Music have managed to wrestle away mainstream music video distribution from MTV, attracting deep-pocketed advertisers such as McDonald's by mandating across-the-board censorship standards and other content gate-keeping measures only possible on a highly customizable platform such as YouTube (Sandoval). Advertisers each have their own list of inappropriate words and questionable content they do not want to be associated with, and since YouTube is organized by individual videos rather than a succession of totally unrelated music video genres—such as a video block on MTV that might feature hard rock, gangster rap, and pop—then Vevo can cherry pick advertising to go with each video, or vice versa. When users come across Vevo's YouTube channel, they are met by a targeted thirty second advertisement before music videos even begin. Vevo videos feature annotations and links to other Vevo content: there are boxes inside boxes, delays on top delays. Web 2.0 is the professional distributor's advertising nirvana. The freedom for users to experience content whenever they please is tempered by the paradoxical truth that online media grants as much power (if not more so) to the producer to mediate that experience.

It goes without saying that advertising is rampant and egregious on YouTube. What differs on Vevo's channel, as far as the YouTube platform goes, is the level of community engagement, both in relation to the videos and external to them. User comments on UMG's top music video of May 2013, will.i.am's—"Scream & Shout ft. Britney Spears," are akin to a series of baseless non-sequiturs. Some users, such as omar suliman, repeat lines of lyrics for posterity, but primarily these comments are like a pathological shout-box for whimsy. Two users agree that at the ten second mark in the music video, there is a reference to the Illuminati. There are multiple spam comments by various users advertising porn sites. There is lots of disjointed, misspelled sexist and racist rambling; after all, "trolls and haters" are "normalized in the cultural system of YouTube" (Burgess and Green, *YouTube* 96). What is interesting about the hateful comments is that this is a professional video users are hating, which means they will not receive a response from the uploader or producer, but only incite community conversation within the comments section. Yet on professional videos, comments rarely engage hater rhetoric in any meaningful way, so hateful users oddly fan the flames of a fire that is not burning. In this way, commercial videos might as well not have a comments section at all: the consumption activity reflects that which goes on with TV, as there is little or no Web 2.0-style participation beyond video embedding. Key to the Web 2.0 ethos is paratextual intrusion into the central text—in this case, the actual YouTube video—user comments and "user reviews," which manipulate or distract from the central media experience, generally do not influence professional content. This supplements the trend in amateur content being the "most discussed" on YouTube; attention within the service should be measured by varying notions of popularity.

Alternatively to Vevo's channel, Paytotheorderofofof2's account manages to catalogue a reflexive relationship between producer/uploader and the userbase following Emily's vlog entries. While it is true that Bree of Lonelygirl15 does acknowledge user comments in some of her earlier videos—for instance, when users comments request she reveal more about herself, Bree does so— the conceit that her videos convey something different from a top-down viewing experience is dropped once the evil, occultist plot bubbling beneath Lonelygirl15 is exposed. Emily not only participates in long, engaged conversations in the comments sections of her videos, but has also, from 2006 to the present, maintained a recursive dynamic, as the comments inevitably shape the content of her successive vlog entries—meaning, that since vlogging is inherently about some form of personal expression, tied to a tangible world outside the YouTube medium, YouTube, then, serves to shape this external world as it locates itself back in it. In Emily's case, something comes through the other side of the screen and back again. After moving from her small, conservative town in North Carolina to Portland, Oregon, Emily gradually explicates more politicized topics in her vlogs, and starts calling herself "Rembrandt," as well as confessing the details of her bicuriosity and polyamory. This, of course, riles up the YouTube community, as any threat to normative ideologies means that reliably excitable anonymous users will run in droves to leave hateful comments or question motives.[6] And Emily does not seem to mind interacting with her sometimes hostile userbase, often relying on humor to deal with her detractors. On December 9, 2011, Emily posted a video ("Polyamory: No, I'm not confused") in reply to an unnamed user who had left a judgmental comment after Emily casually referenced her polyamory in a video she had posted the day before. Emily admits from the outset, "It's been a rough night," because she had not slept due to what the user had said to her. "I've been up angry," she says. "Last night, somebody made a comment on my latest video about my polyamory. They basically said it's not something I should be proud of. I'm lost. I'm confused. I don't know who I am … it makes me angry."

What follows is one part didactic vlog about the definition of polyamory— the word "ethics" is deployed frequently—but also a divulgence of her idiosyncratic investment in the concept, recalling her three boyfriends from first grade: "AJ, Anthony, and Eric, probably the first clue I wasn't keen on monogamy." The fact that a real, material consequence came out of this virtual community interaction, and that it had an immediate creative impact on her personal life, is something diametrically opposed to what occurs on TV or other top-down media. She was engaged by the community, then made it a point to engage the community back, and, most importantly, remained the focal point of the conversation—a feat of production/consumption only achievable on YouTube. And the user comments are right on point with "Polyamory: No I'm not confused"; there is no ad spam and no inconsequential shout-outs or conspiracy mongering, just interaction with the message being delivered in full motion by Emily. Equally interesting is that this video, and all of Emily's videos, subvert popular preconceptions regarding entertainment or media consumption that American culture has held onto throughout the 20th century's various mass media. On paytotheorderofofof2's YouTube channel, there is no escalating dramatic tension, no explicit basis for direct, prolonged attention, and Emily is not a YouTube partner, even with nine thousand (plus) subscribers.[7] She is just one human trying "to connect with other subjects across time and space" (Biressi and Nunn 32). When a subject makes the choice to upload for the sake of affinity, unfettered by monetary interest, and genuinely engages the online social community, there is the chance for increased depth orientation, complexity, and authenticity, as Emily conveys.

Parsing out value to the subject on YouTube is a matter of consumer behavior, not producorial behavior. Consumers should take the constructive qualities of savvy viewership spent on reality TV, the analytical ones concerned about representation and stakeholding, and inject them into their online consumption habits because, amidst the conflicting cultural dynamics of YouTube, there is the potential for *something* authentic, however qualified the level of authenticity. The danger is to accept all Internet consumer creators as authentic because the prevailing participatory ethos dictates they be so; on the other hand, to dismiss all vloggers as Lonelygirl15-style opportunists is equally fraught. This hyperbole is a reappropriation of the cheap reality TV polemic, "Reality TV is not real!" YouTube is about the continuum, which also contains fraud and commercialism, yet that is not its ultimate determiner, and to conclude such weighs on the consumer not the product. Assuming YouTube does not switch over entirely to an on-demand subscription service, then YouTube will retain its potential for subjective expression, the scope of which has much to do with its model for accepting content. While advertising is the foremost concern of television, considered prior to production and distribution, generally, the opposite is true of YouTube: any and all uploaded content is accepted, no questions asked, on a probationary basis. As long as it does not exceed length constraints or is not pornographic, an admittedly fluid descriptor, odds are the video will permanently reside on YouTube. Once on the service, videos are taxonomized according to usage, after which a system of highly contestable, user-created tags are suggested or assigned. These tags are informed by video content and metadata easily accessed by uploaders which gives a clear picture of who is interested in their videos— Google analytics even provides uploaders the exact geographic location their viewers can be found on a global map. This certainly offers greater agency for the amateur, but, yet again, these powerful gratis features are just as helpful for corporate professionals.

YouTube's technical structure suggests that, while "the content favored by advertisers on mainstream television is already crafted to be compatible with the consumerist messages that support it," YouTube's content can remain unshaped by advertising need, so its workforce of amateur videographers and vloggers can upload free of hierarchical sway (Andrejevic, "Exploiting YouTube" 413). Advertising on YouTube occurs after the fact, as interested corporations agree to videos and YouTube channels for their advertising based on the assumption that their associated message is not in opposition to the advertiser's own, though ads will be pulled retroactively as content and sensibilities shift. The question for advertisers then is "not whether amateur content can generate revenue, but whether accepting such revenue means ceding the type of control over content to which advertisers have grown accustomed" (Andrejevic, "Exploiting YouTube" 413). What this all means is that YouTube, similar to the Internet in general, is a comparably *inefficient* advertising platform. Google and YouTube have developed automated content-detecting software such as AdSense and ContentID to try and put wary advertisers like McDonald's at ease, but the vast majority of videos, which are amateur, profane, and sometimes in direct conflict with one or another copyright law, cannot be used for advertising. Appropriately enough, the most ad heavy videos on YouTube are uploaded television commercials because they are the only ones that can guarantee on-message content. In fact, McDonald's own YouTube channel is essentially an archive of their television ads. Emily's YouTube channel, paytotheorderofofof2, unsurprisingly, is free of advertising. Given all this, and the power to embed YouTube videos elsewhere on the Internet, it is clear that the largest percentage of uploaders do so out of some desire that exists *external* to the YouTube medium. Reality TV subjects, for instance, are predicated on their mediation within reality TV; the same is not always true of a YouTuber.

Burgess and Green, in fact, assert that the "ideal" YouTuber is an "ordinary, amateur individual, motivated by a desire for personal expression or community" ("The Entrepreneurial Vlogger" 90). And while YouTube is a nice showcase for the individual subject, it has its limitations. Emily is deeply conveyed on YouTube, aided by her active participation within the community and her willingness to expose herself before the camera, but her "YouTube personality," as uploaders sometimes refer to themselves, is hinged upon her creative labor. This is not reality TV; the cameras do not come to amateur uploaders, they have got to press record themselves. If Emily's life gets in the way of her participation with the platform, as it already has numerous times, then what the viewer gets in return seemingly suffers, too—in order to maintain interest in a channel, uploads have to be reliable and consistent. A person who casually uploads a few uninteresting videos, then drops off the map for a year, then returns, will obviously garner low viewership/ engagement by the community. The average YouTube video length is fairly short, around three to five minutes, so it is true that some *quantity* of videos is needed to flesh out vloggers. As far as content goes, there is an obvious attention bias on YouTube that generally swings toward sex, ideology, sensationalism, or humorous/"slice of life" content.[8] Some very successful YouTube channels, such as Smosh, have a set schedule for new video releases, similar to a traditional television channel, distributing uploads on particular days of the week and during certain times; when YouTube channels become fully monetized, they functionally *remediate* television (the "Tube" in YouTube).[9] Breadth and frequency of uploads really do matter on YouTube, at least that is what popular perception has led YouTubers to believe. The prevalence of metadata (viewing numbers, popularity graphs, etc.) on the platform instantiates an ideological drive in uploaders to engage YouTube's "attention economy," through which *numerical values are inscribed with emotional value* (Jenkins, "What Happened Before YouTube" 116). But attention is not necessarily the only guarantee for engagement on YouTube and this is also a relic of hierarchical media thought.

Emily's total number of videos, over eight years, is a comparably small 103, but despite that lack of participation she seems to thrive with her small, close-knit viewing community. In a plea video from February 22, 2013, she chronicled some of the issues she had been having with her dental health:

"I've been blessed with teeth problems," she says. "And I've been experiencing them." Hesitant because of her lack of insurance, she finally broke down and went to a Portland area dentist, but was served with a quote for $4,288 in order to fix her laundry list of ailments. One of her subscribers, and off-screen friend, Savannah Rae, helped create a site to raise money for her dental bills,[10] which was capped by Emily after reaching $2,775, as she consented to have a couple of teeth pulled rather than do a root canal. Her userbase rallied to pull together the funds and left messages on the donation page, confessing their dedication to her YouTube channel. Along with leaving a twenty-five dollar donation, subscriber Lauren Campos writes, "[Emily], I hope this doesn't sound creepy but I've been subscribed to your YouTube since waaaay back in the day.... You've always seemed like the type of person I would've loved to be friends with. I think you're pretty rad." During the donation period, Emily participated in conversations within the comments section of her plea video, thanking users personally for their donations and further detailing her need.

However different Emily's visual product and motivation to upload is from a commercial uploader's—she does seem to be seeking affinity as a subject among other subjects—remnants of the televisual hierarchy remain. Emily is not ignorant of her power position within her reception community, and this is visible in her request for money. With nowhere else to look for monetary aid, as her parents had already sent her even more money than they could afford, Emily reflexively petitioned her subscribers for help. Emily functions within the "continuum of cultural participation," by which genuine forms of engagement co-mingle with profit-driven impulses; ones which can contaminate mediated subjects in their indulgence, and are endemic to YouTube's paradigm of usage. The point here is not to equate Emily with Universal Music Group, however. While Emily stopped at this monetary waypoint along the continuum, she quickly returned to her usual intimate/everyday style of vlogging by July 2013—the kind which have endeared her to her userbase. She even started a new vlog channel "sortaspooky," on which she has vowed to more actively upload in deference to her dedicated reception community. Emily proves that the core ambition of a vlogger is not guaranteed to be the mythical YouTube partnership. Yet, the fact that she was able to accrue the monetary backing necessary for her dental work through YouTube may well prove to be the ideological turning point for her engagement. Her pursuit to open a new vlogging channel, for instance, communicates the potential for future monetization.

Emily's future with YouTube aside, Lauren Campos and the other subscribers who left Emily personal messages on her donation page did not do so out of celebrity cultism, an ongoing cultural feature of postmodernity according to theorist Chris Rojek. Campos, instead, is compelled to speak as a consequence of an everyday American problem—finding the means to pay for healthcare. This is not a product of YouTube's "attention economy," a quality tied to the celebrity, but rather of empathy derived from genuine connections established over time. America's celebrity obsession is part and parcel to reality TV participation, especially considering how many eyes are looking in on the reality TV participant. The endgame, on many reality shows, is to elevate the participant to something extraordinary, resembling those celebrity idols. And when celebrities participate in reality TV, they are attempting the reverse. Chris Rojek, in considering the celebrity in today's secular postmodern consumer society, asks, "Why do so many of us measure our worth against figures we have never met?" (10). What has happened in Emily's case is antithetical to this popular conception of consumer society. She accrued a following by means of her unrepentant ordinariness, the common denominator tying her to her userbase, because after more than eight years of uploading, she had not defied that ordinariness and had not desired to do so (until her new YouTube pursuits, that is). Additionally, by keeping her subscription community manageable, she transgressed the notion that the people consumers watch on-screen are ones they will never meet. Thanks to Emily's fully-actualized social representation within the YouTube community and visual embodiment, she is someone her userbase has conceivably met, barring the virtual constraints.

Paytotheorderofofof2's YouTube account has a low viewership compared to some other popular vloggers, like Shane Dawson or Greg "Onision." One of Emily's original videos from 2006 drew a high of 119, 652 views, but her current totals are much lower, averaging around 2,000 views. This has not hurt YouTube's reception of her or her reception of YouTube, which she claims is the "most rewarding thing" in her life. Given this, YouTube should not be considered along the same reception lines as television, which tends to be focused on its ability to garner "live" and massive audiences. DVRs, streaming services, and illegal downloading have threatened television irreparably, and with this digital destabilization, consumers can effectively pull TV programming away from its original context and inscribe whatever meaning they want to it. The result of this upheaval often damages the television content received. For instance, particular TV shows malfunction outside the narrative beat structure required by commercial breaks. Certain dramatic, serialized shows do not have the same impact if watched back-to-back in a couple sittings as opposed to on a weekly basis. Of course, on-demand is radically divergent from TV's referential goal for the consumer: to be an imposition on their time and their symbolic world, so that they must serve it and accrue meaning by its terms (i.e., producer controlled flow). YouTube resembles TV if TV were designed first and foremost for DVR-style consumer agency ("on-demand"). And YouTube's idiosyncratic taxonomies and signification are coded by this foregrounded media ideology: "[YouTube's] embrace of flow is selective and user-generated; and its sense of community is networked through recommendation, annotation, and prompts" (Uricchio 35). Despite metadata provided by Google which extolls the contrary, YouTube's amateur value should not be indexed by number of views or subscribers, but rather the depth of engagement by the community with particular videos. Universal Music Group's YouTube channel cannot maintain a dedicated userbase for eight years in the way Emily's account can, which speaks to a deeper, more affective form of engagement between user and uploader.

Within the amateur mode, YouTube is more like the version of mass media McLuhan imagined when conceiving the notion of mass media alongside automation. It is not about "the size of their audience" but of an "instant inclusive embrace" because "everyone becomes involved in them at the same time" (McLuhan 349). Emily uploads her videos as an open invitation to her userbase to consume her, appreciate/denounce her, and subsequently comment on that experience. YouTube, as a platform, does not discriminate consumer agents, and thanks to its on-demand availability, accessible interface, and system of taxonomy based on usage and not top-down interference, the service itself reflects the subjectivity of the ordinary humans who use it. As such, amateur YouTube is a "structure of feeling, neither unique to YouTube nor synonymous with web culture or popular culture more broadly," an idiosyncratic, open environment that can be utilized as a complex medium for human representation, both in terms of reception and distribution (Burgess and Green, *YouTube* 51).

Where the Corporate and the Amateur Co-Mingle

But while Emily attempted an authentic form of engagement through the YouTube platform, she is an exception that proves the YouTube medium *could be* more valuable to human subjective representation than it actually is. In truth, YouTube complexity does have a lot to do with frequency of uploads, but frequency endangers authenticity, because the more uploads, the more attention uploaders will inevitably receive, and the greater the chance they will become YouTube partners. And once their content is monetized, then drops in subjective value are inevitable in order to placate the Google hierarchy and a userbase that expects content from partners to resemble more professional, corporatized work. This is not to say that money somehow moots all subjective value, as evidenced by Emily and her dental episode, but that it certainly troubles it.

Videos that find themselves straddling the line between non-commercial and full-on monetized content prove the most challenging in terms of assessing subjective value, and their similarity/proximity to more authentic content on YouTube muddies the waters of subjective expression for the *entire* platform. In the case of Smosh, Hecox and Padilla's channel successfully transitioned from open-distribution amateur content to corporate professional content, with no in-between confusion; this was aided by the fact that the genre of Smosh's videos rarely intimated affective self-expression, but instead resembled Saturday Night Live skits. However, as was the case with Lonelygirl15, the vlog form—direct, persistent engagement with fellow users—signals authenticity for the YouTube audience, and can be deployed by amateurs whose goal of enabling a consumerist agenda is integrated into their personal expression. And while consumption is key to 21st-century subjectivity, uploaders like Emily promote false hope for the salvation of human beings from their late capitalist subjectivities. There is some truth to be had in the hysterical optimism cyber-futurists such as Kevin Kelly impose upon social networking and online interaction for the future of humanity, but all the Emilies on YouTube are met by an army of uploading *consumer subjects*, content to see their reflection in commodities.

Haul videos on YouTube personify the uneasy tension between consumer subjectivity and mediated subjectivity conceivably removed from the consumer capital designation, such as vloggers seeking human affinity through the platform. The typical form of a haul YouTube video is quite similar to a vlog, though many haulers will host their own personal vlog YouTube channels elsewhere—the content between a haul channel and an offshoot vlog channel run by the same uploader tends to be somewhat blurry. Visually, the haul uploader takes up the center of the screen in their videos, usually restricted to head and torso. Haulers address the camera and community directly. For the most part, these videos are shot in bedrooms, the going filmic space for vloggers, and occasionally content will incorporate personal details from their life. The majority of a haul video's content, however, is dedicated to the "haul" itself: meaning, these users' recent purchases. And an entire wing of YouTube is occupied by these videos, some with remarkably high viewership. Haulers will go through their purchased goods one-by-one, placing them near the camera so viewers can see the details in each object, and often making observations and recommendations as they go along. Within YouTube's haul discourse, there remain two prevailing types of haul videos: sponsored and unsponsored. Sponsored haul videos are part of viral marketing campaigns funded by department stores, such as JCPenney, or smaller retailers looking for cheap advertising solutions. Unsponsored haul videos are supposedly free of corporate funding beyond a YouTube partnership, though Google's relationship to an uploader proves troubling in and of itself. And the consumer has to take haul video uploaders at their word that they are not sponsored—there is no immediate way of confirming this beyond what they relay in their videos or express in their comments sections.

For its reception community, the distinction between sponsored and unsponsored hauls is a matter of agency. Yet this agency is underwritten by a consumer impulse either way. When haulers show off their possessions, they are letting the viewer know what they chose to purchase with their own money, and their recommendations (or denouncements) are taken on good faith as their authentic taste/opinion. When corporations or the producer interfere by supplying the monetary backing for the haul, then content suffers in the minds of the userbase. The consequent affront for the haul audience is that the haul video actualizes an uploader through *consumption* then *display*; it is very much an expression of postmodern consumer subjectivity. William Deresiewicz's channels Lionell Trilling in positing that "if the property that grounded the self, in Romanticism, was sincerity, and in modernism it was authenticity, then in postmodernism it is *visibility*" (emphasis added, 308). It is not enough to buy commodities and feel for them and through them, but also to display those commodities and establish a relational paradigm of subjectivity by means of them: YouTube can provide subjects that particular visibility through the haul genre. In these videos, to be sure, the consumer object foregrounds the subject displayed. And when JCPenny bankrolls the video production, then considerations of socioeconomics, fakery, and bias become the focal point of user comments as opposed to subjective choice or brand quality. Arguably, though, this qualification is mere nuance in a YouTube genre thick with depthlessness. Haul videos are consumer capitalism run amok because meaning rests on the minutiae of value that remains after consumers have taken a trip to the mall—does it matter so much who put the money in their hands? In the minds of the consumer subjects viewing, this is of the *utmost* concern; that one conceivably small element distinguishes an entire ocean of meaning, and certainly speaks to a profound, if albeit niche, cultural intelligence.

Whereas Patricia Lange ascribes emotional/subjective "affinity" to amateur content free of the consumerist agenda, haul videos communicate *consumer affinity*. The haul genre is a potent metaphor for the late capitalist sensibilities of today's digital subject—what is more, haulers are uniquely enraptured by the consumer paradigm, both through their active acquisition of monetary backing (by means of Google ad revenue) and also their content which is reliant upon that money for purchases. Many haul videos dupe their audience into believing they are not, in fact, the Web 2.0 equivalent of QVC or the Home Shopping Network (HSN), but in execution haulers reflect those televisual referents. The significant difference, though, is that the amateur serves as the bottom-up creator of a top-down capitalist enterprise. Rather than having subjects be co-opted by the producer as on reality TV, appropriately enough, that effect is created by the consumer on YouTube. How this is achieved has to do with the continuum of YouTube participation. The subjects engaging with and uploading onto YouTube have mutated by the means of these juxtaposed forms of participation (production for profit/production for affinity)—thus, many YouTubers are interpellated by an ideology which no longer senses any tension between the drive for capital gain and the drive for subjective fulfillment: the two modes co-mingle harmoniously. In these cases, Frederic Jameson's *unnerving dissonance* felt by those subjects unmutated by late capitalism has not just dissolved, but has been overridden my new affective consumer formulations. Highly-manufactured reality TV shows signified the end of this dissonance, giving way to the mutation in the subject Jameson feared, and haulers signify the subjectivities which come after that key mutation.

The Fowler sisters, Elle (user AllThatGlitters21) and Blair (user juicystar07), are fixtures among the hauling community on YouTube. They call themselves "beauty gurus" and specialize in makeup products and accessories, having set the benchmark for many other uploaders. View totals for their most popular videos have hit the multi-millions. The sisters have made nationally televised appearances on shows such as ABC's *Good Morning*

America. As a result of their popularity, the comments on their videos are regularly littered with other uploaders trying to launch their own haul channels. User BeautybyAndriana commented on one of Elle's June 2013 videos with a link to her own channel, saying, "I recently started my own beauty channel, but have been finding it hard to get my videos out there." This comment was flagged as spam, as well as numerous others of a similar nature. BeautybyAndriana's channel, by the way, is a note-by-note recreation of the haul style the Fowlers have perfected. The Fowlers and their rabid userbase meticulously flag each of these self-promotion comments as spam to presumably uphold the singularity of the Fowlers' YouTube presence; meanwhile, the sisters have launched their own product line, shilling custom iPhone covers and clothing, all spurred by the success of their multiple YouTube channels. Elle, the older of the two, has a haul channel and a gossip channel, her younger sister Blair also has a haul channel and a traditional vlogging channel. But the sisters only habitually update their haul channels, which are inundated with ads from Clairol, Tampax, and other feminine beauty and hygiene products, a result of their YouTube partnership that includes targeted advertising enabled by Google's Content ID.

Included in the description of each Fowler sister video is a disclaimer, usually mentioning something about the "distinctness" of their opinions and how they managed to pay for the items they are displaying. A video in which Elle shows off the beauty products in her bathroom, titled "♥ Bathroom Tour and Organization ♥," has an interesting disclaimer because, while the sisters are adamant about buying all of the products in their hauls, conveying that crucial sense of consumer agency key to this YouTube genre, Elle confesses that some of her belongings were not purchased by herself with her own money. She writes, "This video is not sponsored. Most of these products have been purchased by me, however there are so many that I'm sure *some have been sent for consideration....* All opinions are my own!" (emphasis added). This is no slippage. This is a very purposeful move on Elle's part to add meaningful texture to the inventory of goods comprising the postmodern subject. Her keen awareness of a discourse of ownership here invites Elle's userbase into a system of meaning wherein each individual belonging in Elle's bathroom—in their own bathrooms—can be ascribed with its own measure of value. As such, nothing is innocuous or inane. Consumers can value every bar of soap, every loose chapstick hanging out at the back of a drawer. And by the parameters she is codifying, the viewer can infer that the items bought by Elle herself have more value than the ones provided to her for "consideration," especially since she and her sister have expended so much energy asserting their consumer agency, an issue their userbase spends much time commenting on; their audience analyzes every recommendation the Fowlers make, trying to pinpoint insincerity. On some level, this high degree of scrutiny could trouble Elle and Blair's YouTube personas, but Elle's apparent straightforwardness about the items she did not buy in this video seemingly works to appease criticisms on the reception side. But certainly not before their viewers scuffle over the particulars.

Regarding the bathroom video, the point of contention for the userbase revolves around Puffs Ultra Soft & Strong facial tissues. Both sisters had been displaying the product and recommending its use in their videos, appreciating its durability and thickness. In a previous video ("My Morning Skincare Routine!"), Elle admits outright that she had been provided a box of tissues for her consideration, but that she had bought more boxes of Puffs after she found out she actually liked the tissues—notice that ever important shift in agency, accentuated by the performative: "I bought this." Elle's prefacing did not matter much to her userbase, who quickly criticized the sisters regarding their Puffs sponsorship. User koolaid52810: "The last few weeks she and her sister have been blatantly advertising Puffs brand tissues in every video, because they are paid to. It's funny at this point." While koolaid52810's comment is promoted by other users, its response from user GlambitionGirl19 receives three times the backing from the community: "I mean, even if Elle mentions those tissues in her videos and she's paid to, who cares? I'm not gonna go out and buy tissues just because Elle uses them.... I agree it is getting annoying but the fact that people feel the need to point it out is more annoying than the presence of Puffs in her vids." User Rachel Vice, in another well-received comment, self-reflexively adds, "If puffs was paying me to give them a five second mention in a video, I would eat the tissues if they asked me too. Let's be real. [Elle and Blair are] still doing beauty and tour videos." The commenters' discourse here points to two notions which conflict as they cohabitate on the Fowler sisters' channels. First, that sponsorship takes away meaning from the haul video, which the sisters acknowledge, and, second, that sponsorship does not matter so much in the grand scheme of things, especially considering that, in the first place, the content of their videos is about buying consumer products.

If Elle had left her "blatant" advertising unmentioned, then her userbase would have happily denigrated her digital facade, but she smartly preempts criticism through (some) transparency. The visible discrepancies in consumer agency then serve to call attention to greater cultural issues—the comments section on a YouTube haul video is an inexplicable place for cultural criticism, no doubt, and the lexicon is most assuredly muted and shallow. User Elena Klein asks Elle Fowler, "Why do you need soooooo many products?!" to which user missbeautyandsexy replies, "consumerism makes me sad :(" Then, user Angie Sharma says, "What does consumerism mean?" End of conversation.

While user Rachel Vice admits she would "eat" facial tissues if she was paid to, she does a disservice by minimizing the importance of consumer agency in postmodernity. In fact, Rachel Vice's apathy is exactly the sort of complacent attitude unsponsored haul videos are meant to correct. The cultural niche fostered by haul videos sanctions their viewers' right to be mad over some seemingly insignificant facial tissues. Ultimately, the distinction between sponsored and unsponsored videos is valid because caring about sponsorship in a haul video is tied to cultural concerns that precede YouTube. If postmodern subjects formulate their subjectivity through consumer goods, then it is the goods that matter, and everything that goes along with them— where the goods originated (brand/label), how they were paid for, what they mean to each consumer individually. In contrast, consumer apathy about those details means that a producer hierarchy dictates the composition of the postmodern interior self. While Jameson and Baudrillard would argue that in consumer culture the producer dictates the meaning of the objects they create without challenge, democratic technology and its byproduct of greater consumer capitalist literacy have done much to overcome this critique—Millennial culture has assuredly produced more informed varieties of critical consumerism. What postmodern subjects buy is what they are, and, nowadays, they know quite a lot about the things they buy and haul videos are evidence of this fact. Future civilizations will uncover these videos and be in awe of Millennials' extensive knowledge of enzyme exfoliators and different brands of mouthwash. This is the condition James Twitchell is referring to when he posits that "the happy consumer seems to be the one who makes objects come alive, while the unhappy one lets the producer generate meaning" (45). Subjects have to generate meaning for the objects that populate their bathrooms and not have it generated for them, or else (in their minds) embody the consumer drones Baudrillard imagines them to be—an outcome savvy consumers know full well. Knowledge of the objects consumers purchase helps to deter this outcome, but agency is of even greater importance. In light of this albeit contrived nuance, the critical hurdle, then, is not to believe that just because there has been a financial transaction somewhere along the line that nothing meaningful can follow. Yet the *degree* of meaning in these shallow circumstances is negotiable.

In consideration of this nuance, the Fowler sisters vacillate between submission and transgression to the corporate producer, sometimes in a single breath, and the attendant *meaning* for the viewer shifts as well. Outside postmodern subjectivity and actualization, and the gratis "for consideration" commodities, the ostensible point of an unsponsored haul video is, quite simply, letting other YouTubers know whether something is worth buying. In a video titled "High End Products I WON'T Repurchase!," Elle Fowler denounces some major makeup manufacturers such as Chanel by identifying products she considers overpriced and underperforming. This video is a sincere unsponsored haul; Elle even brings up the exact prices of each item so the userbase can appreciate her criticisms—one of the ongoing complaints of the Fowler audience is that the sisters avoid discussing prices because of their various sponsorships. Price, then, is a value of audience determination. The sincerity of this particular video, however, has to be measured alongside the sisters' deal with Puffs and other manufacturers who send them goods to "consider." Incorporating this content gap into the larger Fowler schema, their agency is clearly troubled: hence, the endemic paranoia percolating among their userbase.

However, Elle and Blair's self-consciously reflexive relationship with their consumer capitalist status, and very blatant gestures to shill their own product line, result in a unique learning opportunity for their userbase to accrue cultural knowledge and media literacy—the Fowlers are working *counter intuitively* to make their viewership savvy, a truly postmodern move as this subverts their position as commentators and/or salespeople. All involved in the Fowler paradigm, both in terms of reception and creation, are alerted to the fakery from the outset—the cinéma vérité production trickery employed on truTV, for instance, is left by the wayside—so users, akin to Rachel Vice, will apply their savvy but admittedly reductive logic to ward off any naysaying about the content of the sisters' haul videos: "Why is it an issue if a couple seconds is taken out of [their video] to make some money?" Vice says about the Puffs controversy. "Quit bitching at them for doing their job." This valuation is remarkably familiar to that in which the cheapest criticisms of reality TV reside ("reality TV is not real!"), and this clues us to the valleys of meaning that separate users like the Fowler sisters and paytotheorderofofof2's Emily. The Fowler sisters, according to Vice, are "doing their job," not reaching out through the YouTube interface into the hearts of their userbase. Mediations of the self in postmodernity are steeped in questions of authenticity, referents, stakeholding—interestingly, much of what users comment on in the Fowlers' videos has little or nothing to do with the actual content. And it is never a question of authenticity on the part of the Fowlers' mediation, similar to the Lonelygirl15 incident, but instead the larger problematic of YouTubian culture, much of which is a direct result of its technical structure. McLuhan would be proud because, among the Fowler sisters' video comments, the medium truly is the message. The distracting pieces of meat of the 20th century, however, exist in equal stride on YouTube alongside all these reflexive consumer subjects. But their discovery is predicated on algorithms, a palpable force within the YouTube medium.

The Tyranny of Algorithms

Google's success as a search engine has much to do with its ability to herd large volumes of content—the black hole that is the Internet—in a way that allows its users to get favorable returns for often imprecise search terminology. Additionally, with the aid of smart algorithms, cookies, and thick search histories, Google tracks user behavior and creates an online environment finely tuned to the user's interests, advertising and all.[11] When applied to YouTube, these algorithms point users to content they might be interested in given their previous viewing behaviors. For instance, after watching beauty gurus Elle and Blair Fowler over the course of a few days, YouTube's algorithm suggested to me a dense accumulation of makeup haul videos of varying quality, ultimately favoring popularity over relevance. Haul videos with millions of views were privileged over ones with tens of thousands of views. Videos with only a hundred or so views took some work to access, many of which I had to find through separate, more specific searches on YouTube, or just by scanning the flagged comments on the Fowlers' channels. So the fledgling creators of YouTube's beauty/haul community are subjugated by the very system they are trying to break into—it is no surprise, then, to see these desperate pleas by fledgling haulers in the Fowler sisters' comment sections. This is YouTube's attention economy at its most conspicuous, as uploaders of lesser stature are harder to find while YouTube partners garner more and more subscribers and ad revenue; the algorithmic hierarchy that pushes the most popular content to the top perpetuates its dominance. It is clear that algorithms, however "user-friendly" they make users' online interactions, can also be tyrannical in that they keep users in tightly controlled bubbles of interest, ones they have unwittingly helped to create but also have had created for them, divergent from the amateur ethos. This, coupled with YouTube's famously aggressive user moderation that "preempts" the "expression of minority perspectives" and hides "unpopular and alternative content from view," results in a kind of participatory media that has little to do with democracy (Jenkins, *Convergence Culture* 290). Under the algorithmic paradigm, what unwary netizens experience is selective exposure that eludes them as it works its magic on their computer monitors and their minds.

Employing the appropriate search terms and being of a certain critical mindset, if a user were so inclined (and they often are not), they *could* find a wealth of videos that serve to subvert the Fowler sisters and the entire haul community. Some of these videos are created simply out of spite. For example, the numerous videos which claim both sisters received nose jobs, which feature poorly edited side-by-side comparisons of old Fowler sister videos to new. Indeed, on YouTube there is a vast conspiracy regarding the sisters' apparently numerous cosmetic surgeries—these arguments are mostly founded on a departure both sisters made from YouTube at similar times in late 2010. Some users' preoccupation with the minutiae of their physical appearances, however, says more about the conspiracy mongers than the object of their theories. And some videos are downright abusive: One uploader who refers to the Fowlers as the "qvcsisters" uploaded a two minute rant called "'Blair' and 'Elle'—how much more stupid can they get??," but this kind of negative video-making is part and parcel to the normalized system of "haters" on YouTube. The sisters have uploaded a number of videos addressing their haters directly; Elle's infamous "Red Hot Rant," for instance, which she eventually removed from her channel, has been redistributed by a number of her detractors who have analyzed every word of that video looking for an offhand admission that she did, in fact, receive a nose job. Among these detractors, the more rhetorically important videos are the ones that take Elle and Blair's chicanery and shamelessness to task. Savvy user LusciousPout, who uploads her own haul and fitness videos, admits in January 2011's "Why I Hate *some* Beauty Gurus" that "YouTube has a dark side," one that is rooted in corporate manipulation. "Some of the videos about specific products," she says, "are being paid for.... I think the beauty gurus need to keep in mind that we [the userbase] can tell if you're not sincere about the product."

LusciousPout's apt criticism of the most popular beauty gurus is that YouTube makeup haulers very often tout expensive makeup brands as opposed to cheaper drug store alternatives, which perpetuates a harmful model of consumer spending. And amidst a recession in the United States economy, LusciousPout rightfully posits that the kind of example the Fowler sisters set is irresponsible. "Drugstore options are the most affordable, and it makes the most sense to spend less money on makeup when you're struggling in other areas," she says. "But the beauty gurus, I don't know if they take that into consideration, or if they just think that they can be the girl next door and be relatable [even] if they're using high-end products, which I don't understand." This is edifying criticism of the haul community, and does well to elucidate loyal Fowler viewers—in total, all four Fowler YouTube channels boast over three million individual subscriptions. But in order to view LusciousPout's poignant video, first I had to take it upon myself to seek out these criticisms on YouTube; my agency mattered. If I had never managed to type "Fowler nose job" into the YouTube search bar, then YouTube's algorithm would have only suggested to me other haulers who shared Blair and Elle's consumption modus operandi, of which there are many.

When they work for the consumer, democratized media platforms give them the tools to educate themselves. Wikipedia articles, for instance, are regularly scanned for bias and flagged if there appears to be any overt infraction; alternative viewpoints, therefore, must be incorporated into highly-trafficked articles or be rebuked by the Wiki community. Conceivably, YouTube's system of user moderation is meant to function the same way, pointing out flagrant ideological and copyright abuse. However, with YouTube, the democratic designation works against the consumer; the term "democracy" is deployed as a means of advertising trickery—and the algorithm's axiomatic presence on the service interferes with any contrary interfacial structure.

The ideal of democratic, Web 2.0 media and its attendant technologies is availability and accessibility, and algorithms have taken a considerable amount of this away from free and open platforms such as YouTube—"free and open" should not be a tenuous descriptor. Jonathon Zittrain theorizes that, as the Internet has developed into more of a consumer capitalist enterprise, it has gradually shifted from a "generative" system to a "closed" one. Zittrain defines generativity as "a system's capacity to produce unanticipated change through unfiltered contributions from broad and varied audiences" (70). Apple, for instance, has spearheaded the movement to "close off" digital consumer products in an attempt to accrue greater financial returns. It is no coincidence Apple has shifted from focusing on the sale of personal computers, which offer far greater customizability and freedom for their owners, to tethered mobile devices such as smartphones; its proprietary hardware (iPods, iPhones, iPads) and software (iTunes and the App Store) have established the new standard by which other corporations have followed.[12] And Apple has *confined* its customers under the guise of that dubious notion "user-friendliness." iTunes is so user-friendly, in fact, that a three-year-old can empty out their parents' bank account on an iPad in the name of micro transactions, referred to in various legal suits levied against Apple as "game currencies" (Stern). In the same vein, an algorithm's job is to filter content for the *benefit* of the user, at least that is what Google's marketing language on the concept has relied on, but in practice the algorithm has proven to be representative of an older hierarchical media ethos, efficiently working its way into the position of Internet hegemony, with the user ambivalent as its underling. What is happening now online is that a "broad and varied" audience, also contributing creatively, have been superseded by a smaller, more homogenous one selected by number of clicks as opposed to relevance—without a doubt, what is most relevant to the producer is not what is most relevant to the consumer.

In the wake of algorithms, there is an apparent censorship of attention on the YouTube platform, one which prioritizes monetized content, especially for the haul viewing audience. Despite the agency-driven ethos which stands as the structural base of Web 2.0 digital platforms, advertising revenue increases when herding the user toward a viewing experience of similarly-themed content. The Fowlers best serve YouTube and its sponsors when their content stands alongside other advertiser-friendly videos of a similar nature, not subversive or condemnatory content such as LusciousPout's—the point is to keep viewers engaging particular videos in order they be assigned a particular marketing demographic, in which ad-enabled videos (and TV shows) are taxonomized. In light of LusciousPout's anti-haul videos, if YouTube can manage to edify users of a particular mindset, their own viewing habits can also disable that potential. The paradox of the Internet's massive volume of content is that such volumes can also result in a deprivation of media literacy for the consumer, not unlike when the producer dictates content on conventional TV. YouTubers only know the content that they have been offered. Comparably, though, because conventional TV denies consumers viewing agency, then those consumers are potentially exposed to media content they might not have otherwise—if for no other reason other than sheer boredom. Since Internet engagement is left to consumer agents, and the algorithms working behind the scenes to mold their choices, "creative consumption" can be just as deleterious as it is liberatory.

Though much has been said here about the *creative* promise of YouTube as an uploading service for actualizing subjectivities, the majority of users who participate in the service do so through *experiencing* content not necessarily *creating* it. In fact, over the years, the percentage of users who upload their self-produced videos to the service has hovered around only ten percent; though around twenty-three percent in total will upload videos, much of that content is not their own creative property (Ingram). As is the case elsewhere on the Internet, "surfing" is the dominant mode of YouTubian participation. Strangely, though, on Web 2.0 platforms this kind of participation tends to be looked down upon or labeled "lesser" than the act of creation. Burgess and Green note that "dominant discourses around participatory culture (including the very idea of a gap in participation) appear to frame *passive engagement as a kind of lack*, continuing to affirm and reward those who speak more than those who listen" (emphasis added, *YouTube* 82). Among netizens, however, consumption is just as important as creation, arguably more so. The fundamental problem with defaming "surfers" is that online communities such as YouTube are "co-creative" environments in that its participants "at various times and to varying degrees [are] audiences, producers, editors, distributors, and critics" (Burgess and Green, *YouTube* 82). Which is why shout-out videos and the like are so prevalent on YouTube—much of the vlogging community, for instance, feasts on its self-reflexivity, reveling in their esoteric feuds, crushes, and gossip that could take only exist within the confines of their codified visual discourse community.

For instance, in May 2006, Emily, user paytotheorderofofof2, posted a video ("For my Whiney") in which she confesses her "massive Internet crush" on Canadian YouTuber thewinekone, whom she pet names "whiney." Tony (thewinekone) had achieved fame in the early days of YouTube for his hyperactive persona which appealed to the service's youthful early adopters—he was later featured on a special CNN Democratic presidential debate that used questions posted via amateur video on YouTube as the driving gimmick. Tony's question, which CNN played in the debate's introduction for a laugh, never mind his Canadian citizenship, had something to do with eighty-eight percent of Californians electing Arnold Schwarzenegger governor because they thought he was a cyborg who could fend off nuclear war—certainly a hint at who thewinekone's target audience might be. After Emily's confession video, amid all the heartbroken user comments on her channel, a bevy of male users uploaded reply vlogs explaining to Emily why they were more suitable lovers than thewinekone, creating a new string of content to go along with the original video. Consequently, a veritable mythology of YouTube videos and comments grew out of this event, spanning numerous YouTube channels and off-site blog entries. So Emily uploaded another video addressing her new suitors, called "The Love Square," playfully inciting increased romantic hysteria. She starts the video by saying, "A lot of people know about my Internet love life," explaining how she had found her confessional video on a foreign website and could not figure out what they were saying about her. Emily follows that by playing a clip from thewinekone's own confession, reciprocating her crush on him. She then addresses her new Irish suitor, Adam, calling him "the cutest thing ever," then calls some American kid named Jeff "adorable," then asks the userbase to choose which of these guys she should go with. The "love square" never officially ended, according to Emily, who never managed to settle on any of the three, despite her userbase excitedly weighing in and helping to create a very dense log of Internet interaction.

Emily's userbase, the one that has followed her throughout the years, the same which helped to pay her dental bills, has *actively* followed her. Maybe they stumbled upon her in some offhand search. Maybe they found her through an algorithmic suggestion, though her (current) lack of monetization makes that avenue of discovery unlikely. But her userbase has followed her nevertheless. She was not on billboards, or bumped onto the bottom of prime-time TV shows, or force fed to users through advertising. If YouTubian textual consumption is reliant upon a sort of selective viewing, and in the case of this "love square," active participation by those selective viewers, then ascribing greater value to creation is a fallacy. As such, it stands to reason that viewers can, depending on their level of engagement, accrue subjective value alongside YouTube creators. Given that the percentage of passive surfers far outweighs the percentage of contributors, YouTubers learn more about their own subjectivity by watching other YouTubers as opposed to making their own seen—it is what Burgess and Green call "creative consumption," with the creative act constructing human interiority (*YouTube* 14). Creative consumption operates within the continuum of participation on YouTube. On the one hand, agency has increased since top-down, 20th-century analog media. But this increased agency is a *horizontal* style of agency; while consumer content selection online is basically endless, that selection is consumable only if it can be discovered in the first place. So, the digital agent has a wealth of content to view, but the selection of that content generally rests on constructs of automated reasoning such as algorithms. To be fair, today's digital consumer is comparably more creative, but not as creative as the Web 2.0 ideal promises. However negotiable the attendant agency, passive digital consumption still retains more subjective richness than the paradigms of content distribution and selection on radio or conventional TV. Paytotheorderofofof2's Emily is reaching out to a userbase who accept her affection, who have chosen the videos that she takes full ownership of creatively, and this is a more meaningful action for the consumer than switching between television channels.

Admittedly, passive consumption is antithetical to the digital culture and/or postmodern trend of putting the self on display for the sake of subjectivity, as is the case with many reality TV participants or avid social media users. How this difference in engagement should be read is as *reactionary* to the postmodern tendency of putting the self on display, especially in regard to sweeping criticisms levied by baby boomers against Millennials, these accusations of newfound heights of narcissism.[13] Watching the most intimate YouTube videos, there is a kind of transferrable desperation tinged by a repressed desire, unarticulated, but driving the YouTubian creative and receptive acts. This is what happens when reality TV logic festers long in the minds of savvy consumers—amateurs, weary of the ubiquitous celebrity complex, content with their ordinariness, produce and distribute videos that have nothing to do with themselves but everything to do with subjectivities on the other side of the screen, who are consuming theirs. Different from vlogging, and miles away from the haul genre, these videos eschew any dominant preconceptions regarding visual media. And they are a selfless act of creation and display, lacking the barefaced narcissism supposedly teeming throughout Millennial culture.

A Return to the Repressed and Fluid Ethics

ASMR YouTube videos embody this kind of creation. ASMR, an acronym for autonomous sensory meridian response, is the highly contested medical phenomenon associated with people's physiological responses to external stimuli. When someone stands behind another person and places his or her fingers on top their scalp, opens them slowly, and claims it is an egg cracking, and the experiencer miraculously feels the cool liquid flowing down his or her head from inside that nonexistent egg, then they have experienced an ASMR. Some commentators refer to it as a "brain orgasm" (Simons). Again, ASMR's scientific backing is matter of conjecture, so similar to hypnotism, for an ASMR to work, the appropriate emotional and mental conditions must be achieved first by the experiencer. But YouTube creators do not seem to be too concerned about the necessary conditions on the other side of the screen. In fact, they are glad to film these niche video experiments for whoever might enjoy them, in whatever manner. And, if the comments are to be believed, quite a few users do.

Sometimes referred to as "whisper" or "role-play" videos, YouTube ASMR content ranges from paradoxically relaxing visits to the orthodontist, to make believe haircuts, to a close-up of hands massaging wads of sand on the beach; presumably, the sound of the sand is meant to be therapeutic. The videos are all down tempo, and have a bit of a gender slant, as women creators dominate the most popular ASMR videos, though this is common throughout the YouTube medium.[14] Many ASMR videos employ binaural microphones to create three-dimensional sound so the viewers can hear every rustle, mouth movement, and whatever else might appear on screen; many ASMR creators will recommend their viewers wear premium headphones to get the full experience. The majority of these videos resemble vlogs aesthetically in that they feature a close up of the creator's head in the middle of the frame, but rarely will personal details ever become part of the equation—it is all about the performance of the video's particular theme, and it is important to note here that overt performance is pretty unusual for amateur YouTube content. Generally, amateur performativity on YouTube hinges upon a performed lack thereof, which is a decidedly *anti-performance* variety of performance, but ASMR negotiates the amateur along a trajectory of conventional "acting." Indeed, the performance cues of ASMR videos are established in very much the same way as theatrical drama. The most popular ASMR uploader is GentleWhispering, whose top video has achieved more than 2,886,679 views, an astounding feat for what some critics have called a YouTube "fetish" (Hudelson). The video, titled "*_* Oh such a good 3D-sound ASMR video *_*," interestingly lasts about sixteen minutes, twice as long as YouTube's standard video length. So the userbase is willing to accept deviations from the norm in order to watch/experience/enjoy these ASMR videos.

And if vlogs are inane, then ASMR videos are incredibly so. One ASMR

I watched was a five minute whispered description of a scented candle as it was waved in front the camera repetitively. YouTuber VeniVidiVulpes, a self-proclaimed ASMR "artist," posted a video with half a million views in which all she does is brush her hair and, even by her admission, "ramble" for forty-five minutes. The specifics of her rambling primarily have to do with her microphone falling over and how the viewer is supposed to be relaxing now. An entire minute goes by with only the sound of the hairbrush to keep the viewer company. In a thirty-four minute video, VeniVidiVulpes "whisper reads" the children's book *The Velveteen Rabbit* while a close-up shot of her left hand stroking her pet bunny loops for the viewer's relaxation. User acquiesce022 tells VeniVidiVulpes on the rabbit video, "I can't thank you enough. I have so much trouble sleeping (friggin insomnia) and your videos help, and I appreciate you so very much!" Light Cyrus comments, "Your voice moves me." PufferBluntMan says, "I feel like a fluffy cloud…" To a lesser degree, other users will rightfully argue the merits of ASMR's existence, and yet others will try to decide whether their sexual response to the ASMR is founded: "I know this thing isn't meant to turn u on but this turned me on a little bit," says user James A. The internal experience ASMR videos evoke is indicative of the affective value possible for consumers to acquire and transfer through YouTube's "low barriers," amateur "structure of feeling." What constitutes this value, and where it emanates from, is decidedly postmodern.

Most apparent in the ASMR genre is the shift in structure away from sensible, or even coherent, narrativity. ASMR videos truly are anti-entertainment, in a way that vlogs, even with their denial of dramatic structure, are not; the complete dismissal of prescribed video lengths, the lack of dialogue or direction, and the emphasis on visual/auditory facets as opposed to any intelligible engagement with the audience are just a few reasons why ASMRs are distinct even within the content pastiche that is the YouTube medium. It is helpful, then, to consider ASMR videos as a cultural reaction, similar to some forms of reality TV participation/production. If reality TV is meant to reclaim embodiment lost in the digital age, poignantly expressed on daytime TV such as *Maury* (see Chapter 1), then ASMR videos are trying to reclaim *affect* lost under the same circumstance. Lange's YouTubian notion of "videos of affinity" suggests some of the logic behind this, except that ASMRs take the visual affective encounter far beyond a display of the personal. Narrativity manages to get in the way of emotion in the minds of ASMR creators; this is their attempt at mediating a "purer" experience of affinity. In a larger context, ASMR videos function as a reaction to "the waning of affect in postmodern culture" Jameson sees happening aesthetically in contemporary art and architecture (10). Indeed, ASMR creators are experimenting with a wild new visual form here, except that form has no intrinsic meaning beyond its visual/auditory existence. Indeed, the creators are aiming for a particular "physiological" response from the audience. And many users, such as acquiesce022, use ASMR videos as sleep aids, meaning content is not meant to be obtrusive, mentally stimulating, or (deeply) meaningful. ASMR is not the direct engagement of a subject with others, as in vlogging, but rather the unspoken knowing of some great emotional loss, evidenced by the ostensible desire to make others "feel," whether those feelings are substantive or not. ASMR videos, similar to postmodern art, signify a "return to the repressed, a strange, compensatory, decorative exhilaration" (Jameson 10). And they truly are "decorative," in that forty-five minutes dedicated to the video and sound of a woman brushing her hair only serves to *decorate* a digital space, not make it meaningful.

Just as media theorists in the last half of the 20th century such as McLuhan granted television viewing with particular emotional, subjective, and identity formation abilities, here stands YouTube, with its immeasurable density of human expression. Richard Grusin, in considering the disparity between television and YouTube, suggests that YouTube "not only functions as a 24/7, global archive of mainly user-created video content, but it also serves as an archive of affective moments of formations, much as television has done for decades" (66). Grusin, though, does not parallel YouTube and TV in their ability to shape their audience—an affective moment of formation on YouTube is vastly different than TV because television imposes its content and structure upon the viewer. Despite the tyranny of algorithms and the other various elements that might impede consumer agency already mentioned here, YouTube still has the potential to be a substantially more liberatory viewing experience than TV. So when a user, after selecting a return from a given search or algorithmic suggestion, chooses to watch a particular video from start to finish, which is pretty rare on YouTube, then that proves to be an even more memorable consumption activity as consumer agency plays such a significant part in the consumption exercise. TV happens to consumers, but consumers happen to YouTube.

And because of that, consumers interact with YouTube's service from a decidedly self-aware vantage point, so, as was the case with the Fowler sisters, YouTube's juicy pieces of meat never distract them from the medium itself. In contrast, the system of interaction required to use television never has to be "learned"—it seemingly occurs as a perpetually flowing electrical field in the foreground of a viewer's consciousness, and pressing the "power" button has evolved into an automatic action. Parents cannot place their toddler in front of YouTube and expect that baby to be mesmerized hands-free in the same fashion that they would in front of TV. YouTube must be paid attention to, clicked. User engagement is tinged by self-awareness. Remarkably, within its user community, YouTube is the subject of conversation regarding the medium and not its content; this translates to a system of checks and balances for potential uploaders, who must meet communal demands dictating that YouTube's status quo be maintained or else have their videos be in danger of removal or be labeled taboo by the userbase. The YouTube citizenship vehemently upholds a strange kind of civics for their platform, typified by ethical boundaries which are continually "co-created, contested, and negotiated in YouTube's social network" (Burgess and Green, *YouTube* 21). And these ethics have changed over the years.

One of YouTube's infamous qualities is its knack for welcoming sometimes racist, sexist, and inflammatory content with open arms—this is undoubtedly a consequence of the freedom the platform offers uploaders in regard to questionable content, even if anything remotely "pornographic" is quickly removed from the service. Jenna Marbles, one of YouTube's most subscribed uploaders, has made a name for herself by offering a woman's perspective devoid of Women's Liberation-style feminist discourse—she sexualizes herself for her userbase, denigrates the plight of women, and casually refers to herself as a "slut" and sex object, with little rebuke from her viewing audience. Without explicit acknowledgement, Marbles has helped to influence a bevy of popular YouTube channels which propagate strict formulations of postfeminism. This manner of inflammatory content was normalized in the formative days of YouTube, back when its democratic aspects meant active defiance against a prevailing system of mainstream entertainment that was considered too "politically correct" for its own good. Over time, though, ethical standards for content have shifted from defying political correctness back toward upholding some measure of it. Another well-subscribed YouTuber, user Greg "Onision," has earned a dedicated Goth fan base enraptured by his nihilistic commentary and humor videos pertaining to suicide, something he has admitted attempting himself. In a skit video uploaded on February 28, 2013, called "10 Reasons to Stop Cutting," channeling his on-screen character "Rod Danger," Onision makes a backhanded attempt at humor therapy which, at varying points, calls suicidal people weak, undesirable, homosexual "idiots." One scene features Onision failing to seduce a woman because of the scars on his wrists—he plays both the cutter and the woman, in an emblematic YouTubian casting choice. Many in the YouTube community, however, were none too pleased with the video, despite its content not deviating thematically from Onision's past five years of creative labor. Now, Onision is the subject of a long string of complaint videos, chastising his crass position on suicide and, alternatively, deepening his own popularity; in particular, his feud with user MrRepzion, a longtime Onision hater, is the subject of many videos from a variety of uploaders keen to weigh in on the controversy.

What the contestable ethics of YouTube communicate is that the service is fluid. YouTube is a medium that manufactures boundaries to play outside them and defy them, creating new ones in the process, only to eventually defy those. This is the kind of unstable, experimental system to which early postmodern thinkers such as Jean-François Lyotard ascribed great artistic value. As long as the conventional top-down hierarchies that define television are restricted to a minority presence on YouTube, then it has the potential to remain a depth-oriented, fluid, and meaningful outlet for the exploration and expansion of late capitalist human subjectivity. But that potentiality has already begun to corrode, thus YouTube's continuum of participation. "A postmodern artist or writer is in the position of the philosopher," Lyotard tells us. "The artist and the writer, then, are working without rules in order to formulate *what will have been done*" (emphasis Lyotard's, 81). Savvy YouTubers philosophize on human depth, on meaning where there should not be any; in so doing, they create meaning. But if Jonathon Zittrain and other techno-critics are correct in that the Internet is ceding all its democracy for the sake of profit, then YouTube will succumb to the same fate as other Internet services, e.g., long-dead social networking platform MySpace—obsolescence through Wall Street relevance. But for now, in the early 21st century, YouTube is the Marianas Trench of visual media. "The number of videos on YouTube is almost too large to comprehend," Richard Grusin writes, "experiencing the YouTube sublime, the mind is unable to conceive the immensity of the YouTube universe even while it is empowered by the experience of an affective awe in the face of such immensity" (61).

Conclusion

Beyond Reality TV,
Facebook and YouTube

> Given the central status of deception in relation to the symbolic
> order, one has to draw a radical conclusion: the only way *not* to be
> deceived is to maintain a distance from the symbolic order, i.e., to
> assume a *psychotic* position. A psychotic is precisely a subject who
> is *not duped by the symbolic order.*
>
> —Savoj Žižek, "How the
> Non-duped Err" in *Looking Awry* 79

In 1984, Frederic Jameson isolated a *cultural reaction* among baby
boomers, an "unnerving dissonance," and this emotional incongruity was
keeping burgeoning consumer media platforms at arm's length, away from
subjective interiority. It was a distancing effect, no different than that associated with a traumatic moment alerting people of their habitation in the
symbolic order. And this critical distance served as a catalyst for *resistance*
to consumerism, which is waning or lost in today's technocratic consumer
culture. Baby boomers considered consumer technology the servant of its
human operators. Nowadays this technology is no longer a "consideration,"
but instead a determiner of ultimate truth. The solution, then, is not to revel
in the inability to achieve the distance necessary for literacy (i.e., "savvy
ambivalence") but to instead reassess the notion of today's subjectivity. First,
it is important to redefine *interiority* among the digital regime; the "interior"
self is challenged by the digital, as identity and subjectivity blur. Indeed,
privileging interiority among selfhood speaks to a tendency for subjective
"stability" and consolidation which social media disallows—nowadays, subjectivity, like identity on Facebook, is about *proliferation* and *extension*, destabilizing the self such that an "inner self" ceases to matter. To be sure, many
selves trump whatever depth orientation people can achieve. By decrying the

discursive invention of "inner" and "outer" spaces in order to question gender normality, Judith Butler asks, "How does a body figure on its surface the very invisibility of its hidden depth?" (183). Digital tech provides the answer.

Consider again the MySpace Angle mentioned in Chapter 2: Social media users take a photo of their body at an angle which purposefully masks some aspect of their physical self. But the angling of a camera lens is only about assisting insecurity insofar as the body matters online, which it does— a person's photo is commonly accepted as the most valuable piece of indexical evidence online. Yet once an "inner self" is challenged, the MySpace Angle takes on new significance. Separated from technological mediation, the physical (outer) form is a given and the inner self is hidden; by-in-large, even in postmodernity, this is still a cultural axiom, no matter its efficacy. The MySpace Angle, then, is a reversal on what happens externally of digital spaces; it masks the physical self so that the *intangibility* associated with interiority can occur online. Users employing that angle are making up for a lack of interiority on-screen (and inadvertently off-screen) by devising new ways to hold onto something that is theirs alone (i.e., "the interior life" as corporeally limited). Strategic use of a camera allows users to *make visible hidden depth* onto photos which might otherwise reveal *all that they are* in the digital age. The MySpace Angle, though, has a specious reputation on the Internet; many netizens take its use as an outright fraud, a way of perpetuating the illusion of attractiveness. This reaction, too, is related to interiority, in that as digital spaces have instantiated dissolution of an "inner life," then any attempt at withholding aspects of the corporeal is the same as telling a real world lie. Inner motivations have surfaced to the flesh in the form of social media profiles.

The very invocation of "the subject" implies something occurring inside, not readily visible, but the depth orientation of subjectivity's articulation varies. Without interiority, though, subjectivity must be rethought. Since people still believe in their interior existence off-screen, that desire, like the desire for authenticity, is all that is required for subjectivity to persist. Subjectivity in the digital era is postmodern, assuredly, but also takes on the attributes of the various interfaces and technologies consumers interact with; on the one hand, subjectivity faces a cultural mutation of postmodernism which dictates its content, and on the other a technological mediation which exacerbates the postmodern and adds new complications, new idiosyncrasies to the self. In accordance with postmodernity, subjectivity nowadays is surface-oriented, fragmentary, unstable, and typically free of any knowable referent. But it also carries attributes of the Internet and digital media—one such attribute is Nicholas Carr's idea of "bidirectionality," which says that people online "can send messages as well as receive them" (85). As consumption is now a "read and write" activity, subjectivity has mirrored that effect. Paytheorderofofof2, Emily, submitted her subjective value to her YouTube viewer base through affective encounters, informing her selfhood by means of those exchanges. Subjectivity is no longer static, but bidirectional in that the kind of isolation and privacy that once signified a rich, interior life has been replaced by the participatory environments of Web 2.0.

Certainly this rearticulation of the self is an ideological activity, a "hailed" interpellation, not something pursued outright. Again, the insistence of people in postmodernity that an inner life *still exists* communicates that fact. And the proliferation of subjectivity should not be taken as a de facto flaw. Selfhood is now modal, flexible, and up for debate. This does well to remove *undue* ontological value placed upon the inner life. Subjectivity is no longer concrete. Of course, there will be those who wax nostalgic for a substantive kind of subjectivity, and danger lay in complete surface orientation, but a multiplicity of selves removes the mystification (and subsequent sanctity) of selfhood which is exploitable by some structures of power, such as religion. In this vein, digital subjectivity can be quite transgressive. What is more, these new formulations of selfhood, while not concrete, have the backing of a multitude of platforms as a sort of protection against invisibility; the subjective expression of minorities and the marginalized knows many digital outlets nowadays, with new ones emerging on a daily basis. Online, no voice goes unheard, and no marginal self can be made inert or objective. It is a truism that netizens seem impervious to the machinations of power—this is not to argue that they really and truly are impervious, but that netizens are, at least, incredibly vocal in their opposition to power. Reddit's ever-deepening flame war against religious institutions, and the complicated meaning of Internet atheism, explicates that resistance.[1] Oppressive ideologies cannot withstand the lengthy debates happening on Internet message boards, yet the questionable authority and intent of mediated users can devalue even the most prescient of critiques.

Caveats aside, surface orientation mostly engenders a disjunction for the self because a multiplicity of selves *guarantees* a lack of depth. Surface sees the mutation of the subject such that an ASMR YouTube video can appease psychic needs once belonging to the off-screen world. McLuhan's preoccupation with technological "extension" and prosthesis spoke, firstly, to the corporeal. Twentieth-century techno-apologists and phobics both preached about humanity's future as Cyborgs, physically one with the machine. It is apparent now that the prophesied technological prosthetic *did not* turn out to be of the physical; digital consumer tech has facilitated the universal adoption of *psychic prosthesis*. Social media and the Internet extends the inner life, stretches it out like putty across a multitude of platforms, such that it loses its substantive richness. Critical distance, then, is a preventative to spiraling surface orientation—distance achieved through the baby boomer's reflective mode of unnerving dissonance.

How to garner dissonance nowadays is a matter of consumer mentality. When critically evaluating their own behavior, consumers oftentimes see themselves as *distinct* from larger cultural trends, which they themselves are also propagating, despite their protestation to the contrary. For instance, in an example from Chapter 3, YouTube user missbeautyandsexy comments on a Fowler sister haul video by saying, "consumerism makes me sad"; this video ostensibly implicates that Elle Fowler is part of a sponsorship/advertising scheme extraneous to her YouTube partnership. Missbeautyandsexy's statement, at first glance, suggests a dissonance, but that statement exists on YouTube, which is also a consumer capitalist platform (albeit a contestable one). It is a much harder conceptual act for people to admit that they are complicit, that they foster the same kind of consumer practices which subvert the affective moments also achievable on YouTube. What if missbeautyandsexy had said, "I am helping to create this!" in response to that video? Surely that would have evoked a strong dissonant reaction because that means she is implicating herself—I am willingly aiding a system I *already know is harmful*, she would be saying, which seems like lunacy. And this is new dissonance: Engaging subjects traumatized, and traumatizing others, by the awareness of their own complicity. They are, then, ostensibly subverted by the prevailing consumer system, and once in that zone, they are able to *reflect* on it more fully since they are no longer "equal" participants in the consumption exercise, as Web 2.0 ideology has interpellated them to believe.

When subjects are complicit in their surface orientation, they undoubtedly resist it—Facebook dispenses this lesson amid the trauma of catfishing. In the moment of revelation on MTV's *Catfish: The TV Show*, the duped parties are alerted to a wealth of lies they willfully accepted, fostered, and took pleasure in. Even if these people cannot say it aloud, their emotional response to their dupery says, "I helped to create this!" Unsurprisingly, the duped will usually stop using Facebook, while others will swear off social media entirely;

this is an extreme reaction, especially since now they actually know better, but sometimes dissonance demands that kind of response. The point here is not to assert that people should not use social media or engage the digital regime, as they really have no choice to the contrary, but that they should never forget their complicity in their own duping.

Duping the Literate

Available on both Apple's iOS and Google's Android operating systems, Snapchat is a smartphone application that advertises a comparably safe/private means by which to share photos. The app allows the sender to determine how long a recipient can view a sent photo. That photo is also tethered to the application, meaning it cannot be readily copied and used with another application. Snapchat is primarily geared toward the young, with a median user age of eighteen, as of January 2014 (Colao "Inside Story..."). Its practical function is to make sure users can take and send whatever photo they like without worry that it might haunt them on social media or, worse, on darker corners of the Internet; the app's mascot, coincidentally, is a cartoon ghost named "Ghostface Chillah" that floats atop a yellow background (Colao "Snapchat..."). The ghost, though, is meant to communicate the promised ephemerality of Snapchat's photo distribution service, not the scarier idea of digital specters that it also evokes. As a consumer platform, Snapchat serves as a response to the dangers of social media, something many students are lectured on ad infinitum within secondary education nowadays. Indeed, Snapchat is what comes after users believe they are digital skeptics, properly distrustful of the Internet, because the application *outwardly acknowledges* and *professes to rectify* privacy problems with content shared through digital spaces.

And, of course, Snapchat has been abused and is the subject of some controversy regarding its data retention practices—according to its creators, Snapchat photos are deleted from its corporate servers not long after their determined time for viewing expires, so avoiding abuse means consumers have to trust Snapchat's service claims and employee background check policies. The problem is that many smartphones have a "screenshot" or "screen capture" function which allows users to take a photo of whatever is on their screen at any time, whatever application they are using, thereby overriding Snapchat's privacy measures. This specific software breach is what initiated a December 2013 Canadian child pornography case, where the teenage boys involved demanded their girlfriends send them sexually explicit photos through the service. The girls, by their admission, thought they were safe because of Snapchat's ethos of privacy. After screenshots were produced, the boys then shared those illicit photos online (CBC News). In a widely-reported May 2014 settlement with the Federal Trade Commission, the company was forced to publicly acknowledge to their userbase that the app's privacy capabilities were exploitable, and that they should not use the service as a safe means of sharing intimate photos. But Snapchat's reputation for ephemerality precedes and dwarfs that warning.

A popular website called snapchatleaked.com is home to a catalog of images obtained through the application. The website's explicit goal is not to debunk Snapchat's privacy claims, but to be, as they say, a "silly" diversion that abides by "Google's terms and service." Astoundingly, even though the site spreads knowledge regarding an unsafe application which professes otherwise, snapchatleaked.com duplicates Snapchat's own flimsy ethical stance: "We are here to provide a safe social platform to you all," a statement snapchatleaked.com makes on its front page. That the website preying on the security holes of an application which claims to be safe *also claims to be safe* speaks to something deeply ideological. Snapchatleaked.com is part and parcel to a larger online economy of abuse and instability, yet the website, which is obviously reliant on the same skepticism and distrust as its software referent, dutifully propagates the same fraudulence it is isolating. In this case, literacy is both impediment and proponent to new digital forms. From the critic's perspective, literacy is a prerequisite to digital consumption—its appearance should not be considered extraordinary, except that literacy itself is a tenuous, evolving concept online. Some amount of digital literacy points users to the Snapchat app, but too little keeps them using and trusting the service, and snapchatleaked.com feasts on that defeating paradigm of knowledge. Degrees of literacy, then, matter in the cat-and-mouse game of digital consumption. When everyone is comparably savvy, producers must deepen and complicate their ploys in order to grow their customer base.

Similarly to Facebook, the notion that a digital service can somehow rectify the structural problems that its interface is built upon is merely a provocation, not a sound means by which to "trust" that service, as the girls from the Canadian pedophilia case did with Snapchat. Facebook's prevailing truth claim is predicated on the same notion; it states that by means of its privacy measures, and an ethos of accountability, authentic reality can find a way onto Facebook, but that simply is not the case, not always. People do authentically use that social platform, and share authentic moments on Facebook, but to accept Facebook's truth claims without at least some doubt is to be interpellated by an ideology of consumer dupery. And this way of thinking is even less nuanced than the ideology which infects and is dispersed by Snapchat because Snapchat is, in many ways, *responding* to the privacy failures of Facebook and its social media ilk.

In Snapchat's case, what producers/corporations exploit is a tendency in new digital consumption modes toward what Mark Andrejevic calls "savvy paranoia," in which "the debunking of symbolic efficiency results not just in generalized skepticism but, consequently, in the multiplication of paranoiac possibilities," thus creating undue "conspiracy theories" and widespread distrust which dilutes the ostensible *value* of distrust ("Visceral Literacy" 327). And this is why Andrejevic assigns these consumers with the negative descriptor of "paranoid," because this digital distrust is extreme and irrational—Andrejevic's point, then, is not that savviness is bad or impossible, but that when exercised excessively, or in situations it ought not, then savviness results in a consumer who, without good reason, believes they are literate. Indeed, public discourse is nowadays front-loaded with mistrust and doubt about media, which is paradoxically harmful because such skepticism *should* keep in check the truth claims of a corporate entity like Snapchat; instead, this excess of doubt exacerbates the problem because, in their "savvy paranoia," consumers believe they have "the ability to cut through the facade, whether by investigation or intuition" (Andrejevic, "Visceral Literacy" 328). But the hierarchical forces of capitalist consumption also know that consumers believe they are savvy and literate, not dissimilar to production modes for reality TV. Thus, Snapchat invites these "savvy paranoiacs" into a digital space which is *ideologically* satisfying, but *practically* deceitful.

The 21st-century variation of the hipster, whose ardent belief in authenticity and savvy nature have capitulated the reemergence of many archaic technologies and cultures, serves as the model paranoid consumer. Hipsters' obsession with long-forgotten beer brands, unfiltered cigarettes, and single-speed bicycles are all meant to be some kind of remedy against late capitalism; it communicates, in so many words, that they *do not trust* the products which emerge from this digital consumer era. A small subset of hipsters has even spearheaded a subculture of VHS collection, raiding flea markets and second-hand stores in search of tapes from the 1980s and 90s. The collectors admit *outright* that the video and sound quality of VHS is vastly inferior to digital transfers, but that they prefer the enchantment of analog, the materiality of the tapes themselves, as DVD saw a reduction in the physical "presence" of a movie.[2] Essentially, VHS collectors reject digital offerings, even to their detriment, so that they can nostalgically re-live an era untouched by questionable ideas of ownership. Digital distribution and video streaming have eradicated the notion that to own a movie means it must take up shelf space, but most Millennials have argued against the necessity for this aspect of ownership ad infinitum.

One of the most significant byproducts of the hipster ethos has been the cultural restoration of vinyl records. Albums had been produced in vinyl format for the enjoyment of a select few, music producers and DJs and hardcore enthusiasts, but they had not been carried by large scale retailers since the prevalence of compact discs. No longer a cottage industry, vinyl records are now sold in the millions, at a higher rate every year since 2007.[3] Arguments are made to their quality in the face of digital transfer's undeniable fidelity, and in some cases vinyl collectors have a point, but mostly their dedication to this archaic format is an ideological one. And it should come as no surprise that the popularity of MP3 players, which remove the tactility of album collection in its entirety, were met by an ostensible vinyl backlash; this is a paranoid reaction to the digital regime because it signifies a rejection which accepts one consumer truth claim for another, and not necessarily one of any greater ontological value. The tenets of consumerism are not somehow eradicated by the vinyl owner's gesture—they are instead *resituated*, and just as exploitable. In an effort to cash in on this consumer mode, goliath retailers Best Buy and Walmart now carry vinyl records. It is worth noting that vinyl records for new releases cost around double that of compact discs. Here, paranoid reaction is met by consumer culture's own acceptance and facilitation—paranoia is exploitable. In truth, all manner of consumer behavior is exploitable, though VHS will probably never see the same kind of popularity as vinyl due to its high manufacturing cost.

Hashtag (De)contextualization

Reality TV confessionals taped after an episode's filming are often cited as shallow because they lack the immediacy of the on-screen event that they are supplementing, so a person's "confession" seems detached or, in some cases, uncanny. Indeed, these tepid confessionals are discontinuous amid the fiery temperaments simmering on *The Real World*. ABC's *The Bachelor* and

The Bachelorette traditionally film their reunion finale months after taping, when relationships have settled and congealed—thus, the people participating in ABC's intense televisual romance experiment are all very polite to one other. Passive aggression is usually the only emotional poignancy afforded viewers on these reunions, often delivered by host Chris Harrison, whose demeanor is quite flat in the first place. Partly, this is a context problem. These people have been distanced from their experiences and, thus, have lost the full emotional context that made those experiences matter in the first place.

YouTube comments on the most popular corporate content also lack the appropriate contextual relevance; theirs is a lack of affective context, in that thinking, feeling subjects comment on a video with no subjective relevance beyond ad revenue or exposure. On a trailer uploaded to YouTube by Disney for their summer 2014 tentpole movie *Maleficent*, user Saviyon comments: "Much chills. Such wow." Articulated in YouTube's text-based comments section, Saviyon's succinct affective response is informed by a consumer context which does not readily support emotionality. As such, it *surrenders* its real world contextual relevance: Saviyon's corporeal context. Further, decontextualized, pseudo-philosophical Facebook status updates run rampant—to whom, or what, does an unprefaced quote of Mahatma Gandhi's refer? Facebookers can only speculate, or "like" the quote if their heart desires. Among contemporary mediational platforms, decontextualization is one of their overarching symptoms, no secret to anyone, and that is not why it is important here. More interesting is how that contextual void mutates from one platform to the next.

To further demonstrate, probably the most influential digital social medium from the late 2000s and early 2010s has been Twitter; the platform has shaped an entire way of thinking and communicating, in that its emphasis on brevity has also shaped brevity's prevalence outside its use, for better and worse. On Twitter, individual communications, i.e., tweets, are restricted to 140 characters—that is not even 140 words, but the alpha numerical items which *build* signification. And this is very McLuhan-esque in that the Twitter speech act is *dictated* by the medium: Internet speech, among tweets, becomes less about the content than the digital medium which limits it. Other social media outlets have abided by Twitter's standard for brevity to try and replicate its success. For instance, while Facebook-owned social platform Instagram does not outwardly limit applied text, its usage favors photos and images *over* words, thus Instagram seemingly does away with individual "characters" altogether. In fact, the only way to access applied text on Instagram is to click on uploaded images themselves, oppositional to Facebook which makes users' applied text explicitly visible atop every image, clicked on or not. A palpable synonym in the world of online video is uploading service Vine, which constrains video lengths to a maximum of *six seconds*. Vine videos are strictly homogenous in content as those six seconds offer such a limited range of creative expression, duplicated now millions of times over—like Internet pornography, Vine's sense of "variety" is garnered via click through repetition.

Only being able to use 140 characters undoubtedly *hurts* subjective engagement, and some Twitter users will transgress those limitations by publishing multiple tweets successively in order to communicate a longer message; at that point, however, textual communication through Twitter becomes undeniably awkward. Some users incorporate abbreviated Internet slang (LOL, brb, l8r, etc.) into their tweets to also try and counteract these limitations, but the shortening of language is dangerously close to the Orwellian Newspeak many commentators levied against cell phone text messaging in its formative era, around 2000. Surely these attempts to "beat" Twitter must function as a self-reflexive moment for users, where the medium truly does overpower their own desires to speak and feel. None of this is necessarily *new* to the Twitter critical conversation, but is necessary foregrounding to understand its most ubiquitous cultural feature: the hashtag.

A system of digital taxonomy born from the experimentation of Twitter's creators, the hashtag is meant to "group" particular tweets together, contributed by any and all users, so that they adhere to a specific cultural, ideological, or emotional discursive referent, such as the NCAA Final Four or a presidential election "trending" on the service. This means that the tweets with an applied hashtag of #Democrats will all be associated with one another. The problem, then, is what has happened over time, as the hashtag has been appropriated by Twitter's userbase who accept it instead as a linguistic accessory, ambivalent as to whether their message will be "grouped" with other messages. In this hyperreal hashtag ideology, the term "hashtag" extols no technical value, at least not technical value in line with its original utility of taxonomy. Its new form, then, is more abstract, in that it signifies different things to different people. In a more than apt example from November 2012, an American couple legally named their newborn baby girl "Hashtag" (Hoffberger). The idea that the term somehow applied to one or another gender is proof enough of how *distanced* hashtags have become from any referent. And this phenomenon is incredibly interesting, as it speaks to a cultural resignification of consumer techno jargon—hashtag's use in casual conversation outside Twitter promotes the cause of Twitter, but, more often, it has nothing to do with Twitter. In this way, a contextual lack can be liberatory such that consumer capitalists cannot preserve their intended referential meaning. But whatever its place in the popular imagination, the hashtag's technical origin remains, so people abiding by this new abstract understanding of hashtags still employ them in their tweets, and those hashtags are then "grouped" with a series of tweets that all sit next to one another in schizophrenic disharmony. This is emblematically postmodern.

To elaborate, when following the #Democrats tweet stream, users are met by a smattering of disparate ideological/cultural approaches, very different uses of the word "democrat," which means these messages oftentimes contradict and/or conflict with one another. Blue Congress, a public Twitter account promoting liberal Congress candidates, writes, "#Democrats MUST vote! NO EXCUSES!! We MUST stop the GOP from continuing to destroy our country. #VoteBlue2014," asserting a positive referential meaning for #Democrats. But, within the same #Democrats stream, that Blue Congress tweet neighbors one by Lady Sanders, a private Twitter user and Tea Party member, who uploads redneck memes and spouts anti-progressive, anti-liberal Tweets such as "Hollywood libs [i.e., liberals] are just clueless about the real world." Indeed, when following this hashtag string, it is as if everyone is having their own private conversation, with its own idiosyncratic context, its own political value. As such, there is no value to be had because to parse out the context and meaning of each is to guess at something which is already deprived of complexity, as the tweet's 140 character limitation is only space enough to speak (very) tersely about something in first place. Hashtags communicate a destabilization and surface orientation that is so literal, Twitter's interface does not even try to whitewash it, and the hashtag's adoption on other social media means there is a generalized *acceptance* of digital destabilization. Acceptance indicates either savvy ambivalence or outright ignorance.

Relevant to this political example, ideology freed from its context assuredly destabilizes ideology, and this circumstance could be construed as aiding in a beneficial sort of critical distance. But, similarly to discourse online, oppressive ideologies are as unstable as progressive ones. A contextual void online does not safely communicate distance; it more readily promotes the ambivalence which has fostered a wealth of unaccountable media nowadays. When context is obsolete, then ideology, too, can be made obsolete—or, worse, monolithic.

New Contexts, New Meanings

Hashtagged tweets exist outside their original context, and are therefore separated from their referential meaning. This is not to say that they *do not* have context; it is just that this context is far removed from off-screen referents. On-screen context, then, is the most relevant for tweets. More specifically, though, hashtag context is *interfacial context.* Each consumer platform has its own terms of mediation, and its own interfacial idiosyncrasies. And since the schizophrenia of a hashtag stream is significant firstly (if not exclusively) to the Twitter platform, then that is its *most valid* context. And this makes sense because hashtags were supposed to be a device for digital taxonomy, a technical vehicle, in the first place. Interfacial context, though, is not meant to imply that hashtag streams cannot be significant off-screen, but, rather, that off-screen reality must accept the attributes of the interface in order to engender interfacial context significant.

It is no surprise, then, that a technical element to an online social media platform is being used as a person's birth name because that explicates an unstable environment for meaning, a parallel to the referential instability among hashtag streams. As the larger culture has adopted hashtags, culture, too, has been mutated by its means. In conjunction with this idea, Alexander R. Galloway, writer of *The Interface Effect*, believes that "the interface is above all an allegorical device that will help us gain some perspective on culture in the age of information" (54). Indeed, as consumer tech is omnipotent, it must be considered a force which *shapes* culture and its engaging subjects, a point that has been expressed in this project repeatedly. What is more, according to Galloway, "Interfaces themselves are effects, in that they bring about transformations in material states" (vii). Hashtags are not exclusively to blame for the entirety of destabilized postmodern ways of being and thinking, though they are certainly a result and function of them. To be clear, the current off-screen referential question is larger than just Twitter can answer. As consumers shift from one interface to the next, their off-screen thinking shifts too, further complicating already established ideologies and consumer modes. Thus, the Snapchat dilemma: How can consumers, in particular young ones, be asked to challenge a particular interfacial claim, when that claim is *juxtaposed* by a multitude of interfaces of differing uses, of differing signification? Part of the mystification of consumer software, especially with the onslaught of smartphone apps nowadays, is its ability to keep the consumer *asking questions*, not because their interfaces are so esoteric and inaccessible that they must be re-learned again and again, but because they are not. As stated in Chapter 2 regarding Facebook, *ease of use* interpellates media users such that they are not interrogating the truth claims of media producers. As the interface shapes its engaging subjects, if it is easy to use, then subjects have less to ask of it, and so they then accept its claims at face value.

A multitude of applications means consumers *are* asking questions, but those questions have to do with consumer choice as opposed to software ethics—in other words, many consumers are not asking the *right* questions. One of the prevailing issues with Apple's iOS distribution platform (the App Store) is that their quality standards for monetized software content are practically nonexistent, as pornographic material seems to be the most persistent grounds for rejection, similar to YouTube. What happens, then, is that the most popular applications, such as Candy Crush or Pandora Radio, are imitated (literally "cloned," in some cases) by software designers looking to make an easy buck through ad revenue and in-app purchases; make no mistake, this is not imitation as the highest form of flattery but, rather, imitation as consumer gimmick, never mind the litany of copyright and intellectual property abuses. Sifting through this menagerie of fakes is a literacy task on its own, bolstering the *complications* of literacy instead of literacy itself. And this is just one instance of the difficult geography consumers must navigate as they make decisions about their media—the *right* questions are elusive and fluid.

"Safe," "open," "democratic," Web 2.0 thrives on a lexicon which only *tenuously* points to any agreed upon referents, just as hashtag is now distanced from its technical meaning. Consumer capitalists also engage and add to this lexicon, and not just to exploit literate consumers through Snapchat or other smartphone apps; there has been an even greater ideological shift instantiated through language. Nowadays, the discourse of digital consumer technology is built upon language which is (generally) suited to other uses. "The cloud" is the most obvious of recently deployed marketing speak that deludes the actual processes by which digital technology functions. Multiple corporations offer "cloud services," from Google to Apple, which promises that consumers can safely deposit their personal data someplace besides their own devices. "The cloud" metaphor has become so ubiquitous with portable digital technology that the very nature of how cloud storage functions is a matter of conjecture among some consumers. Apple's "Air" products, in fact, are purposefully reliant on the cloud in that their on-board hard drives are comparably deficient. But "the cloud" is simply another physical location to deposit data, servers owned by Google or whoever else, except the metaphor is problematic in that it gives the illusion of immateriality. And, certainly, data which consumers might not want to share, for legal reasons or otherwise, should not be uploaded onto cloud servers, even if they do claim to be "safe" and "private." Corporations are not known to resist turning over data or information which might implicate them—Facebook's complicity with the National Security Administration has been proof positive of that.

Another oft-used term is "ecosystem," deployed by the likes of Sony and Microsoft as a means of tying together various products to make a device seem as if it *requires* others in order to function properly. Sony's electronic ecosystem consists of TVs, game consoles, Blu-ray players, and other such hardware and software. Because it is an ecosystem of products, as opposed to a bunch of unrelated gadgets of varying necessity, then the only sensible thing consumers can do is buy them all, or else their ecosystem might lack some sustaining element. From a more immediate standpoint, Sony deprives smart televisions of some content that can only be accrued by means of a Blu-ray player or game console, furthering the tangibility of this metaphor. As the rainforest is so delicate it requires a variety of natural resources working in tandem, so, too, do Sony electronics need one another in order to provide their owners the richest consumption experience. Quite visible here is the *naturalism* of the "cloud" and "ecosystem" metaphors—consumer capitalists, then, ascribe a referential value to their products that belongs to the natural world. In this light, the ecosystem of Sony consumer electronics "has always been thus," more than just a delicate system, but one that is as omnipotent and unchanging as the sun.

Digital scholars have long speculated on what Web 3.0 might constitute, and have differing opinions on the matter. On his personal blog, polemical thinker Andrew Keen writes that Web 3.0 will be the return of merit-based "authority" to online spaces, oppositional to amateur content creators such as those on YouTube or Wikipedia (ajkeen.com). Some business writers think Web 3.0 is when Internet amateurs and professionals are on equal *economic* footing. For instance, on YouTube, amateur partners would not be beholden to Google for their ad-revenue paychecks, as they are now. More generally, though, people believe Web 3.0 will be a unified system which provides all media content (e.g., TV, video games, news) indiscriminately and from the same Internet-enabled device *through* the Internet; in many ways, smartphones have already achieved this end, with the caveat being a tiny screen for a tiny consumption experience. But the prevalence of the "ecosystem" metaphor communicates the resistance of corporations to Web 3.0's potential endgame. The more products to buy, the greater the return, so a "unified" consumer platform is enemy to the consumerist agenda. However, the gradual destabilizing of behemoth cable TV companies by streaming video providers, such as Netflix and Hulu, signifies the potential for a Web 3.0 of this kind.

Romantic Ideology

Cyber-futurists who abide by and propagate an ideology that instantiates digital technology as a solution to problems, especially problems incurred firstly by technology, are technological "solutionists," according to critic Eugeny Morokov (xiii). Solutionism ideals have championed Internet and digital communication technologies as a means of solving human problems since the dot com bubble burst. Whether those solutionists are Bill Gates or Mark Zuckerberg makes no difference because the content of their speeches are underwritten by a solitary and implicit declaration: digital technology is humanity's salvation. A recent instance of solutionism's ignorance (and impotence) was when Google, rather than sending more monetary aid to Africa, proposed to float Wi-Fi balloons over some areas of the country to provide much needed access to the Internet (Talbot). This is not to say that the goal of Google's project was not charitable, but that it mistook its own priorities for those of Africa's. Once everyone on the planet is online, then everyone is, ostensibly, Google's customer. The project, ironically named "Loon," was openly criticized by Morokov and also Gates, as this was apparently not a good example of the kind of humanitarian aid Africa or any other nation might need from a money-soaked technology company. Google's "Loon" project is a nice allegory for solutionism itself—at first glance, it is a nice idea, but lacks a kind of material necessity. Indeed, "Loon" sates an ideological motive firstly.

Technological solutionism, which Morokov illustrates in his book *To Save Everything Click Here* (2013), has proliferated into the consumer imagination, part of the restorative nostalgia directing young people back to the place where they began to solve their problems, in cyclical defeat. A traffic circle does not progress its traveler; the traveler must turn off it. Solutionism, then, is not progressive. More so, there is a popular ideology which casually accepts Web 2.0, participatory Internet as some "default" solution to the capitalist media hierarchy. But this is not the case, at least not easily. To achieve this end on YouTube, for instance, affective creators must rhetorically tip-toe around the larger space of economics which YouTube readily facilitates. Indeed, YouTube is an "engagement, not an interruption" for the corporate world (Miller 429). Participation guarantees no reliable solution to consumer capitalism, but is merely *perceived* to provide that solution.

In a related anecdote, I gave an admittedly condemnatory presentation on Twitter hashtags at a conference not long ago, and, during the question and answer session, a colleague in the audience, as a means of defending hashtags, told me they were the invention of hackers. Twitter hashtags, specifically, are not the invention of hackers or the consequence of hacking. However, hashtags as a taxonomical device for communication were initially employed on an online communication platform called IRC that was, for a long time, run by coders and other netizens who considered themselves hackers, including the creators of Twitter. In fact, Twitter's creators merely duplicated that function of IRC onto their own platform. More important than the historical specificity, here, was the assumption beneath my colleague's statement—because hashtags are associated with *hackers* that somehow distinguishes hashtags from other social media features. This assumption posits that hackers are "one of us," outside of the hierarchical sway, outside consumer capitalism. And that may have been the case in the 1990s or before, when the Internet was not effectively disciplined by consumer capitalism, but this most certainly is not the case nowadays.

Mark Zuckerberg proved his ability as a programmer while hacking Harvard's servers to compile student photos for his infamous Facemash web site. On Facemash, Harvard elites selected between contrasting photos to decide which of their female undergrads were "hotter," a moment in his mythology narrativized in the great 2008 film *The Social Network*. Zuckerberg would go on to use these same "transgressive" skills to compile his billions. From this example, there are two kinds of hackers: transgressive ones and institutional ones, and they, like participation on YouTube, work on a continuum. Hackers, in the ideals of digital romantics, are agent transgressors who invade institutionalized digital spaces to destabilize their paradigms of control. A literary analog is Neal Stephenson's noirish hacker savant, Hiro, from 1992's *Snow Crash*, whose digital exploits are lionized by a future techno-culture that prides itself on anti-establishmentarianism through the machine.

Yet hackers can also work for corporations and the government in order to prevent hacking on their end and/or hack other netizens to the gain of their employers. In 2013, Edward Snowden, a computer specialist himself, blew the whistle on the National Security Administration in exposing their surveillance routines, which included the hacking of e-mail accounts and various other online sources belonging to American citizens. Snowden, then, works along the hacker continuum, as he was employed by the NSA to be a part of "institutional hacking," but also transgressed by those means. As such, to axiomatically assume that hackers are working solely for "our" benefit is problematic. In the case of Zuckerberg, a hacker can vacillate fluidly between personal/communal goals and institutional ones, with nary a slippage. The great machine dream professes that humans are liberated by the machine, but the content of that dream is codified by the institutional logic which protects and propagates consumerism and political ideologies. Hiro did not vacillate from one form of hacking to another because the fictional world in which he thrived did not necessitate such a demand, but Stephenson's character, it should be said, still makes his home in a Los Angeles storage locker, on the fringes of society.

This, then, is ultimately postmodern in that ideological hackers, a "noble" group considered exceptional by all accounts, must be weighed alongside institutional ones. As such, the hacker's transgressions are sterilized. As Frederic Jameson says of postmodern transgressions, hackers "no longer scandalize anyone and are not only received with the greatest complacency but have themselves become institutionalized and are at one with the official or public culture of Western society" (4). From here, there is an ambivalence to the potential of digital spaces, as that potential has been squashed by the variety of consumer capitalist desires prevailing online, resignifying that space—resignification which demands from users a literacy that shifts by the day, moment, second.

Nostalgia Impulse

There are different forms of media/digital literacy, many different ones. How one form of literacy does not translate from one medium to the next, though, is ultimately puzzling. For instance, the delusions of Facebook (e.g., catfishing) are quite primitive compared to those on reality TV, which thrives on its fakery, despite their hierarchies of control being fairly similar. Unlike Wikipedia, a democratic knowledge database which relies on its bottom-up configuration even (and especially) to the detriment of its authority, Facebook is explicitly front-loaded with "barriers" impeding its use, all maintained by a hierarchy of clandestine moderation. Users are quickly alerted to what they are permitted to do on Facebook not long after registration—this outwardly identifies that they are situated *beneath* some indeterminate structure of power.

In lectures given by High School counselors, Facebook, Twitter, and Instagram are commonly discussed regarding appropriate privacy implementation and safe/unsafe forms of usage, so it stands to reason that all social media might be similarly perceived in the minds of these listeners. And this is only taking into account the *institutional* education young people receive regarding social media. Their technological education stretches far beyond the parameters of schooling, as smartphones and the Internet are now at the center of cultural maturation; a kid's first smartphone is an equivalent developmental milestone as learning to drive or going to the prom. Despite this, Snapchat still managed to elude dominant privacy standards, as its popularity, for what is simply a banal photo sharing application, was solely initiated by its privacy claims. And Snapchat's consumer dupery is associated with the larger authenticity problem on social media, such as that on Facebook. Young people's subjective articulation is *interlinked* to social media, and nostalgia for a substantive subject flavors the delusions of these young users as they seek out the trustworthy space of digital representation promised to them by consumer capitalists.

According to Svetlana Boym, whose work in nationalism has helped shape the study of nostalgia, "The twentieth century began with utopia and ended with nostalgia. Optimistic belief in the future became outmoded, while nostalgia, for better or worse, never went out of fashion, remaining uncannily contemporary" (7). While not *directly* parallel, along the historical trajectory of this project there are echoes of Boym's stance. Reality TV, at first, stood for an optimistic kind of impediment to the hierarchies which long dictated television production. Eventually, though, that optimism was stamped out and mutated into a savvy ambivalence to the format (e.g., truTV). These savvy viewers, then, suffer from "restorative nostalgia" in that their perception of reality programming is steeped in self-defeating conspiracy—televisual realistic representation can never accurately represent reality, so then why believe in it at all? This position, though, assumes an absolute, unattainable kind of truth or reality. For Boym, restorative nostalgia "knows two main plots: the restoration of origins and the conspiracy theory. The conspiratorial worldview reflects a nostalgia for a transcendental cosmology and a simple premodern conception of good and evil" (14). Indeed, that "everything is broken" does not effectively communicate the futility of all things, but, rather, the futility of contemporary culture to abide by an impossible premodern conception of reality. MTV's first seasons of *The Real World* tapped into a Generation X viewing audience crying foul on TV representational standards, but as people have grown dismissive of reality TV, they have inadvertently helped to protect "absolute truth" (13). So while restorative nostalgia protects the absolute truth, "reflective nostalgia" calls it into doubt. Gen Xers were *reflecting* on the television medium, thus identifying specific problems which could be addressed by Bunim and Murray's reality experiment, for instance the use of "ordinary people" as on-screen characters.

When young consumers turn to self-mediation through Facebook and YouTube, trying to correct the shortfalls and manipulations of media hierarchies, that nostalgia impulse is driven not by reflection but instead by restoration. Their error resides in the assumption that digital platforms controlled and distributed by capitalist consumer enterprises might be able to overcome the failures of TV or film to achieve some absolute truth. "Re-flection means new flexibility, not the reestablishment of stasis," says Boym. "The focus here is not on the recovery of what is perceived to be an absolute truth, but on the meditation on history and the passage of time" (15). For media literacy, it is *reflection* which enables literacy to translate from one platform to the next. Nineteen ninety-four's *The Real World: San Francisco* demonstrates that even a failure of truth can achieve a human victory—it must, however, be predicated on the understanding that no irrefutable *absolutes* can be produced. After all, reflective nostalgia "reveals that longing and critical thinking are not opposed to one another, as affective memories do not absolve one from compassion, judgment, or critical reflection" (Boym 15). Season three of *The Real World* did not distance itself from its contrived televisual boundaries, yet still managed an affective encounter between its on-screen subjects and their off-screen viewers. In Boym's nostalgia model, cynicism is easy, too easy, because it says *nothing* can ever be good enough, so nothing is.

Where the youngest of consumers, such as those that use Snapchat, align with Boym's position on nostalgia is as restorative in that their usage ahistorically accepts unstable, fragmentary digital spaces as absolutist, unruptured ones. That a truth claim by a Silicon Valley startup might be taken as sacrosanct is wildly restorative because *technology* is the absolute in that equation, and technology, social media in particular, has already dispersed lessons which explicate the contrary, as evidenced by all the state-mandated digital literacy propagated in schools nowadays. Again, turning to technology to solve some problems with technology is a quintessential non-solution, ignoring what consumers already know. Consumerism instantiates a drive away from historical meditation; Fredric Jameson's view of postmodernity is not coincidentally ahistorical but fittingly so. And Boym affirms this: "The rhetoric of restorative nostalgia is *not* about 'the past,' but rather about universal values, family, nature, homeland, truth" (emphasis added, 13). When some consumers keep turning to social media for an *absolutely* authentic, truthful, and safe social experience, history repeats itself—the past is ignored. The authenticity quotient promised by Web 2.0 media cannot be "restored" because its appearance relies on a historical reality which never existed in the first place.

In contrast to this particular result of restorative nostalgia in young people, however, is the gradual shift in consumer usage away from strict privacy settings on social media. From 2008 and on, as Twitter has become popular, so has a new form of explicitly *public* social media participation. Twitter's interface is designed in such a way that public use is encouraged because Twitter communication strings are not segregated as easily as on Facebook. Thus, participating in these strings means users' tweets will exist outside individual Twitter profiles, to be accessed publicly within and outside the service. It is still possible to privatize all tweets, but once users have done so, they defy the service's standard of use. So, in order to get the full Twitter experience, users have to participate *openly*. Instagram has also seen a new breed of consumers who favor a public kind of engagement, sharing personal photos visible across the *entirety* of the Internet. At one point, this kind of sharing was universally considered taboo, and many netizens still believe it is reckless. Denying privacy settings is part and parcel to the restorative problem associated with savvy reality TV viewership: If safety/privacy can never truly be achieved, then why bother trying for it at all? Twitter's popularity arrived well after Facebook's mainstreaming, so privacy settings already mattered to social media. But to dismiss the potential for *any* privacy communicates a similar consumer trajectory as reality TV, toward savvy ambivalence.

Hipsters try to restore the past while rejecting the present; their insistence that history can remedy the present day's ontological void depends on a variety of cultural solipsism which the Internet has extinguished. Culture is no longer insulated or privileged. Many Millennials embrace digital consumer technology with absolute skepticism or blind restorative faith, articulating a consumer binary of self-defeat. So reflective nostalgia remains a forsaken mode of late capitalist consumption. To reflect nostalgically on digital media is to achieve a critical distance. Consumers are then implicated and complicit, able to deepen their engagement. As such, they can possess a new literacy for the self defined by fluidity, instability, and emergence. Submitted to YouTube or Instagram or Twitter, the machinations for selfhood are *re*configured. Digital subjectivity fragments across a multitude of platforms, ever changing, itself a determiner for new modes of thinking and feeling.

Chapter Notes

Introduction

1. While these distinctions more thoroughly divulged in individual chapters, baby boomers are, here stated, the generation birthed out of America's economic affluence following the World Wars. Generation Xers are baby boomers' offspring. Millennials are the subsequent generation, generally thought to be born from 1980 through the year 2000.

Chapter 1

1. The "Digital Native" is Marc Prensky's oft-used media studies term referring to Millennials—i.e., people born into the current era of digital consumer technology whose relation to digital tech tends to be like second nature. Their alternate is the "Digital Immigrant," born prior to the 1980s, who must "learn" digital technology and tends to be somewhat alienated by the idea of it.

2. This is Jameson's notion of "late capitalism," or capitalism at the tail end of the 20th century into the new millennium, though Jameson's designation has more in common with Baudrillard's "consumerism" than a traditional notion of capitalism.

3. "Producorial" denotes a layer of television program mediation that is not *technological*—that is its own consideration—but instead devised by content creators. This is not to say technology and production concerns should be considered distinct (often they work in tandem), but that the two are front-loaded with their own set of ideological biases and other technical idio-

syncrasies. The considerations made by producers as they shape televisual representation range from advertising, to audience, to television censorship guidelines, etc.

4. Conceivably ad-free networks like HBO, for instance, are not exempt from this dynamic, though the dynamic articulates itself in a different way. Since consumers are paying a monthly fee for access, HBO's life blood, the end result is the channel's slavish dedication to the consumer instead of the advertiser; and the consumer can often be more needy and fickle. In the case of David Milch's *Luck*, which ran for one season in 2012 on HBO and had a tiny show order of nine episodes, critical acclaim and an Oscar-winning cast, including Dustin Hoffman, proved little motivator to renew the show; viewership numbers paled in comparison to HBO's supernatural and fantasy juggernauts *True Blood* and *Game of Thrones*, and as such *Luck*'s screen time was deemed better spent on reruns or episode previews for these more popular shows. Toward the end of its nine episode run, when *Luck* was criticized by animal rights groups as consequence of its use of retired race horses—the show was about race track gambling and the seedy folks associated—HBO quickly cut *Luck* from its lineup. For a network that prides itself on quality television that is not always appealing to a large audience, it seemed a cheap way to leave an otherwise strong show by the wayside.

5. The specifics of these emotions are discussed at length later in this chapter with regard to the long-running, salacious talk show *Maury*.

6. Season nine, *The Real World: New Or-*

leans (2000), infamously featured a Mormon twenty-something from Brigham Young University, Julie Stoffer. Her ideological difference proved one of that season's ongoing points of conflict. And her sometimes negative portrayal meant widespread Mormon backlash against MTV.

7. Michel Foucault elaborates on the therapeutic value of the confessional in *Discipline and Punish*, saying it is "a ritual in which the expression alone, independently of its external consequences, produces intrinsic modifications in the person who articulates it: it exonerates, redeems, and purifies him; it unburdens him of his wrongs, liberates him, and promises his salvation" (62).

8. This varies depending on the show, network, and the degree of illusion being maintained; the more present tense used in confessionals, the more illusory the show, the less present tense used, the less illusory. Obviously, using past tense will bring light to producer intervention, but sometimes that is the desired effect.

9. Nicole "Snooki" Polizzi, one of the stars of MTV's *Jersey Shore*, told *Rolling Stone* in 2011 that being on the show—*Jersey Shore* has an identical fishbowl, fun-with-strangers format to *The Real World*—was akin to "prison, with cameras."

10. When Anastasia and Averey realize they both have alcoholic fathers, which they quickly reveal upon meeting in episode one, they give each other high fives in the kitchen. It seems the confessional has bled out into the open, into the roommates' every speech act.

11. *The Hills* had succumbed to universal hatred during its run because cast relationships on the show sometimes did not reflect those that were happening off-camera, and the idea that MTV was selling a complete contrivance as opposed to something that occurred at a crossroads between truth and fiction rubbed many viewers the wrong way. What made the show insufferable was the distinctly over-produced style: cameras were rarely handheld, the footage was unnecessarily high quality, the lighting was too good, and scene staging felt forced. It was

reality TV embracing its unrealness, and when devoid of the illusion of actuality, the format loses its unique charm.

12. This may not be the case some years into the future, as everyone's favorite box in the living room is phased out, but cyber-futurists have been declaring the end of TV for some time now, so who knows when and if it will happen. There is nothing quite like crowding around a big screen with others all experiencing the same show, whether it be *Maury* or some erudite program on PBS.

13. TV does now possess some participatory/prosumption elements to it like those that dominate the Internet, for instance the voting component on Fox's *American Idol*, which Henry Jenkins does well to explicate in his book *Convergence Culture* (2008). But there is no mistaking TV for the Internet, both in terms of style of consumption and content—again, TV is still comparatively much more regulated and top-down.

14. Indicating "stigmatization" does not take into account ironic appreciation for reality shows. Here, the analysis' only concern is with genuine appreciation of reality TV or genuine distaste, certainly not camp viewing, "hate-watching," or savvy viewing.

15. While Channel 4's *Big Brother* dominated Britain in the early 2000s, the term "reality TV" struggled to make its way across the Atlantic. British commentators and producers were highly resistant to what they saw as a cheap Americanism, its claim on reality considered dubious and harmful to viewers, replacing it with the designation "docu-drama" instead. Their resistance to the term did not last long, as "reality TV" is now widely employed by the Brits, though they do tend to distinguish between degrees of constructedness in their media lexicon better than Americans do. On American shores, all reality TV (whatever the content) gets lumped together in one indiscriminant pile.

16. Often, those practicing camp in the 21st century confuse genuine appreciation for ironic appreciation, and because everyone is already confused, especially about what "irony" constitutes, no one is the wiser.

Confusion seems to be the dominant characteristic of cultural knowledge acquired through the Internet. It is also interesting to note that the 1990s are considered by some the highpoint of irony in pop culture and that 9/11 is the "end of irony."

17. To make the production process visible, as it is in *Lizard Lick*, conceptually mirrors 1960s French documentary vérité in that making the reality of film production "seen" somehow staves off any questions of believability—paradoxically, quite the opposite has proven true.

18. Currently, fictional vérité makes up a measurable percentage of popular media. Famous examples include monster flick *Cloverfield*, BBC and NBC's *The Office* (a mix of direct cinema and vérité), and, surprisingly, many foreign and American horror movies, the most economically successful being *Paranormal Activity*. The immediacy of the style makes for conceivably better horror fare.

Chapter 2

1. Henry Jenkins' "black box fallacy" states that it is fallacious to assume a piece of tech that transfers content is singular in its relation to the larger media spectrum, or even, and especially, the future of media. Facebook is not about the "black box" of a personal computer, per se, but any and all future digital communication technology (*Convergence Culture* 15).

2. To expand on the idea of postmodernity's relationship to contemporary theory, it is useful to consider contemporary theory's pursuit of "truth" from Frederic Jameson's *Postmodernism, or, The Cultural Logic of Late Capitalism*. "But what is today called contemporary theory—or, better still, theoretical discourse—is also … itself very precisely a postmodern phenomena. It would therefore be inconsistent to defend the truth of its theoretical insights in a situation in which the very concept of 'truth' itself is part of the metaphysical baggage poststructuralism seeks to abandon" (12).

3. Child pornography, for instance, remains one of 4Chan's most prevalent issues. In a court case from March 2012, a Detroit man named Thaddeus McMichael was posting on 4Chan's infamous /b/ message board and began a flippant conversation regarding the complicity of children in pornography. He then went on to admit possessing some illegal images of his own. McMichael was quickly detained by the FBI, who had been monitoring his activity after some suspicious comments McMichael had previously made on Facebook. The FBI raided his home and found a computer loaded with child pornography. The irony was that all the illegal photos the FBI found on McMichael's computer were traced back to 4Chan (*U.S. vs. McMichael*).

4. The "Violentacrez" debacle spurred reaction all over the web regarding Internet ethics, an issue that many Redditors were unwilling to discuss because they sided with Brutsch in the midst of the Anderson Cooper exposé. Crosscut.com referred to the incident as a byproduct of the "creepy uncle" nature of anonymous online spaces. Feminist blogs were discussing the privileged male ideology tied to anonymity. Forbes.com figured Brutsch was prying out a "new manners" for the Internet. Indeed, the "Violentacrez" username is part of a much larger conversation of the cultural value of Internet anonymity.

5. For instance, social network Twitter implements a system of association to categorize user posts they call hashtags, which is a seemingly limitless and subjective means of taxonomizing communication. Hashtags are not restricted or predetermined by Twitter's interface, but are instead composed of any imaginable word or phrase preceded by a "#." Attaching a hashtag to a communication associates it with any other communication with the same hashtag, which is discussed further in the conclusion. Users primarily moderate hashtag creation. For example, attaching #fruitloops to "Kellogg's makes the best cereal" will align that comment with a universe of Fruit Loops lovers, so that this community of common interest could conceivably keep talking about Fruit Loops until the sun comes up, simply by using the same hashtag. Facebook found Twitter's hashtags so effective, in fact, that

they adopted a hashtag system of their own in the summer of 2013, and many other social networking platforms, like YouTube, have done the same.

6. According to Alexa's analytics regarding Facebook, over thirty percent of Facebook's overall global usage comes from Western countries, with India taking the largest percentage otherwise, at around seven and half percent. The country with the largest Facebook usage percentage is the U.S. with around twenty-one percent.

7. Celebrities and politicians will use intermediary off-screen users to moderate their Facebook profiles. It is well known that social media can function as successful publicity. For instance, Vin Diesel has helped reinvigorate his image after a number of pitfalls in his acting career partly through very active, public participation on Facebook (he currently has over 44 million plus likes). However, celebrities and actors, such as Justin Bieber, will use Twitter more often than Facebook nowadays, as Twitter tends to be less reliant on personal information, so Diesel's fanbase has benefitted from his juxtapositional openness regarding his personal life.

8. Turkle does not explicitly say when she joined Facebook, but alludes to the psychic struggle she had over the decision (*Alone Together* 182).

9. For reference, readers should turn to Ben Mezrich's book *The Accidental Billionaires: The Founding of Facebook, A Tale of Sex, Money, Genius, and Betrayal* (2009) and the excellent David Fincher film on which it is based, *The Social Network* (2011). Zuckerberg has contested the biographical account of both the book and film in various venues, but they are very intriguing nevertheless.

10. Turkle reiterates throughout *Alone Together* that accepting friend requests (or having our own accepted) has the emotional weight of sitting at the "cool kid" table in high school; thus, this action carries a feeling of acceptance.

11. Through online polling, Facebook conceivably allows its users to decide what the service can and cannot do with their personal information—except it really should not be a question whether the privacy of its users ought to be maintained, as it is a founding philosophy of Facebook. In June of 2012, for instance, Facebook held what they called a "governance vote," inviting users to decide if their private information could be distributed to marketers and other interested parties without their consent. Obviously, the userbase voted to uphold the old, seemingly "rigid" privacy standards.

12. From late 2012 to 2013, Google encouraged users via alerts to retroactively modify their YouTube usernames to read as their real world names, information they can provide secondarily across Google's various digital platforms (Gmail, YouTube, Drive, Play). And it does behoove users to provide their actual identities through e-mail, especially for work prospects and the like. But it goes without saying that many YouTubers Google alerted, including myself, chose to stick with anonymous usernames on the service. This was foregrounded by their November 2013 rollout of stricter YouTube commenting standards.

13. On the show, a Google reverse image search will usually suffice as the primary means of catching a catfish. This will reveal the location online from which the catfish has stolen their profile pictures, exposing the catfish's fraud outright. In some cases, the images the catfish steal are so commonly stolen (like pictures of attractive models, for instance) that the photos will be posted on Internet watchdog websites, alerting people who might be curious about someone they are chatting with online to certain image's heightened potential for inauthenticity.

14. Ihab Hassan, in understanding the disparity between Modern and Postmodern eras, figures that modernity is focused with "depth" and postmodernity "surface," taken from "Toward a Concept of Postmodernism," *The Postmodern Turn* (1987).

15. Many of the religions of Facebook's userbase emanate from disputes in identifying various wings of "mainstream" religions. There are the obvious varieties of Christian Catholicism, "Roman" and "Greek," but also

some more obscure varieties of Christianity, like "Bible Baptist" versus "Southern Divinity Baptist." Other interesting religions include, "To Each Their Own" and "I Don't Believe in Religion I Believe in GOD."

16. For reference, a prolific example is Mark Bauerlein's book *The Dumbest Generation*, in which he considers digital insularity part of the Millennial generation's paradigm of "non-learning" (113).

Chapter 3

1. Thanks to its impact on streaming video, other Internet video services exist in relation to YouTube, not on their own merit. Vimeo.com, for example, has a higher quality standard of video than YouTube, and is popular among more traditional film-oriented and artistic uploaders for that reason, but its social community is lackluster. Video platform Vine, a Twitter property, restricts videos to six seconds long (or shorter), perfect for the newspeak-esque Twitterverse, even shorter than the shortest popular videos on YouTube. So Vine is happy to serve as an alternative to YouTube, but it is not the same caliber of content provider as Google's service. Also, YouTube offers live video streaming to established uploaders, something it was criticized for not providing in its formative years—meaning, audience demand has shaped the service overtime.

2. Close to the final manuscript submission for this book in 2015, Google unveiled a pay-per-month ad-free version of YouTube called "YouTube Red," in the vein of other streaming services such as Netflix. The ad-enabled version of the service, though, remains untouched.

3. YouTuber "Weird" Paul Petroskey (user weirdpaulp) claims to be the "original" vlogger. He uses as proof home movies he had filmed as a child in the 1980s which resemble, note-for-note, the format and substance of many contemporary vloggers, with that distinctly vlog-style direct address to the camera. There is a video of Paul's, for instance, where he ruminates on the "art of eating waffles," in which he mostly just ha-

rasses his mother instead of actually showing how to actually eat a waffle—I am curious what audience he thought he was filming for back then. In a video from 1984, he reviews the McDonald's breakfast, holding the items up to the camera very similarly to many contemporary YouTube food and merchandise reviewers.

4. Daniel is a consistent character in the Lonelygirl15 universe, appearing in seasons one, two, and three, unlike Bree, played by actress Jessica Lee Rose, who departs after season one. It is worth noting that Lonelygirl15 is also a pretty sexist series of videos; only men can save the young women being hunted down by the occultists—a sexy young woman in distress appears to be the only central plot point allowed to push the story forward, when these same women are not rolling around in beds or getting drunk scantily clad. To their credit, the producers knew what content was required to achieve high YouTubian viewership.

5. Standards for amateur production on YouTube have evolved over the years, and uploaders who disavow these standards have become increasingly inexcusable by the userbase. Simple visuals prevail. Dead air is edited out of vlogs, evidenced by the frequent jump cuts nowadays. Sound must be audible, with little to no background noise. But beyond at least some practical visibility, filmic lighting on amateur YouTube videos is still an afterthought.

6. As of November 6, 2013, YouTube has attempted to do away with the lack of accountability amongst its commenters by tethering YouTubers forcibly to a Google+ account, which controls Google Gmail and other services that, very often, have a close relation to their real world operators; this conceivably denies anonymity. Also, YouTube's interface now emphasizes "most popular" (most "liked" and replied to) comments as opposed to the "most recent" in the hopes of sifting out throwaway ad hominem comments and the like. But this tactic does not guarantee the proposed outcome of accountability, just makes it more difficult for trolls and haters to function, as they can easily sign-up for dummy

Google+ accounts to enact their anonymous abuses.

7. Emily is not an overt Internet entrepreneur. She does have a live journal, but it is not associated with a business venture and has not been updated in a few years. Some uploaders use YouTube as a means of accruing traffic for their ad-enabled blogs, or Tumblr sites, or fledgling online businesses. This is not the case with Emily. Before leaving North Carolina, she dropped out of high school and got a GED, then floated around for a bit in Oregon. As far as she has explicitly said in her vlogs, as of early 2013 and on, she is employed as a restaurant hostess in Portland. Emily does keep some particular details about her life private, especially her relationship with her immediate family, though she has alluded to its contentiousness.

8. In regards to ideology, the atheist/believer conversation remains the densest on YouTube, as it does on much of the Internet. In the 2010s, Reddit serves as of a microcosm for the larger ideological debates that happen online; without resorting to hyperbole, Reddit's ongoing message board war between belief and non-belief is the stuff of Internet mythos.

9. This is a reference to Jay Bolter's concept of "remediation." According to Bolter, in order for a piece of media to rightfully be considered as such, it must be part of a historical process of remediating older forms of media—in this case, YouTube remediates TV, while TV remediates radio, etc.

10. The URL for Emily's donation page is http://www.gofundme.com/24kb78.

11. However defeatist it may sound, in the case of Google, it is best to table the obvious points of discussion regarding personal privacy and surveillance because contemporary society, on practically a global scale, seems to have done the same. There is now a universalization of citizen submission wherein large measures of privacy are sacrificed for access to the digital technologies which dominate 21st-century consumerism, creativity, and social interaction. To double-back at this juncture stunts the conversation regarding these new technolo-

gies. Indeed, the prevalence of on-screen experience has been ideologically imposed by this 21st-century truth.

12. In reference to Jonathon Zittrain, if the corporate producer has their way, the future of Internet technology and services will be dominated by unhackable "sterile appliances," meaning restrictive devices like Apple's, "tethered to a network of control" (3). Zittrain offers the democratic online encyclopedia Wikipedia as an "open" solution to the growing problem of proprietary digital consumer offerings. Zittrain's argument is not impervious, however, as iPhones and other Apple products can be "jailbroken" by hacker programs, though performing this operation does void hardware warranties and sometimes conflicts with cellular telephone contracts.

13. As an example of this critique, take the May 20, 2013, issue of *Time* magazine with "The Me Me Me Generation" on its cover. "Millennials are lazy, entitled narcissists who still live with their parents—Why they'll save us all," says its tagline. But the narcissism critique is larger than just one *Time* article, literally endemic to all of digital culture rhetoric. Mark Bauerlein's now oft-cited book *The Dumbest Generation* (2008) finds the locus of tension in Millennials' personal struggles resting upon their incredible narcissism. The pertinent discursive move when discussing digital spaces, then, should not rely on "narcissism," however much an axiom it is to the current culture, but instead to ask what has arisen out of that narcissism, or what is now responding to it? Digital narcissism is a cultural trend, here stated, not a point that needs to be asserted ad infinitum.

14. Within YouTube, an entire attention economy has been dedicated to uploaders colloquially referred to as "Reply Girls," attractive women who post reply videos to already-popular videos uploaded to the service, thereby maximizing their viewership (and potential for ad revenue). Their view totals are reliant upon video thumbnails that entice users by showcasing copious cleavage. Reply Girls are one of the reasons YouTube now gives more weight to subscribers than total views.

Conclusion

1. For reference, refer to subreddits /r/ atheism, /r/DebateAnAtheist, or /r/atheism-rebooted, all of which maintain a fairly complex understanding of Information Age atheism.

2. VHS collectors are the subject of a 2014 documentary, *Adjust Your Tracking: The Untold Story of the VHS Collector*, which unmasks an insular community of obsessives not dissimilar to many of the niche eBay auctioneers who have helped color a newfound sense of "antique."

3. Though vinyl records account for less than five percent of total album sales, their profitability and growth have proven appealing even for prickly retailers like Walmart. Regarding their growth, in 2007 vinyl records sold less than million units in total. In 2012, they sold over four million units (Cheredar).

Bibliography

Abdul-Jabbar, Kareem. "How the *Real House-wives* Have Made America Better." *Huffin-gton Post*, 22 Apr. 2013. Web. 29 Apr. 2013.

Abram, Carolyn. "Welcome to Facebook, Everyone." *The Facebook Blog*. Facebook, 26 Sept. 2006. Web. 1 Aug. 2013.

"Alexa Top 500 Global Sites." *Alexa Internet, Inc.*, July 2013. Web. 28 May 2013 and 31 July 2013.

"All Good Things..." *The Hills*. Perf. Kristen Cavallari and Brody Jenner. MTV. 13 July 2010. Television.

Andrejevic, Mark. "Exploiting YouTube: Con-tradictions of User-Generated Labor." *The YouTube Reader*. Eds. Pelle Snickars and Patrick Vonderau. Stockholm: National Li-brary of Sweden, 2009. 406–423. Print.

_____. *Reality TV: The Work of Being Watched*. Lanham: Rowman & Littlefield, 2004. Print.

_____. "Visceral Literacy: Reality TV, Savvy Viewers, and Auto-Spies." *Reality TV: Re-making Television Culture*. Eds. Susan Murray and Laurie Ouellette. New York: New York University Press, 2009. 321–342. Print.

Bakioğlu, Burcu S. "Exposing Convergence: YouTube, Fan Labour, and Anxiety of Cultural Production in Lonelgirl15." *Con-vergence*. Forthcoming.

Barthes, Roland. *Camera Lucida: Reflections on Photography*. New York: Hill and Wang, 1981. Print.

Baudrillard, Jean. *The Consumer Society*. Trans. Chris Turner. London: Sage, 1998. Print.

_____. *Simulacra & Simulation*. Trans. Sheila Faria Glaser. Ann Arbor: Univer-sity of Michigan Press, 1994. Print.

_____. *The Spirit of Terrorism*. Trans. Chris Turner. New York: Verso, 2003. Print.

Bauerlein, Mark. *The Dumbest Generation: How the Digital Age Stupefies Young Amer-ican and Jeopardizes Our Future*. New York: Penguin, 2008. Print.

_____. "Introduction." *The Digital Divide*. Ed. Mark Bauerlein. New York: Penguin, 2011. vii-xiv. Print.

Bazin, André. "The Ontology of the Photo-graphic Image." Trans. Hugh Gray. *Film Quarterly* 13.4 (Summer 1960): 4–9. Print.

Benjamin, Walter. "The Work of Art in the Age of Mechanical Reproduction." *Illu-minations: Essays and Reflections*. New York: Schocken, 1969. 219–253. Print.

Biressi, Anita, and Heather Nunn. *Reality TV: Realism and Revelation*. New York: Wallflower Press, 2005. Print.

Blascovich, Jim, and Jeremy Bailenson. *In-finite Reality: Avatars, Eternal Life, New Worlds, and the Dawn of the Virtual Rev-olution*. New York: William Morrow, 2011. Print.

boyd, danah. *It's Complicated: The Social Lives of Networked Teens*. New Haven: Yale University Press, 2014. Print.

Boym, Svetlana. "Nostalgia and Its Discon-tents." *The Hedgehog Review* 9.2 (2007): 7–18. Print.

Brodie, Anne. "Catfish Creators Tell Us If It's Real or Not." *Moviefone*. Web. 16 Sept. 2010. 8 Jan. 2013.

Bruzzi, Stella. *New Documentary: A Critical Introduction*. London: Routledge, 2000. Print.

Burgess, Jean, and Joshua Green. "The En-trepreneurial Vlogger: Participatory Cul-ture Beyond the Professional-Amateur

Divide." *The YouTube Reader.* Eds. Pelle Snickars and Patrick Vonderau. Stockholm: National Library of Sweden, 2009. 89–107. Print.

_____, and _____. *YouTube: Digital Media and Society Series.* Cambridge: Polity Press, 2009. Print.

Butler, Judith. *Gender Trouble.* New York: Routledge, 1990. Print.

Carr, Nicholas. *The Shallows: What the Internet Is Doing to Our Brains.* New York: W. W. Norton, 2011. Print.

Catfish. Dir. Ariel Schulman. Universal, 2011. DVD.

Cheredar, Tom. "Despite Pandora & Spotify, Total U.S. Music Sales Grew in 2012." Venturebeat.com, 4 Jan. 2013. Web. 17 July 2014.

"Child Porn Charges Laid Against 10 Laval Teens." *CBC News,* 14 Nov. 2013. Web. 18 Mar. 2014.

Childish, Bill, and Charles Thomson. "Remodernism: Towards a New Spirituality in Art." *Stuckism Documents.* Stuckism International, 2000. Web. 7 Aug. 2013.

Colao, J.J. "The Inside Story Of Snapchat: The World's Hottest App or a $3 Billion Disappearing Act?" Forbes.com, 20 Jan. 2014. Web. 18 Mar. 2014.

_____. "Snapchat: The Biggest No-Revenue Mobile App Since Instagram." Forbes.com, 27 Nov. 2012. Web. 18 Mar. 2014.

Corner, John. "Performing the Real: Documentary Diversions." *Reality TV: Remaking Television Culture.* Eds. Susan Murray and Laurie Ouellette. New York: New York University Press, 2004. 45–62. Print.

Deery, June. *Reality TV.* Cambridge: Polity Press, 2015. Print.

Deresiewicz, William. "The End of Solitude." *The Digital Divide.* Ed. Mark Bauerlein. New York: Penguin, 2011. 307–317. Print.

Disney Movie Trailers. YouTube Channel. *Disney's Maleficent—Official Trailer 3.* Web. 18 Mar. 2014. http://www.youtube.com/user/DisneyMovieTrailers.

Dünne, Jörg, and Christian Moser. *Automedialität: Subjektkonstitution in Schrift, Bild und neuen Medien.* Munich: Fink, 2008. Print.

"Episode 312." *Lizard Lick Towing.* Perf. Ron "Ronnie" Shirley. truTV. 27 Aug. 2012. Television.

Fowler, Blair. YouTube Channel. Web. 17 June 2013. http://www.youtube.com/user/AllThatGlitters21.

Galloway, Alexander R. *The Interface Effect.* Cambridge: Polity Press, 2012. Print.

"Google Closes a $2b YouTube Deal." *Reuters,* 14 Nov. 2006. Web. 28 May 2013.

Griffin, Drew. "Exclusive Interview w/ Man Behind 'Jailbait'—Ex-Reddit Troll Michael Brutsch." CNN.com, 18 Oct. 2012. Web. 12 Sept. 2013.

Grusin, Richard. "YouTube at the End of New Media." *YouTube: Digital Media and Society Series.* By Jean Burgess and Joshua Green. Cambridge: Polity Press, 2009. 60–67. Print.

Hartley, John. *Television Truths.* Malden: Blackwell, 2008. Print.

_____. "What Happened Before YouTube." *YouTube: Digital Media and Society Series.* By Jean Burgess and Joshua Green. Cambridge: Polity Press, 2009. 126–143. Print.

#Democrats. Twitter Hashtag. Web. 18 Mar. 2014. https://twitter.com/search?src=typd&q=%23Democrats.

Hassan, Ihab. "Toward a Concept of Postmodernism." *The Postmodern Turn.* Columbus: Ohio University Press, 1987. Print.

Hayles, N. Katherine. *How We Became Posthuman: Virtual Bodies in Cybernetics, Literature, and Informatics.* Chicago: University of Chicago Press, 1999.

_____. *My Mother Was a Computer: Digital Subjects and Literary Texts.* Chicago: University of Chicago Press, 2005. Print.

Heffernan, Virginia. "Comic Shorts, Home on the Web." *New York Times Online,* 4 April 2006. Web. 27 May 2013.

Heffernan, Virginia, and Tom Zeller. "'Lonely Girl' (and Friends) Just Wanted Movie Deal." *New York Times Online,* 12 Sept. 2006. Web. 27 May 2013.

Hoffberger, Chase. "Parents Name Their Newborn Daughter 'Hashtag.'" *The Daily Dot,* 21 Nov. 2012. Web. 18 Mar. 2014.

Holmes, Susan, and Deborah Jermyn, eds. *Understanding Reality Television.* London: Routledge, 2004. Print.

Holpuch, Amanda. "Reddit User Violentacrez Fired from Job after Gawker Exposé." *The Guardian* 16 October 2012. Web. 31 July 2013.

Hudelson, Joshua. "Listening to Whisperers: Perfomance, ASMR Community and Fetish on YouTube." *Sounding Out! Blog*, 10 Dec. 2012. Web. 12 June 2013.

Ingram, Matthew. "On Social Networks, Most Just Like to Watch." Gigaom.com, 28 Sept. 2010. Web. 12 June. 2013.

Jameson, Frederic. *Postmodernism, or, the Cultural Logic of Late Capitalism*. Durham: Duke University Press, 1990. Print.

jawed. "Me at the zoo." YouTube. 23 Aug. 2005. Web. 10 June 2013.http://www.youtube.com/watch?v=jNQXAC9IVRw.

Jenkins, Henry. *Convergence Culture: Where Old and New Media Collide*. New York: New York University Press, 2006. Print.

_____. Afterword. "Reflections on Politics in the Age of YouTube." *Convergence Culture: Where Old and New Media Collide*. New York: New York University Press, 2008. 217–194. Print.

_____. "What Happened Before YouTube." *YouTube: Digital Media and Society Series*. By Jean Burgess and Joshua Green. Cambridge: Polity Press, 2009. 109–125. Print.

Jenkins, Henry, Sam Ford, and Joshua Green. *Spreadable Media: Creating Vale and Meaning in Networked Culture*. New York: New York University Press, 2013.

Jermyn, Deborah. "'This is about Real People!' Video Technologies, Actuality, and Affect in the Television Crime Appeal." *Understanding Reality Television*. Eds. Sue Holmes and Deborah Jermyn. London: Routledge, 2004. 71–90. Print.

"Jerrod & Abby." *Catfish: The TV Show*. Perf. Nev Schulman and Max Joseph. MTV. 10 Dec. 2012. Television.

Johnson, Steven. "The Internet." *The Digital Divide: Arguments for and Against Facebook, Google, Texting, and the Age of Social Networking*. Ed. Mark Bauerlein. New York: Penguin, 2011. 26–33. Print.

Keen, Andrew. *The Cult of the Amateur: How Today's Internet Is Killing Our Culture*. New York: Random House, 2007. Print.

_____. "Web 1.0 + Web 2.0 = Web 3.0." ajkeen.com, 25 April 2008. Web. 18 March 2014.

Kenneally, Tim. "Ratings: *Duck Dynasty* Finale Draws Nearly 10M Viewers." *The Wrap*. MSN Entertainment, 25 April 2013. Web. 29 April 2013.

Lange, Patricia G. "Videos of Affinity on YouTube." *The YouTube Reader*. Eds. Pelle Snickars and Patrick Vonderau. Stockholm: National Library of Sweden, 2009. 70–88. Print.

"Lauren & Derek." *Catfish: The TV Show*. Perf. Nev Schulman and Max Joseph. MTV. 16 July 2013. Television.

Leidl, Dan. "American X: The Ironic History of a Generation." *Research in Cultural and Media Studies: Generation X Goes Global*. Ed. Christine Henseler. New York: Routledge, 2012. xiii-xxiii. Print.

Lonelygirl15. YouTube Channel. Web. 13 June 2013. http://www.youtube.com/user/lonelygirl15.

LusciousPout. "Why I Hate *some* Beauty Gurus" YouTube. 2 Jan. 2011. Web. 17 June 2013. http://www.youtube.com/user/LusciousPout.

Marinucci, Mimi. "You Can't Front on Facebook." *Facebook and Philosophy*. Ed. D.E. Wittkower. Chicago: Open Court, 2010. 65–74. Print.

Matyszczyk, Chris. "Poll: Teens Migrating to Twitter over Facebook." *CBS News*. 22 May 2013. Web. 31 July 2013.

Maury. Host Maury Povich. Syndicated. 9 Sept. 1991–present. Television.

McHale, Brian. *Postmodernist Fiction*. New York: Methuen, 1987. Print.

McLuhan, Marshall. *Understanding Media: The Extensions of Man*. Boston: MIT Press, 1994. Print.

Miller, Toby. "Cybertarians of the World Unite: You Have Nothing to Lose But Your Tubes!" *The YouTube Reader*. Eds. Pelle Snickars and Patrick Vonderau. Stockholm: National Library of Sweden, 2009. 424–440. Print.

Morokov, Eugeny. *The Save Everything Click Here: The Folly of Technological Solutionism*. New York: PublicAffairs, 2013. Print.

Muhr, Sarah Louise, and Michael Pederson.

"Faking It on Facebook." *Facebook and Philosophy*. Ed. D.E. Wittkower. Chicago: Open Court, 2010. 265–275. Print.

Nakaso, Dan. "YouTube Providers Could Begin Charging Fees this Week." *Silicon Valley's MercuryNews.com*, 7 May 2013. Web. 24 May 2013.

Nichols, Bill. *Introduction to Documentary*. Bloomington: Indiana University Press, 2001. Print.

O'Reilly, Tim. "What Is Web 2.0." *The Digital Divide*. Ed. Mark Bauerlein. New York: Penguin, 2011. 215–229. Print.

Onision. YouTube Channel. 27 June 2013. http://www.youtube.com/user/Onision.

Parental Control. Ex. Prod. Michael Canter. MTV. 6 Feb. 2005–2010. Television.

paytotheorderofofof2. YouTube Channel. Web. 10 June 2013. http://www.youtube.com/user/ paytotheorderofofof2.

Peters, Katherine, and Andrea Seier. "Home Dance: Mediacy and Aesthetics of the Self on YouTube." *The YouTube Reader*. Eds. Pelle Snickars and Patrick Vonderau. Stockholm: National Library of Sweden, 2009. 187–203. Print.

Postman, Neil. *Technopoly: the Surrender of Culture to Technology*. New York: Knopf, 1992. Print.

Rice, Lynette. "Thursday Night's All Right for Fighting." *Entertainment Weekly* 585 (2 March 2001): 22. Print.

Rojek, Chris. *Celebrity*. London: Reaktion Books, 2001. Print.

Rosen, Christine. "Virtual Friendship and the New Narcissism." *The Digital Divide*. Ed. Mark Bauerlein. New York: Penguin, 2011. 172–188. Print.

Rushkoff, Douglas. "The People's Net." *The Digital Divide*. Ed. Mark Bauerlein. New York: Penguin, 2011. 116–126. Print.

Ryan, Johnny. *A History of the Internet and the Digital Future*. London: Reaktion Books, 2010. Print.

Sandoval, Greg. "Universal, YouTube Near Deal on Music Video Site." CNet.com, 4 March 2009. Web. 30 May 2013.

Sarachan, Jeremy. "Profile Picture, Right Here, Right Now." *Facebook and Philosophy*. Ed. D.E. Wittkower. Chicago: Open Court, 2010. 51–64. Print.

Seasons 3 and 28. *The Real World*. Creator(s) Mary-Ellis Bunim and Jonathon Murray. MTV. 21 May 1992–present. Television.

Sessions, Lauren F. "'You Looked Better on MySpace': Deception and Authenticity on Web 2.0." *First Monday*. 14.7 (2009): 1. Print.

Simons, Hadlee. "An Orgasm for Your Head?" *iafrica.com*, 16 Aug. 2012. Web. 12 June 2013.

Snickars, Pelle, and Patrick Vonderau. Introduction. *The YouTube Reader*. Eds. Pelle Snickars and Patrick Vonderau. Stockholm: National Library of Sweden, 2009. 1–16. Print.

Sontag, Susan. *On Photography*. New York: Picador, 2001. Print.

Stern, Joanna. "Parents Sue Apple for In-App and In-Game Purchases Made by Kids." *ABC News Online*, 20 April 2012. Web. 28 Oct. 2013.

Talbot, David. "African Entrepreneurs Deflate Google's Internet Balloon Idea." *MIT Technology Review*, 20 June 2013. Web. 18 March 2014.

Turkle, Sherry. *Alone Together: Why We Expect More from Technology and Less from Each Other*. New York: Basic Books, 2011. Print.

_____. *Life on the Screen: Identity in the Age of the Internet*. New York: Simon & Schuster, 1995. Print.

Twitchell, James B. *Lead Us Into Temptation: The Triumph of American Materialism*. New York: Columbia University Press, 1999. Print.

United States vs. Thaddeus McMichael. 2:12-mj-30147-JU. Eastern District Court of Michigan. 2012. *U.S. Archives*. Web. 30 July 2013.

Uricchio, William. "The Future of a Medium Once Known as Television." *The YouTube Reader*. Eds. Pelle Snickars and Patrick Vonderau. Stockholm: National Library of Sweden, 2009. 24–39. Print.

Vena, Jocelyn. "Brody Jenner Reveals Alternate *Hills* Ending with Lauren Conrad." *MTV News*. MTV.com, 14 July 2010. Web. 24 Apr. 2013.

VeniVidiVulpes. YouTube Channel. Web. 23 June 2013. http://www.youtube.com/user/VeniVidiVulpes.

will.i.am. "Scream & Shout ft. Britney Spears." Vevo (YouTube). 28 Nov. 2012 Web. 10 June 2013. http://www.youtube.com/watch?v=kYtGlldX5qI.

Wittkower, D.E. "A Reply to Facebook Critics." *Facebook and Philosophy*. Ed. D.E. Wittkower. Chicago: Open Court, 2010. xxi-xxx. Print.

Zittrain, Jonathon. *The Future of the Internet—And How to Stop It*. New Haven: Yale University Press, 2009. Print.

Žižek, Slavoj. *Looking Awry: An Introduction to Jacques Lacan through Popular Culture*. Cambridge: MIT Press, 1991. Print.

Zúñiga, Homero Gil de, and Sebastián Valenzuela. "Who Uses Facebook and Why?" *Facebook and Philosophy*. Ed. D.E. Wittkower. Chicago: Open Court, 2010. xxxi-xxxvii. Print.

Index

Index